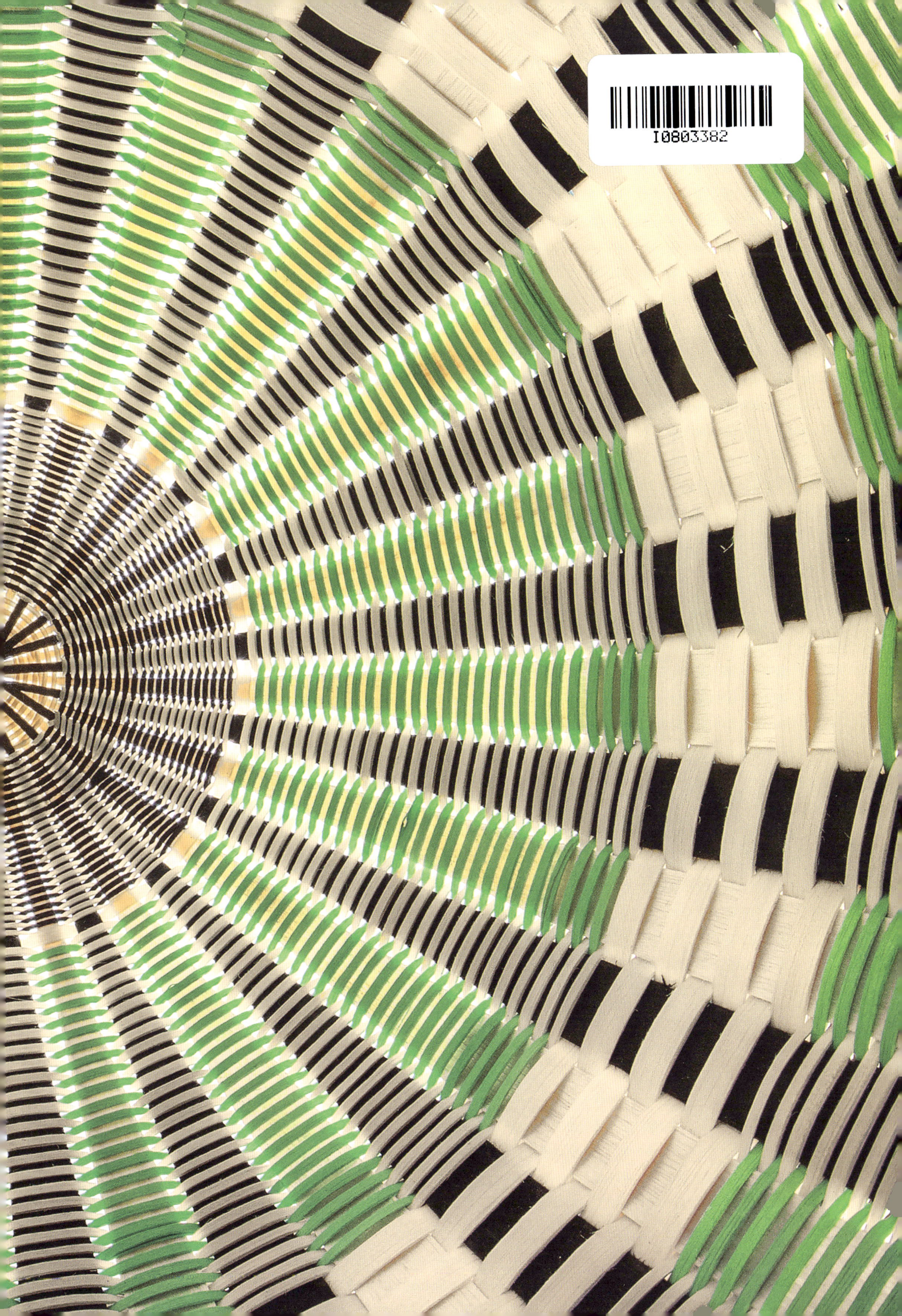

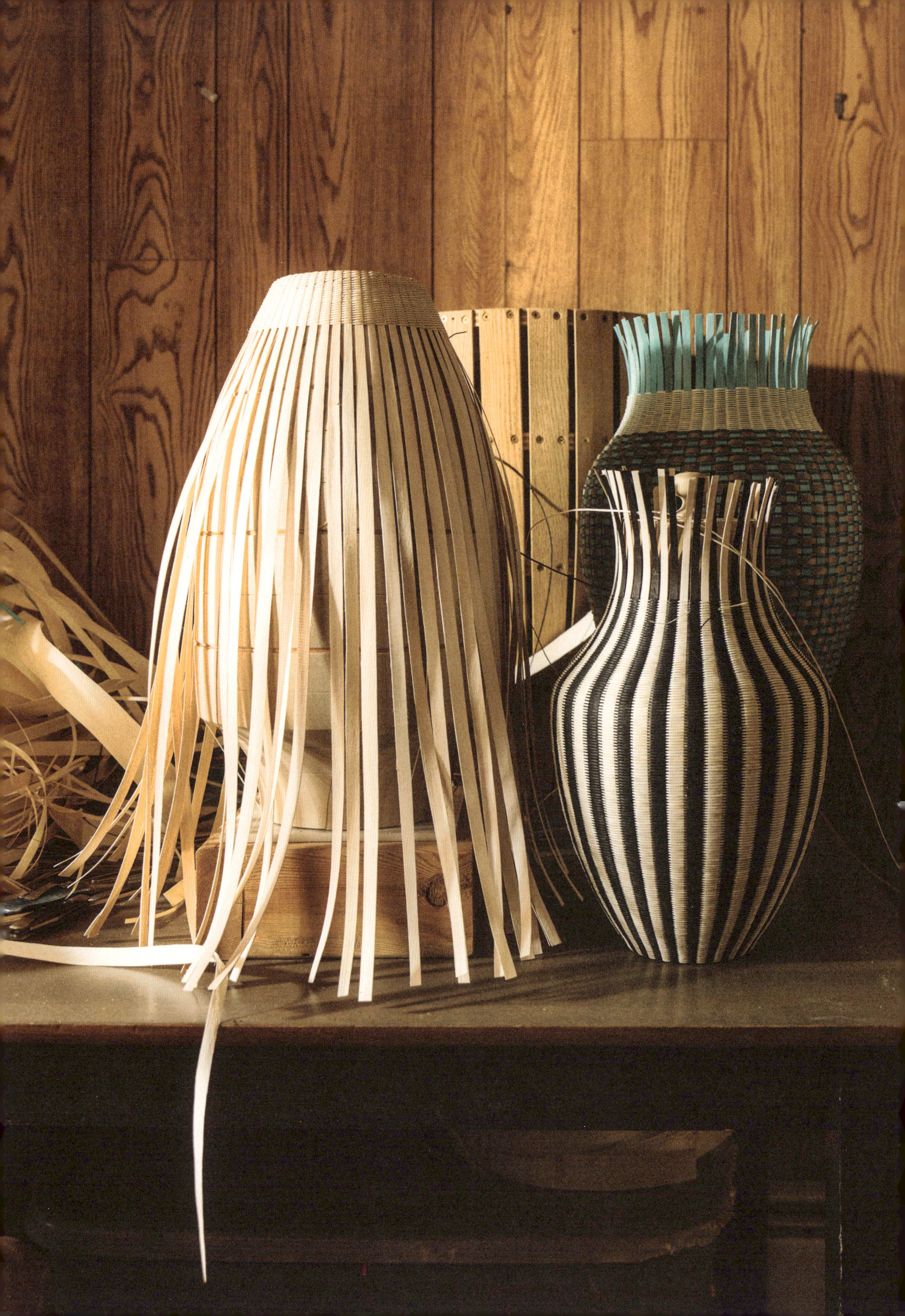

Jeremy Frey

Jeremy Frey
Woven

Edited by
Theresa Secord
and Ramey Mize

Contributions by

Theresa Secord
Andrew James Hamilton
Dakota Hoska
Jaime DeSimone
Ramey Mize

PORTLAND MUSEUM of ART

Rizzoli Electa

Contents

Artist Acknowledgments

Thank you, first and foremost, to my wife, Ganessa Frey—an incredible artist in her own right—who has supported me from day one. I am grateful beyond words to her and our children for their love and encouragement.

My mother, Gal Frey, first taught me to weave, and I am forever thankful to her for sharing and cultivating this art with me. She has nurtured my creative pursuits since I was young, and I would not be the artist or person I am today without her. My uncle Moose went out of his way to teach me how to harvest my materials; his teachings were seeds that grew into the foundation of my practice.

My sincere thanks to Theresa Secord, who has been an invaluable mentor and friend to me. Theresa's work through the Maine Indian Basketmakers Alliance was instrumental in making my path to basketry possible. It was also Theresa who first pushed me to go to the Santa Fe Indian Market, which proved to be an essential platform for my career. Again and again, Theresa opened opportunities for me that I wouldn't have otherwise had. I am deeply grateful to her for her clarity of vision, generosity, and belief in my work.

I would like to acknowledge the support network provided by the Santa Fe Indian Market, organized by the Southwestern Association for Indian Arts, as well as the Heard Museum Guild Indian Fair and Market in Phoenix. These venues bring important visibility to the work of countless Indigenous artists, mine included. Similarly, the Artist in Business Leadership Fellowship that I received from the First Peoples Fund in 2012 made a major difference in my life, coming at a critical point when I needed financial support for the tools I use in my art. I will never forget their help at a formative juncture in my development. A USA Fellowship from United States Artists in 2010 was influential in my trajectory as well.

I am grateful to Jaime DeSimone for bringing the idea of this exhibition to life, and to Ramey Mize for her contributions in bringing it to the finish line. The team at Karma gallery has facilitated these efforts and expanded the audience for my art, and I deeply appreciate their support. Finally, thank you to the Portland Museum of Art for giving me the ability to express my gratitude through this project and to share such a diverse representation of my work with the wider public.

There are countless other people, institutions, and organizations that have had important impacts on my work along the way. Though space prevents me from listing everyone by name, please know that you have made all the difference.

— Jeremy Frey

Evolution of an Artist and the Oldest Art Form in New England

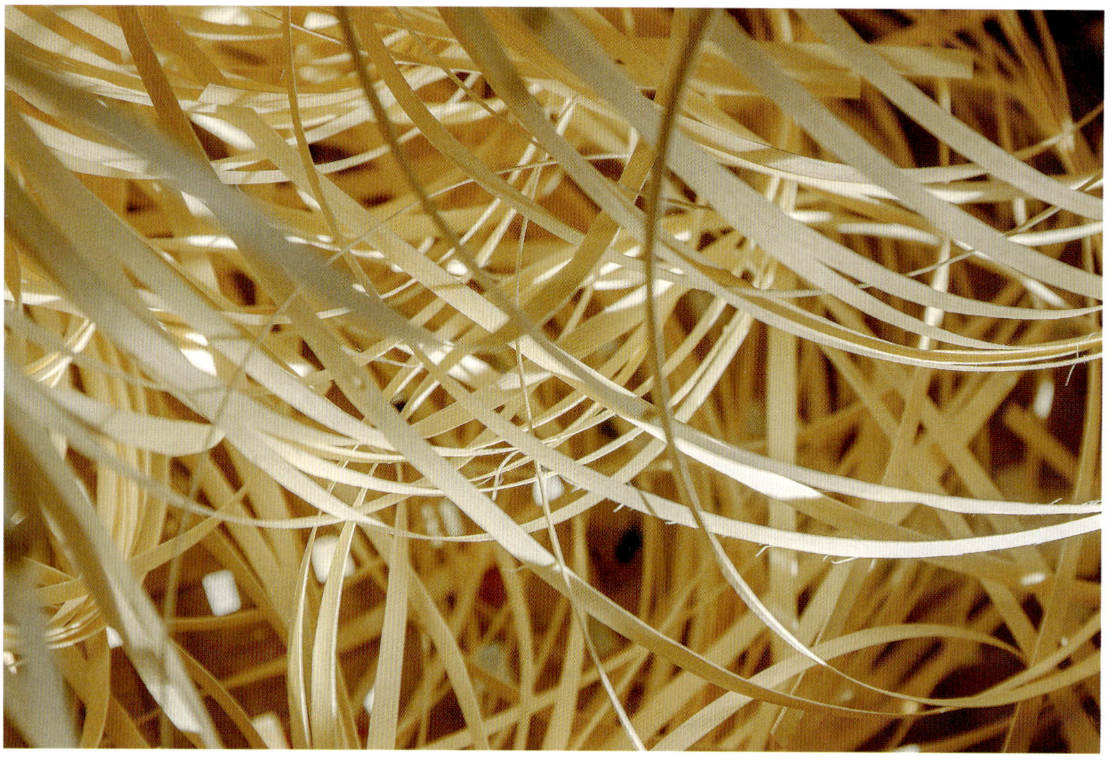

Theresa Secord
(Penobscot)

Glooskap came first of all into this country . . . into the land of the Wabanaki, next to sunrise. There were no Indians here then. . . . And in this way he made man: He took his bow and arrows and shot at trees, the basket-trees, the Ash. Then Indians came out of the bark of the Ash-trees. —Molly Sepsis, Passamaquoddy, 1884[1]

Opposite Ash weavers, 2023

Introduction

I'm honored to share my perspective regarding the evolution of a remarkable artist and the support system that helped him and others transform an ancient art form. Jeremy Frey descends from at least seven generations of ash basket makers from "the land of the Wabanaki, next to sunrise,"[2] at the easternmost point in the continental United States. He hails from a family of creatives, as his mother, brothers, and maternal grandparents are or were renowned basket makers and culture bearers in the Passamaquoddy community.

Jeremy's contemporary baskets were not anticipated by the founding members of the Maine Indian Basketmakers Alliance, yet his innovative basketry has forever changed the tradition and the way our art is perceived. Most of us were still weaving our "grandparents' baskets" when Jeremy began working in the medium around 2000. Historically, traditional utility or work baskets were primarily woven by the men, and the Victorian style of artistic "fancy baskets" were woven by the women. Work baskets represent the oldest art forms in Maine. Pack baskets, still woven today, are shaped to be worn on the back for hunting and fishing, and similarly, to tuck into the bow of ancient birch-bark canoes. The more artistic fancy baskets originally evolved from eighteenth- and nineteenth-century baskets, woven for use in colonial homes (such as sewing baskets) and further refined in the mid- to late 1800s Victorian period with fanciful shapes and forms, such as handkerchief baskets and glove boxes. These baskets were sold as tourist items for use in the large so-called cottages at the coastal and inland resorts in Maine, including those at Bar Harbor, Kennebunkport, and Poland Springs, to name a few.

The Maine Indian Basketmakers Alliance

The Maine Indian Basketmakers Alliance (MIBA) was founded in 1993 by Indigenous basket makers from the four federally recognized (Wabanaki) tribes in Maine: Houlton Band of Maliseet Indians, Aroostook Band of Mi'kmaqs, Passamaquoddy Tribe, and Penobscot Nation. As a young Penobscot basket maker, I became the first director. The approximately fifty-five founding members of this all-Indigenous arts organization set out to save the endangered art of ash and sweetgrass basketry—and did. Through the implementation of more than two decades of programming, including apprenticeships, tribal community basketry workshops, and intensive marketing efforts, the MIBA is credited with lowering the average age of basket makers from sixty-three to forty and increasing numbers to approximately 150. The teaching programs and marketing efforts of the MIBA created an environment for the young, next-generation basket makers, like Jeremy, to learn and thrive in.

1. Charles G. Leland, *The Algonquin Legends of New England* (Boston: Houghton, Mifflin, 1884), 19.
2. Ibid.

In the mid-1990s, Jeremy's mother, Frances "Gal" Frey (Passamaquoddy, born 1957), was one of the first apprentices in the Traditional Arts Apprenticeship Program, originally administered by the Maine Arts Commission. Already an extraordinary beadwork artist, she was mentored by the late Sylvia Gabriel (1929–2003), a great Passamaquoddy basket maker and founding MIBA board member. This transfer of intergenerational knowledge had been taking place naturally in the tribal communities for generations, yet the institution of this program gave the MIBA basket makers and our efforts a significant boost. One can still see the influence of Sylvia's basketry in the "porcupine weave" or "points" in Jeremy's award-winning basketry today (fig. 1).

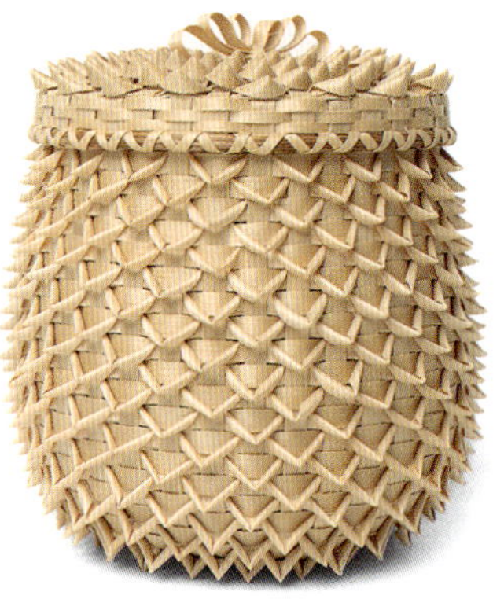

Fig 1 Sylvia Gabriel (Passamaquoddy, 1929–2003), *Fancy Basket*, 2000, ash and sweetgrass, 7 × 6¼ × 6¼ inches. Hudson Museum, University of Maine, HM8633

Jeremy, the third of Gal's four sons, has roots in the Sipayik Passamaquoddy community. There, his renowned grandfather Fred Moore Sr. (Passamaquoddy, 1933–2014) was a prolific pack basket maker and wove many other work baskets used by both the "old-time" Indians and non-Native Mainers in the region's woods and waters. Traditional Passamaquoddy baskets for hunting, fishing, gathering, and ceremony have been woven for more than thirteen thousand years, according to tribal and archaeological records.

"It's the Community That Makes the Basket"

I first met Jeremy in 2002 at a large tribal community basketry workshop at Sipayik (the Pleasant Point Passamaquoddy Reservation). The MIBA sponsored annual workshops on each of the five reservations in Maine, which drew upwards of eighty people from the community. As many as twenty basketry teachers from all four Wabanaki tribes would converge for an entire weekend of basketmaking and intergenerational sharing. Participants learned everything from processing the wood to weaving the finished baskets in a variety of styles. Techniques such as pounding the ash log, braiding sweetgrass, and making potato baskets, pack baskets, wastebaskets, and different styles of fancy baskets were taught. Community members joined in to weave, and others came to watch, support, share meals and stories about the old days, and "talk Indian." It was here where tribal community members could also find a mentor and later enter the more formal Traditional Arts Apprenticeship Program (fig. 2).

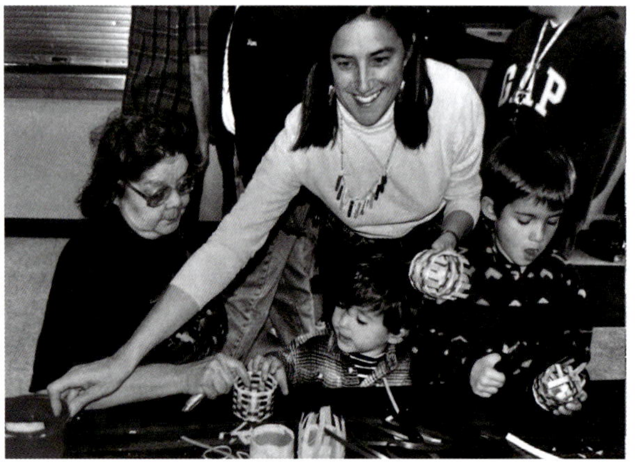

Fig 2 Theresa Secord teaching, with her son Caleb Hoffman (lower right); Tobias Francis, son of the late David Moses Bridges (center); and Clara Neptune Keezer (Passamaquoddy), in Sipayik, ME, c. 1998

The community environment was ideal for networking and cultural socialization. Otherwise, someone might be reticent to knock on the door of a basket maker and ask to be mentored. I remember a workshop where an elderly Maliseet man drove over the border from a First Nations Maliseet reserve in Canada to visit a workshop in the Houlton Band of Maliseets' community. It was his seventieth birthday, and when his family called him to come home for his party that evening, he refused, saying he preferred to stay where "the people were making his baskets and speaking his language." Instead, the MIBA president, Molly Neptune Parker (Passamaquoddy, 1939–2020), led a birthday song in the Passamaquoddy/Maliseet language at the workshop meal that day.

At the Passamaquoddy workshop, Gal Frey asked me if Jeremy could have a helper role to pound and split the ash wood for the workshop baskets in exchange for fifty dollars for the gas to drive from the Motahkomikuk Passamaquoddy community where he was living. I wrote his first artist payment check that day. His mother had been teaching him basketry at home to earn income and to help him stay away from the drugs that were circulating and wreaking havoc on his peers in their small rural community and around Washington County. Later, Jeremy would become a formal apprentice and then a mentor himself, which is our cultural way. The responsibility to mentor once someone was taught was promoted through the work of the MIBA.

Historically, our basketry was not practiced outside of a community context. Still today, most practitioners live on or near the tribal reservations in Maine. The cultural preservation and sustainability of the art of ash and sweetgrass basketry are inextricably linked to tribal community. According to Passamaquoddy medical administrator and author Gail Dana, "It's the community that makes the basket." To paraphrase, she once told me:

> A man and his son (or grandson, or nephew) may hunt for and harvest an ash tree in the deep Maine woods. Next, the son may pound the log to release the wood splints along the growth rings. In the old days, someone else in the family may split the wood, and then use handmade tools to "gauge," or further refine, the splints. Next, in the "work basket" weaving tradition, another person may weave the basket bottoms and still another finish up the sides and bind the tops.

In the days of higher fancy basket production (from the mid-nineteenth to the mid-twentieth century), when many people were engaged in basketry as an industry, a relative (or today a member of another tribe) may pick the sweetgrass at the coast and sell or trade it to the basket makers, by the pound. Until very recently, there were ladies who were paid by the yard to braid the grass for basket makers. So by the time the basket materials had been harvested and prepared and the basket woven, there may have been as many as four to six other people involved. This unique community setting and structure make Jeremy's work and emergence from tradition even more meaningful, as he grew up in this system yet now conducts all these activities on his own. At the time of this writing he has employed his first studio helper, my son Caleb Hoffman (Cherokee/Penobscot, born 1991).

For generations, there has been a small cottage industry around the materials, supplies, and manufacture of hand tools and wooden molds, or forms, used in basketmaking. Jeremy makes all his own tools, including his wood splitter and gauges (fig. 3). Until recently, he even cut the trees to fabricate the large wooden forms and turn stands (needed to hold and turn the heavy forms) for his specialized baskets. Many contemporary basket makers use scissors in some of the cutting work, but Jeremy still uses a knife as his primary tool for cutting and scraping the wood, as is traditional and how he was taught (fig. 4).

Gal once told me Jeremy has always been an artist. For example, as a boy he would build up an elaborate castle in clay,

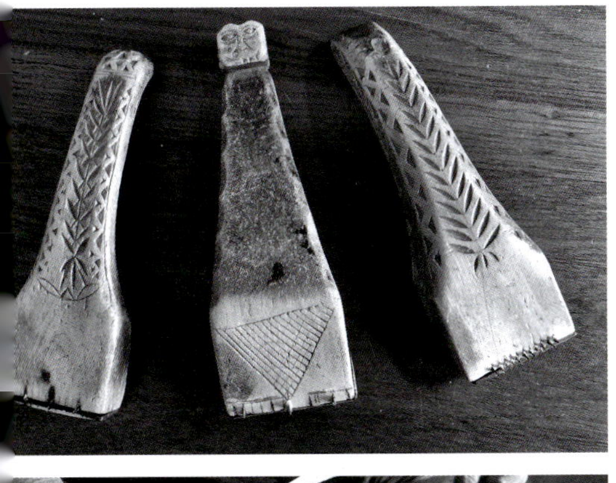

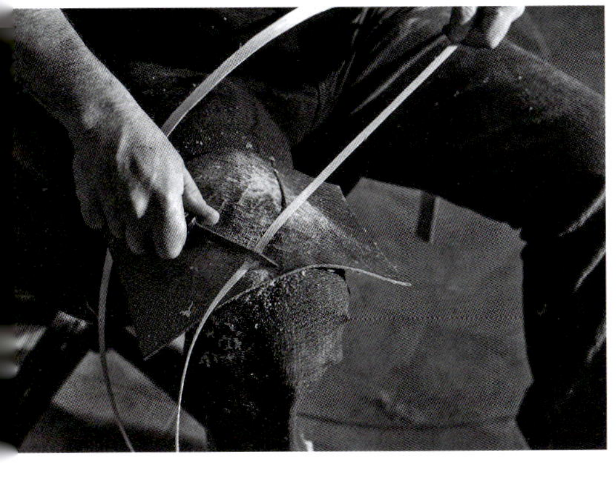

Fig 3 Heirloom gauges from Secord's great-grandmother
Fig 4 Frey scraping ash, 2023

spending the entire day working on it without guides or drawings, only to crush it all down at night and reuse the clay for another creation the next day. As I write this, I think of the metaphor of Glooskap, our Wabanaki "culture hero," making the animals out of rocks and clay, as Jeremy now creates highly complex art and a cultural life out of the wood from the ash trees. Jeremy's cultural life and place in a long ancestral continuum of cultural tradition are poignantly depicted through a recent image of a harvest of ash tree logs together with a bull moose (fig. 5). In fact, hunting for a suitable ash tree to provide for his own art is similar to hunting for a moose to provide for his family.

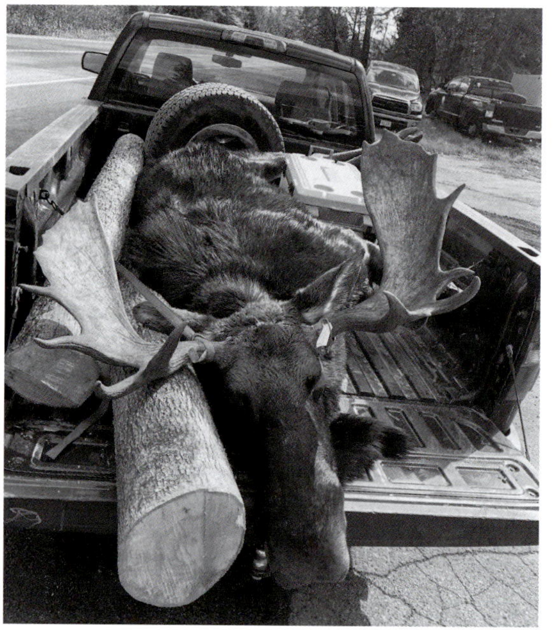

Fig 5 Sustainable harvest of ash logs and moose by Frey and his family. Passamaquoddy Territory, Maine

Glooskap made the first people, who came out of the bark of the sacred ash tree; yet today, the emerald ash borer beetles are coming out of the bark. Wabanaki basket makers are in a race against time to keep the art form alive, as this devastating aspect of climate change is killing ash trees across the continent. In 2023 Jeremy began working with an engineer to build a new, portable prototype of an ash-pounding machine in order to harvest as much wood as possible before all the ash trees are gone. The loss of the ash will mean more than the loss of our ancestral weaving material, as our Wabanaki identity and genesis are encoded in the trees.

Support for the Ancestral Tradition

The Maine Indian Basketmakers Alliance was founded at a time when very few young people were learning the tradition, basket makers were having a difficult time sourcing healthy ash trees, and there were only small, local markets for basket sales. At the time, thirty years ago, the MIBA reenergized the Ash Task Force, bringing the traditional ecological knowledge (TEK) of Indigenous basket makers together with tribal, state, university, and federal foresters to find solutions related to the scarcity of ash wood—well before the term "climate change" was in regular use. In fact, the foresters determined then that summer drought conditions and what they referred to as the flood/freeze of ash tree roots were limiting the quantity and quality of ash trees suitable for baskets. Flood/freeze refers to flooding around the shallow tree roots and subsequent winter freezing of the wet roots, prior to the protective snowfall cover. Meanwhile, access to sweetgrass, harvested at the coast, was and continues to be severely limited due to private property ownership and now invasive grasses, resulting from climate change as more southerly plants move northward and take over sweetgrass beds.

When I first began working with the mostly elderly basket makers in 1993, if the word "artist" was mentioned, they would wonder who I was talking about. This was a generation of basket makers who conversed with one another in their Indigenous languages, particularly the Passamaquoddy, who have kept their spoken language active. Basket makers in that generation similarly had kept the basketry alive, despite great odds and many obstacles. During the prior fifty-year period, they had received little financial return for their labors, and there were no awards, commissions, grants, or fellowships to be found. The elder founders of the MIBA, who were so committed to teaching the next generation, deserve much credit for the success of basket makers today. Ours is the oldest continuously practiced art form in Maine, and its cultural knowledge is still passed on orally through intergenerational mentoring relationships. The harvest and preparation of the materials, weaving instructions, and traditional ecological knowledge are not in written format, which preserves a cultural richness and authenticity and introduces some mentoring challenges at the same time.

Marketing an Ancient Art

Thirty years ago, there wasn't a path for marketing our basketry in the art world, except one that had been established by our ancestors in the 1800s at the resorts on the coast of Maine. So the MIBA began there by reestablishing a market in Bar Harbor, a Wabanaki prehistoric summering ground and a historic selling area. We forged a new path by implementing a series of local annual art markets for the mostly elder basket makers, who were struggling to find better markets at that time. Most basket makers were making and selling baskets to pay their "light" (electric) bills, with a small basket income to supplement their Social Security checks. In 1993, baskets were selling for upwards of one hundred dollars, with most selling for thirty dollars or less. While there were one or two highly skilled basket makers selling baskets for a little higher, the price structure would only slowly change when Jeremy came along. About fifteen years after the MIBA's founding, we would launch our basket makers into the large, national juried Indian art markets in Phoenix and Santa Fe. There, Jeremy would eventually win the top prizes and command the highest prices ever for contemporary Indigenous baskets.

As we reestablished our prehistoric connection in Bar Harbor, our historic selling area (since at least 1840), the MIBA hosted the Native American Festival at the College of the Atlantic beginning in 1994. This became the largest in-state market where we highlighted the MIBA's apprenticeships, which were funded by the National Endowment for the Arts for twenty-one years, from 1993 to 2014. At our peak in the markets, we purchased hotel rooms for upwards of fifty basket makers and their families to participate in the festival. This was the first public market for many of the young basket makers in the Alliance who essentially grew up coming to the festival, including Jeremy. The annual July event at the College of the Atlantic drew hundreds and then thousands of visitors at its peak around the mid-2000s, with some basket collectors flying in from as far away as California. In collaboration with partners, we also established a market at the Common Ground Country Fair in Unity, Maine, and a winter market at the Hudson Museum, the University of Maine, in Orono. In December 2022, the Hudson Museum sponsored the twenty-eighth annual Native art market in collaboration with the MIBA, the longest-running market for Wabanaki baskets and other art forms in Maine.

It was a seven-year dream of the basket makers in the Maine Indian Basketmakers Alliance to open our own retail store for selling baskets. The board members of the MIBA, all basket makers, longed to exercise their own sovereignty, cultural resilience, and economic self-sufficiency through our basketry again. Wabanaki baskets have been sold in Maine for two centuries and traded for many more. In 2000, the MIBA opened the Wabanaki Arts Center Gallery in

Old Town, Maine, next to Indian Island, the Penobscot Nation's ancient village. Here, the gallery manager and MIBA assistant director, Jennifer Sapiel Neptune (born 1969), also a Penobscot basket maker and an art curator, bought and sold Jeremy's and other next-generation basket makers' first baskets. This local marketing effort, combined with outreach and the annual markets, was a concerted effort on the MIBA's part to market the young basket makers' work as they were being mentored in our apprenticeship and workshop programs. We knew they had to immediately find markets for their baskets and earn a living doing so (at least part-time) if they were to carry on the tradition (fig. 6).

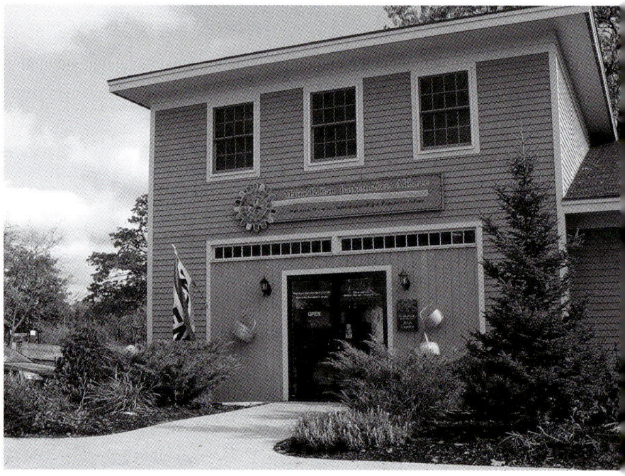

Fig 6 Wabanaki Arts Center Gallery, Old Town, ME (operated by the Maine Indian Basketmakers Alliance)

Initially, Jeremy's basket pricing caused tension among other basket makers in the MIBA, since younger basket makers were historically taught to set prices below the elders'. To do otherwise would be considered disrespectful, paramount to saying your baskets were superior to those of your mentor. Also, basket makers who were accustomed to selling for lower prices thought his price structure would make it difficult for lower priced baskets to sell. The controversy gave way, however, as younger basket makers showed they could earn decent prices for the amount of skill and work involved in the fast-evolving styles of baskets being created. Today, Jeremy—a brilliant marketer in his own right—is among the artists commanding some of the highest prices for contemporary art in the nation.

The comprehensive and successful strategy in the marketing efforts of the MIBA over two decades was to promote the basket makers and baskets at the Wabanaki Arts Center Gallery, in the annual Maine markets, through advertisements and articles in magazines for collectors of Native American art, and with visits by basket makers out to the national Indian art markets. When I reflect on our work together at the MIBA, I'm proud of our self-determining, community grassroots efforts to save our own endangered art and bring forward an entire generation of basket makers.

Innovation: A New Style on an Old Form

It was interesting to many of us in the Wabanaki basketmaking community that Jeremy's early work reflected the so-called fancy basket style, an artistic form traditionally practiced by women in the Wabanaki tribes. Prior to Jeremy, the only male fancy basket maker I knew was Lawrence (Billy) Shay (1912–2000), a Penobscot and the husband of my teacher, Madeline Tomer Shay (Penobscot, 1915–1993). Men, including Jeremy's grandfather (who was alive at the time Jeremy began weaving), were still accustomed to weaving the work baskets, used in hunting, fishing, and other traditional practices. Yet it would be a mistake to think there were or are more women basket makers than men in our tradition, as our culture shows equal participation.

Jeremy's fine weave, sea urchin shape, and porcupine point baskets were his early breakout, signature baskets. Although antique baskets from nearly one hundred years ago had featured the fine weave, it wasn't being practiced anymore. This weave required much time, effort, and skill for the price gained, and these baskets' value had dropped decades earlier. In fine weave baskets, the ash is gauged down to nearly threadlike widths of one-sixteenth of an inch and even one-thirty-second of an inch. For many of the basket makers, selling baskets had become associated with paying household bills, so people were not putting in the time to make the fine weave baskets anymore. The fine weave is often seen in the base of even Jeremy's largest pieces (pp. 152-55).

To my knowledge, no one had ever braided the ash wood or cedar bark before Jeremy wove those materials into his baskets. Only the sweetgrass was pre-braided before being woven over the ash standards. The braiding of the actual wood does not appear in the historical record of some two centuries of baskets in museum collections (p. 113).

Jeremy once shared that he likes to challenge himself in his creative process by designing something that seems impossible at the time, but then expects to spend most of the next two years working to engineer and manifest the concept into a piece. He has innovated many new forms, creating large wooden molds on which to weave and to execute complex patterns and designs, while incorporating traditional Passamaquoddy concepts and figures from the natural world.

The Wabanaki Basket Maker as an Artist and Early Indigenous Influences

Jeremy's first exhibition, and commissioned work, was at the Smithsonian Institution's National Museum of the American Indian in New York, the George Gustav Heye Center; titled *The Language of Native American Baskets: From the Weavers' View*, it ran from late 2003 to early 2005.[3] This was the first major basketry exhibition in the United States that was cocurated by Native American basket makers. Jeremy's work was showcased among three generations of apprenticeship weavers from the same tribe: Sylvia Gabriel, Gal Frey, and Jeremy. As noted earlier, the porcupine weave is a common thread appearing in each of their pieces, and the first time that the weave—still so prominent in Jeremy's work today—was featured in a museum by all three generations of the apprenticeship. During this time, his mother's mentor and a founding MIBA board member, Sylvia Gabriel, passed away. The loss of the first generation of basket maker teachers in the MIBA, within only ten years after the organization's founding, was palpable. In the first decade of work, we were losing teachers (two to three per year due to old age) faster than young basket makers could learn. The net loss of culture, language use, and traditional ecological knowledge (TEK) in our unique weaving traditions, possessed by this generation and the ones before, could not be completely reclaimed.

In 2006, at the Smithsonian Folklife Festival in Washington, D.C., the MIBA supported travel for Jeremy and four other intergenerational basket makers—including Ganessa Bryant (Penobscot, born 1982), Jeremy's future wife—to represent Wabanaki culture among eighty basket makers from all over Native North America. This eye-opening experience, being exposed to other Indigenous basketry cultures and weavers, was life-changing. Jeremy could witness the very high esteem that the basket makers as culture bearers were held in. Here he met Mike Nahoopii (born 1964), a Native Hawaiian weaver who taught him

3. Bruce Bernstein, ed., *The Language of Native American Baskets: From the Weavers' View* (Washington, D.C.: National Museum of the American Indian, 2003). I was one of several Indigenous basket makers who were guest curators, including Lisa Telford (Haida), Pat Courtney Gold (Wasco Nation of the Warm Springs Confederacy), Julia Parker (Pomo), Sherrie Smith-Ferri (Dry Creek Pomo and Bodega Bay Miwok), and Terrol Johnson (Tohono O'odham).

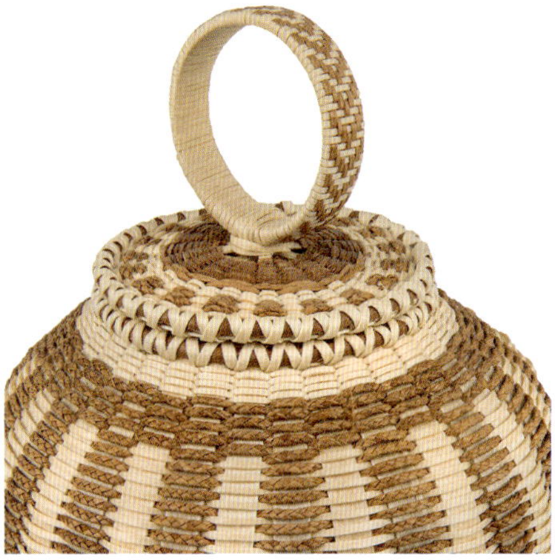

Fig 7 Jeremy Frey, *Fine Weave Vase* (detail), 2015, ash and braided cedar bark, 9 × 4½ × 4½ inches. Collection of Dr. and Mrs. Ari and Lea Plosker

to weave with lauhala materials (leaves of the hala tree). This informal mentoring influenced the unique signature woven ring finials on Jeremy's basket covers, a weaving style used in traditional Hawaiian woven cuffs and warrior armbands (fig. 7 and pp. 126–27). But Jeremy initially found that kind of esteem could be elusive back home, especially among his own generation. After this experience, Gal Frey would say to me, "He's not honored at home in Maine for being sober, let alone for being an artist." By that fall, two of Jeremy's young male peers from his small tribal community of around five hundred would die of drug overdoses.

Although Jeremy has benefited from exposure and friendships with other Indigenous artists at the national level, he's quick to point out that he's always been influenced by his own drive to make his work stand out and be distinguished from that of other artists. His integrity in being true to his own values, ambition, and inquisitiveness play key roles in his artistic process and career.

The Indian Market Artist

In 2009, Jeremy's first year at the storied Santa Fe Indian Market, he was frustrated that he couldn't enter the juried competition because he was in a nonprofit booth and not juried in. The MIBA had been invited by the Southwestern Association for Indian Arts (SWAIA) to introduce our basket makers to the market, the largest juried Indian art show in the world. We sent three generations of basket makers to the show. Prior to this, Jeremy had been gaining attention in the local markets in Maine, sponsored and cohosted by the MIBA. The goal of the Santa Fe Indian Market booth was to encourage basket makers to enter a national stage and later become juried in for their own booths, so they could enter the competition, but Jeremy skipped the market the next year. Then, when he did go to the show on his own in 2011, he entered the competition—and won the ten-thousand-dollar top prize of the entire Santa Fe Indian Market. His winning basket sold for an astounding fifteen thousand dollars, the highest price ever commanded for a Maine Indian basket at the time. To understand this accomplishment in the Native American art world, a few facts should be pointed out. This was the first basket to win Best of Show in the ninety-year history of the Santa Fe Indian Market. Jeremy's basket was chosen from more than one thousand other entries of all kinds of artwork. What's more, he had also won Best of Show earlier that same year among seven hundred artists at the fifty-third annual Heard Museum Guild Indian Fair and Market in Phoenix—the second-largest juried Indian art market. Only one other person in more than five decades had won the top prize in both shows in the same year (fig. 8).

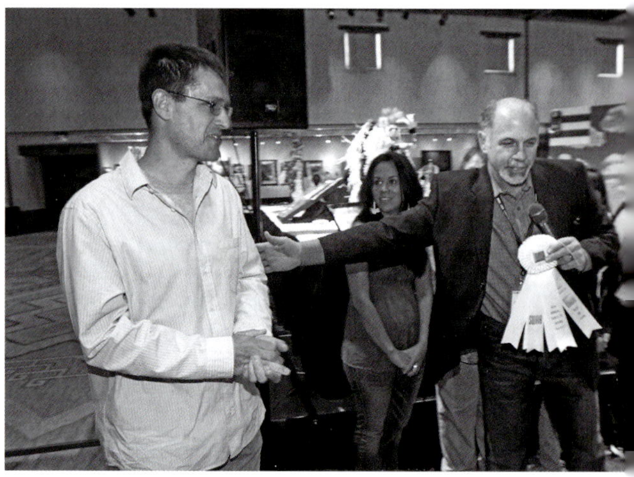

Fig 8 "Jeremy Frey Winning SWAIA Ribbon," *The Santa Fe New Mexican*, August 20, 2011. Presented by Bruce Bernstein, SWAIA Director

As his stature rose in the Indian markets and his work became even more technical and innovative, Jeremy won his second Best of Show at the Heard Museum Guild Indian Fair and Market in 2015, for his *Loon* basket (pp. 68–69). Now he

4. Debra Utacia Krol, "Basketmaker Jeremy Frey: All He Does Is Win," *ICT News*, October 7, 2011, https://ictnews.org/archive/basketmaker-jeremy-frey-all-he-does-is-win. See also "Jeremy Frey Wins Second Best of Show Award at 2015 Indian Fair," Heard Museum, March 6, 2015, https://heard.org/news/jeremy-frey-wins-second-best-of-show-award-at-2015-indian-fair/.

was incorporating great skill in porcupine quill imagery, which he wove in birch bark on the tops of his baskets, combining two ancient cultural expressions. Since then, he has won a number of Best of Basketry classification awards in both markets.

At these two-day art markets, there are thousands of collectors in attendance and much interaction between artists. I believe this interaction influenced Jeremy's development as an artist and how he saw his place in the greater Native art world. He met other young contemporary Indigenous artists, including Pat Pruitt (Laguna Pueblo, born 1973), Jamie Okuma (Luiseño/Shoshone-Bannock, born 1977), and Ken Williams Jr. (Northern Arapaho/Seneca, born 1983), to name a few. These other Best of Show artists were also making and selling art at the highest levels. Prior to Jeremy's entry into the Indian art market world, there wasn't access to other successful young Indigenous artists and mentors in our region. Many of the artists in Santa Fe had been to school at the famed Institute of American Indian Arts (IAIA), an artistic education and network that wasn't as accessible to young Wabanaki artists in Maine. Many contemporary non-Native artist peers went to art schools to earn BFAs and MFAs, again not as accessible. I believe Jeremy's nontraditional path to the contemporary art world makes his success all the more laudable.

Support for a Career and Lifting the Canoe That Carries Us All

By the time Jeremy earned his associate's degree in automotive technology and general technology at Washington County Community College in 2010, the gallery manager at the Wabanaki Arts Center (Jennifer Sapiel Neptune, Penobscot) was making a conscious effort to buy and sell all his baskets. Concurrently, I sought opportunities for his professional development as an artist and nominated him for a 2010 United States Artists Fellowship. When he won, Jeremy became the youngest artist at the time (at the age of thirty-two) to win the fifty-thousand-dollar national award for artistic excellence. Now he and others could see himself and his art in the landscape of other nationally recognized artists who were non-Indigenous.

Jeremy and other basket makers who had been participating in the larger national Indian markets were now drawing collectors to the Maine art markets and shows. His visibility and success were lifting us all up and enabling me to fundraise for the mentoring programs and nonprofit work at the MIBA. At this time, in addition to the workshops and apprenticeships, we were selling the baskets and other art of approximately one hundred Wabanaki artists in the Old Town gallery. For example, Jeremy once represented our organization and the next generation of basket makers in the boardroom of the Ford Foundation in New York. There he spoke about how the MIBA had helped foster his art and career and shared how we were succeeding in our mission. The Ford Foundation, among a number of other local, regional, and federal sources, had been providing important operational funding over the years to support our efforts to save our own basketry.

The MIBA was receiving support from other foundations, organizations, and agencies, including two decades of funding for traditional arts apprenticeships by the National Endowment for the Arts (NEA). Over several years, the NEA would also recognize Wabanaki basket makers with the National Heritage Fellowship, the nation's highest honor in the traditional arts, including Passamaquoddy basket makers Clara Neptune Keezer (1930–2016; Passamaquoddy), Molly Neptune Parker (1939–2020), and later me, a Penobscot.

In 2012, Jeremy received funding support from the First Peoples Fund as an Artist in Business Leadership Fellow. He was selected to receive this grant by and among Indigenous artist peers and has since said that this was among the most meaningful instances of support he has received. The funds and affirmation came at a very important point in his career when he needed to purchase power tools, other equipment, and additional materials necessary to make his own increasingly complex wooden forms to take his art to a new level.

In addition to this recognition and that of other younger basket makers, Jeremy became a success story that the tradition and the organization needed as new life was breathed into this ancient art form and paved the way for the next generation. Jeremy began to take the art form in an entirely new direction and to a higher technical plane, from as early as 2003, the ten-year mark of the MIBA's efforts to bring forward young basket makers. Others of his generation followed his lead and started innovating through their own lenses. This seemed to validate all the hard work of the basket makers of the first decade. Jeremy's success in the second decade of the MIBA helped substantiate and bring support for all as the intergenerational basket makers continued our work together. His awards and innovation indirectly brought us all success, raising our collective canoe.

5. Quoted in Bob Keyes, "Portland Museum of Art Turns to New Participants for Biennial Exhibit," *Portland Press Herald*, April 23, 2015, https://www.pressherald.com/2015/04/23/portland-museum-of-art-announces-artists-for-biennial-exhibit/?auth0Authentication=true. See also Bob Keyes, "In 2015 Biennial, Wabanaki Artists Take Their Place at the Museum," *Portland Press Herald*, October 4, 2015, https://www.pressherald.com/2015/10/04/in-2015-biennial-wabanaki-artists-take-their-place-at-the-museum/.

The Art Exhibition Artist and Wabanaki Basketry as Fine Art

Jeremy's first art exhibition in Maine was *Transcending Traditions* at the University of Maine's Hudson Museum in 2011, which featured five next-generation MIBA basket makers. His baskets and those of three other Wabanaki basket makers, including me, were displayed in the Biennial at the Portland Museum of Art (PMA) in 2015. This inclusion, however, was somewhat controversial as the artists and their baskets were selected rather than juried in. The curator, Alison Ferris, said she included these artists because "their work is exquisite." She further explained, "Artists from the Wabanaki tribes were the first artists in Maine, and the fact that art forms from these traditions are still being practiced thousands of years later is remarkable."[5]

MIBA basket makers were garnering the top prizes in the national Native art markets, selling at what would seem like astonishingly high prices to even our recent ancestors. Jeremy was pushing the envelope of design and creativity, winning awards and setting new standards with his pricing. The 2015 PMA Biennial marked the first time our baskets were shown in a fine art museum exhibition. The baskets that the PMA purchased were among the first major acquisitions of Wabanaki baskets, at full retail price, by any museum. By then, our basket makers had become well-known in the national Native art markets and collectors' circles, yet until the Biennial we were known in Maine only to a smaller group of interested basket collectors. For years, we had been drawing western collectors of Native art and other basket collectors to attend MIBA art markets and visit the Wabanaki Arts Center Gallery in Maine.

The Colby College Museum of Art exhibition *Wíwənikan . . . the beauty we carry*, in 2019–20, was based in a Wabanaki values system,

Fig 9 Making *Color in Winter*, 2019

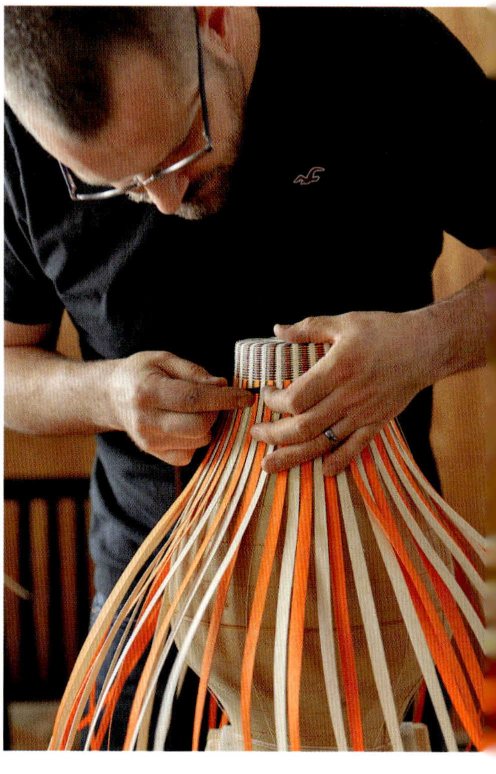

in which community goals, such as language use and revival, climate change, TEK, and a Wabanaki worldview, were highlighted in addition to the art. This was the first time Wabanaki art was shown in a fine art museum as a stand-alone exhibition. It featured the work of twenty-three Wabanaki artists and was co-curated by Jennifer Sapiel Neptune and Kathleen Mundell, with Native advisers from each of the Wabanaki communities. Jeremy's basket *Color in Winter* was a major commission for the exhibition (fig. 9 and pp. 78–79). In 2019, he received the Colby College Museum of Art's prestigious Cummings Award for Artistic Excellence.

Personal Reflections and Friendship

Jeremy is one of the hardest-working artists I know. To me, as a basket maker with thirty-five years of experience, Jeremy's weaving seems perfect, demonstrating the highest level of skill, technical difficulty, and precision. The symmetry in his completed baskets and the optical illusions created in the pieces are unsurpassed (fig. 10).

I have known many basket makers and visited hundreds of ancestors' baskets in museum collections. According to the Maliseet basket maker and MIBA founder Fred Tomah (1951–2018), "Only the creator makes perfect baskets." With that in mind, Fred always wove a small intentional mistake into his baskets. While this concept is noted among belief systems in a number of tribes, Jeremy's work seems to transcend that.

One of my favorite baskets by Jeremy is *Porcupine Urchin* (c. 2012), an urchin shape with a quilled porcupine on the birch-bark top, which he sold in one of his early Indian market appearances. This basket embodies tradition with the historical sea urchin shape, as the Passamaquoddy people live beside the sea, and the innovation with the porcupine or point weave in black and white. It is a touchstone both of the past and of the future. The porcupine image—made with actual porcupine quills—together with the porcupine weave in the same piece is symbolic. I also admire the more recent basket *Malsom*, because he used his own Passamaquoddy language for its title; he won Best of Basketry at the Santa Fe Indian Market in 2021 with this piece (pp. 82–83). Like other Indigenous artists, his work reflects his own value system and that of his community, as his tribe works against the clock to save the oldest spoken language in Maine.

Jeremy and I have been friends since the day we met. Soon after, I began to assume the role of an "artist professional development" mentor as he looked to me, as the MIBA director, to help further his reach with his art career. I was also working part-time for the First Peoples Fund then, holding workshops nationwide to train emerging artists in professional development. I had a national perspective through my own Indigenous artists and weavers circle and my own participation in the Indian markets. I knew Jeremy's work was remarkable and could see avenues where he and other basket makers in the MIBA could gain exposure.

The first step had been to launch the young artists into the juried Native art markets in the West. This is where collectors "discovered us," before museums and galleries did. We plugged into the large art markets where art collectors have been purchasing western Native American art for more than a century.

I have characterized our trajectory as Wabanaki basket makers finding a place in the art world and market as, first, "Indian Market artists." Until very recently, our baskets were excluded from museum exhibitions and our artists were not represented by galleries. This is new territory for our art and artists, having been left out of museum collections, even in New England, for hundreds of years. I often share my observation that Wabanaki basket makers could not donate a basket to a fine art museum in Maine or elsewhere in New England even ten years ago or be taken

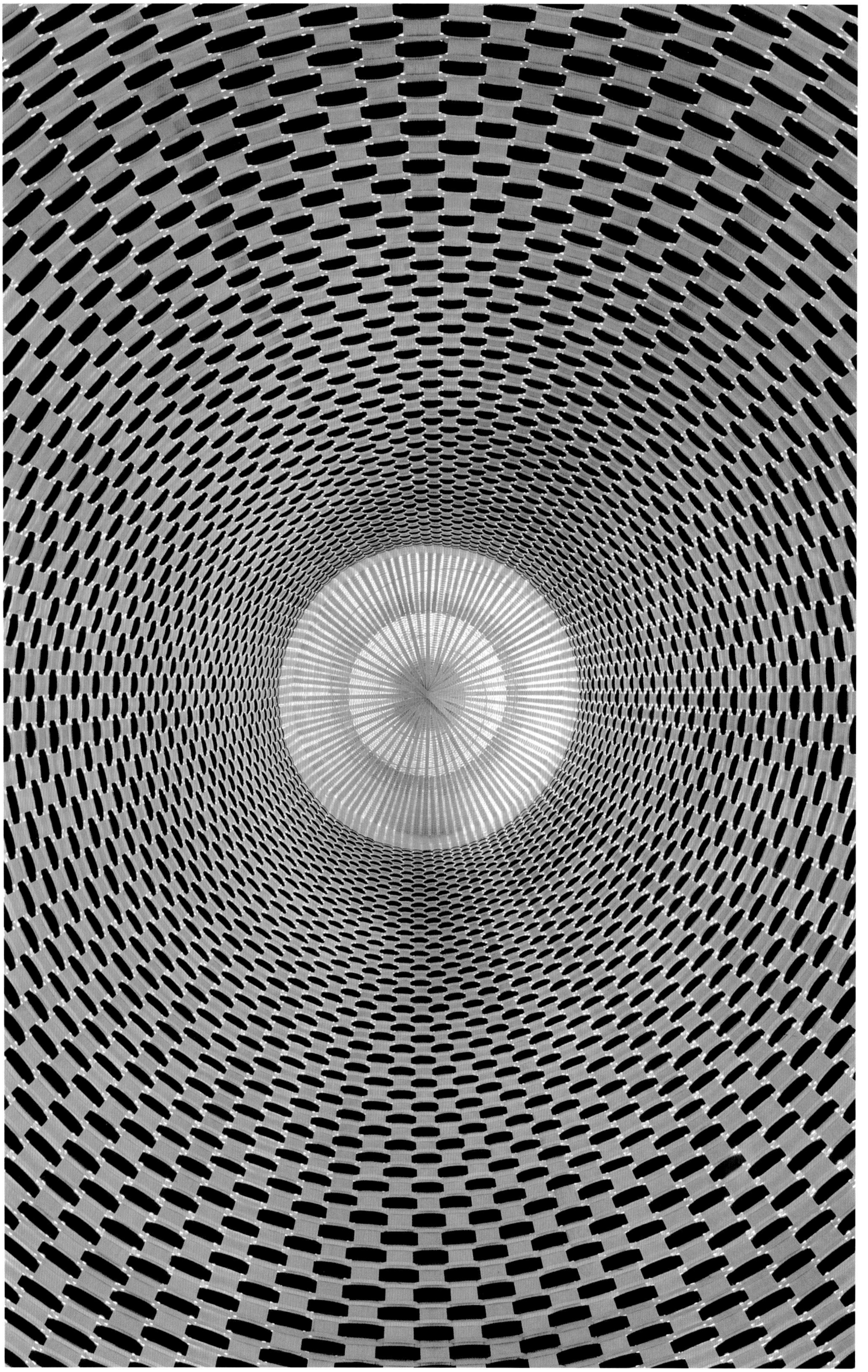

20

seriously when the MIBA first suggested art exhibitions at that time—except at the ethnographic museums such as the Hudson Museum in Orono and Abbe Museum in Bar Harbor. Now artists are being commissioned by fine art museums to weave baskets for permanent collections and hired as curators and advisers on art exhibitions. Basket makers are serving on fine art museum boards and employed as artists in residence and fellows.

As with his art itself, Jeremy is a trailblazer, with many firsts beyond the art show awards in his professional career. He is the first Wabanaki artist to have a solo exhibition in a fine art museum in the United States, organized by the Portland Museum of Art to take place in 2024 and commemorated in this publication. He is the first Wabanaki basket maker to be represented by a gallery in Santa Fe, the mecca of Native American art: King Galleries in 2019. These were among his own recent professional goals. Now he's represented by Karma gallery in New York, which sold one of his pieces at Art Basel in Miami in 2022 and featured a solo show of his work in April–June 2023, the first solo show of a Wabanaki artist in an art gallery anywhere.

Personally, I've been inspired by Jeremy's sense of design and execution as well as his focus and work ethic. His courage to experiment is unique. Being a risk-taker in the art markets can be very costly if the judges and collectors don't understand the vision and the work. As an Indian market artist myself, I understand that showing up at an art market with inventory that may not sell, when that is your primary income source, is very risky. It's far safer to weave baskets that we know will sell. At the same time, Jeremy still works in, and respects, a very specific Wabanaki art values system and process finding balance and harmony. I also believe we all became better basket makers as Jeremy set new weaving standards. For example, my own work became finer, as I've challenged myself and refined my artistry.

Jeremy's path, as I have described, is unique among contemporary artists in his age group, who may have had access to art schools and mentors that are beyond the reach of most young people from an Indian reservation in Maine. This makes his success all the more remarkable. Artists with BFAs and MFAs seem to have direct channels into museums and an art scene and market with many opportunities through their and their professors' university connections and credentials.

My son, Caleb Hoffman, represents a still younger generation of Wabanaki basket makers. He has admired Jeremy for years, growing up being mentored by me and attending many MIBA events. As noted, Jeremy has recently engaged Caleb as an apprentice and studio helper. He is also learning to harvest and prepare the ash so he can help provide materials for me, an elder; a process and exchange that is steeped in ancestral tradition. Although Jeremy and his work now travel in the contemporary art circles of the East Village in New York, in Santa Fe, or at Art Basel in Miami, he retains his deep tribal roots and an associated sense of cultural responsibilities.

Jeremy has made wooden forms for my own basketry, including scaled-down models of my great-grandmother's antique wooden barrel form. We have a reciprocal friendship in which he now advises me on different aspects of the art, the market, and the field (fig. 11). In a recent conversation, I realized he is not pleased with his art or thriving unless he's mentally and creatively challenging himself. I believe the ancestors are proud, as I know his family and his tribe are. So am I, as Jeremy continues to redefine what it means to be a Wabanaki basket maker.

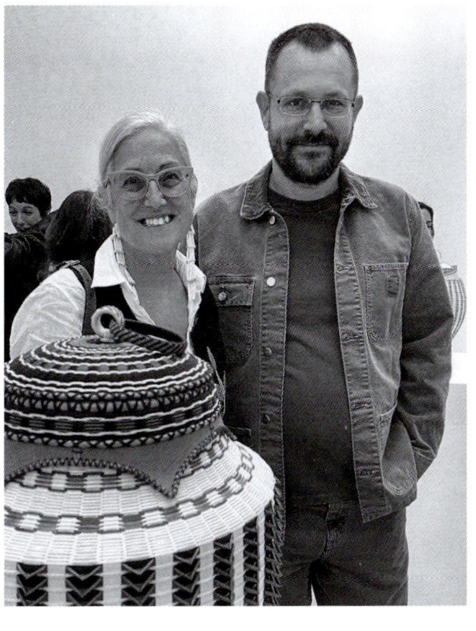

Fig 10 (opposite) *Loon* (interior detail), 2020, ash, cedar bark, porcupine quill on birchbark, and dye, 36 × 23 × 23 inches. Collection of Catherine Stiefel, California (pp. 80–81)
Fig 11 Theresa Secord and Jeremy Frey at the opening of *Jeremy Frey: Out of the Woods* at Karma gallery, 2023

Weaving Wood

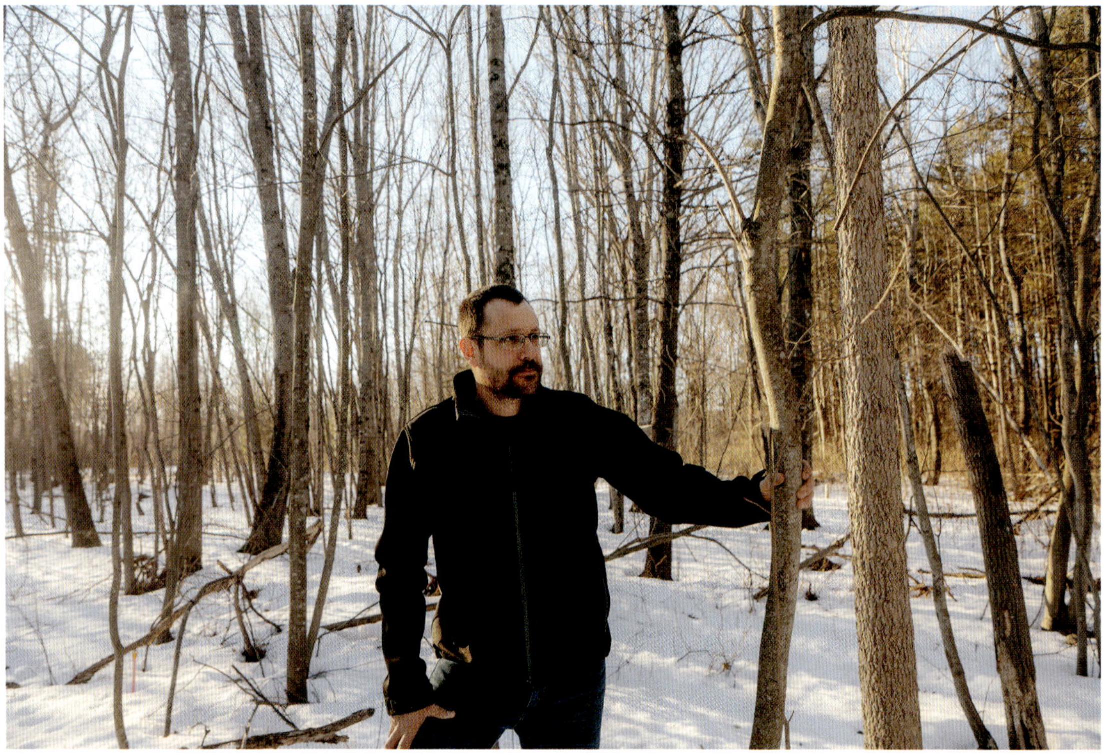

Andrew James Hamilton

Jeremy Frey's baskets are objects of exceptional beauty. Their curved shapes, vivid colors, striking patterns, and densely textured surfaces are rich feasts for the eyes. But Frey is so deft in his art—so precise in his preparation and handling of materials—that it can be challenging to understand just what he has accomplished. Remember, his baskets are made of wood. They were once heavy tree trunks, covered in moss, scampered over by squirrels, and exposed to rain and snow. Like a magician or alchemist, Frey transforms these rigid logs into intricate woven forms. But in spite of their being made of countless strips of wood, each with two ends, none of the ends are actually visible, and how they come together structurally may not be apparent. And while his baskets possess some qualities of textiles, they have the dimensionality and presence of sculptures. Ultimately, their ornate exteriors make it easy to forget that, as baskets, they are hollow. Frey's art is as much driven by structuring surfaces as creating concavities.

Opposite Jeremy Frey in an ash stand, 2023

But what really makes Frey's artistic practice so complex to decipher is that he is a relentless innovator. Every basket he weaves is a reaction to one that came before: a next step, an alternate approach, or a doubling down. What this means for a viewer is that just when you might have figured out how he made some aspect of one basket, you have to start all over again with the next. When I asked him, Frey indicated that technical innovations are his favorite part of basketmaking, but it is also important to understand how critical they are to his identity as an artist.[1]

In his view, there are certain techniques of Passamaquoddy baskets that all Passamaquoddy artists may employ. They are part of a shared artistic tradition. But for Frey to make his baskets his own, he feels he has to innovate not only beyond these common traits but also within them. Frey is careful not to use the inventions of other Passamaquoddy weavers or of anyone from other Native communities; these are their intellectual property. By the same token, he is keen to guard his own discoveries, which he deploys but hides among the array of shared techniques he was taught by his relatives. In so doing, Frey is continually redefining what a Passamaquoddy basket can be in countless subtle ways—precisely what makes his work so significant.

Frey's art begins in the forest (opposite). Walking between the trees, he gives the impression that he is already seeing baskets in them. Frey weaves the wood of a particular species of ash tree. Throughout much of the United States, it is called black ash; within Maine, however, it is referred to as brown ash.[2] Like generations of basket makers before him, Frey "hunts" for trees in the woods as one might hunt for moose or deer. He studies the trees' habitats, which affect the quality of the wood. And from a remarkable distance, Frey can differentiate a brown ash tree from, say, a white ash (the former's bark is softer and corkier, he explains, while the latter's bark has deeper furrows and is lighter in color). What is more, his trained eye, with traditional ecological knowledge (TEK) that has been handed down from many generations, has almost X-ray vision, anticipating the grain of the wood inside the trunk. He recognizes that a slight deviation within the bark signals a crookedness in the underlying fibers. He spots a small knot and knows that the wood skirts it like a river flowing around a rock. Such traits make areas of a tree unusable for his baskets. Frey looks for long, straight trunks that can yield long, smooth strips of wood for weaving—and very few trees meet his exacting criteria. What's more, there is only a limited supply of healthy ash trees to begin with, as the emerald ash borer has already reached Maine and now threatens the entire resource.

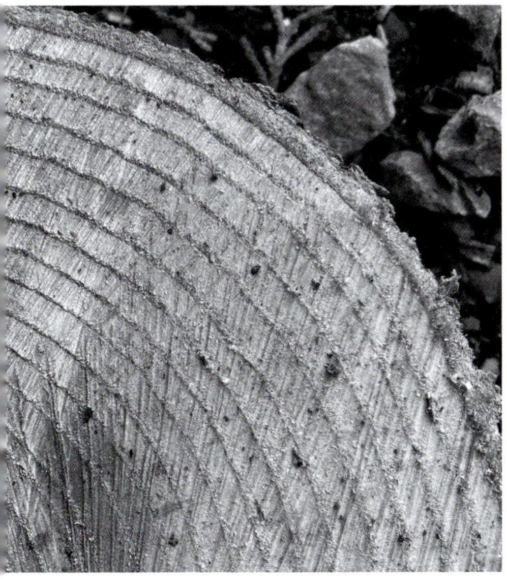

Fig 1 The thin spring and thick summer growth rings of an ash tree, 2022

1. Jeremy Frey in discussion with the author, December 15, 2022.
2. See the entry for *brown ash* in the glossary on page 172.

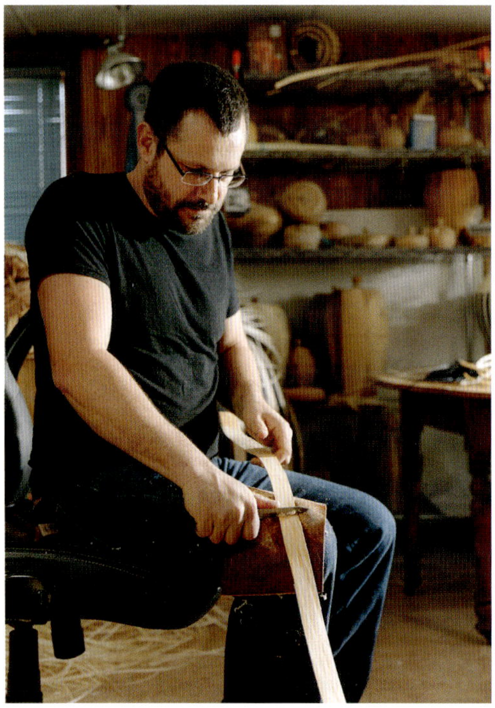

Fig 2 Frey scraping ash, 2023

What makes brown ash so advantageous for basket-making is the structure of its growth rings (fig. 1). The lumber is referred to as ring-porous; that is, the wood that the tree grows in spring has more vascular tissue, so it is spongier than the thicker and denser summer rings. Once Frey has felled a tree and removed its bark, he pounds the log with the butt of an axe; this causes the spring wood to collapse, and the summer wood separates and breaks into segments. The tree's gift is its propensity to yield these strips of wood fiber.

Still, the full depth of a ring is too thick for Frey to weave. To address this, he soaks the splints in water until they are supple. Then he inserts an end of a splint into a device called a splitter and begins to peel it in half. So much of the knowledge of this process rests in his hands. As the long fibers separate, Frey must skillfully control how much force he applies with each hand, depending on how the wood resists, to ensure it splits evenly. Splitting also introduces a new texture to the wood: while the exterior sides of the growth ring are fuzzy, the split sides are smooth. After he divides a splint in half, he may split it again into quarters, even eighths, depending on the size of the basket he is making and what he is using the wood for. Even once he gets the splint to what looks to his eyes like the right thickness, he has to use his fingertips to search for subtle irregularities—and then carefully pare them down with a knife (fig. 2).

In addition to thinning the splints, Frey must shape their widths. He uses gauge cutters with evenly spaced blades that he hand-forms out of tempered steel from old clock springs—a technology that is some two hundred years old (fig. 3).[3] These tools allow him to cut regular strips as wide as five-eighths of an inch or down to a mere one-thirty-second of an inch in width. The scale of the strips plays a key role in the aesthetic of his work. Frey excels at making baskets with very small, tight weaves (pp. 64–65).

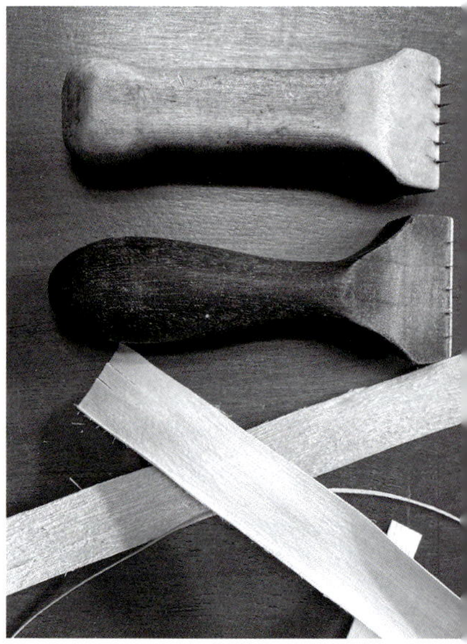

Fig 3 Frey's gauges for cutting ash, 2022

However, not all the splints he uses have the parallel sides that these tools cut. The foundational components of his baskets are called standards—at least, this is the word Frey was taught by his mother, Gal. As he acknowledges, it is possible that the original term was "standers," because they are the splints that stand up, forming an armature for the basket during weaving.[4] (These forms are akin to the warp in cloth.) Frey must carefully hand-cut the standards so that their widths swell at what will become the widest point of the basket, while tapering toward its mouth and bottom. He calculates the correct placements and degree of the tapers and cuts them with incredible precision and consistency, so that gaps do not form between adjacent standards when he weaves. Because Frey's standards are only five-eighths of an inch at their widest point, this allows him to create the fine, dense weaves he is known for.

When ash has just been split, it is pale and luminous. Over time, the wood oxidizes, turning darker. Frey never loses sight of this raw material in his work—its natural state and even scent carry deep cultural meanings.[5] Indeed, he has woven numerous baskets entirely with natural, undyed ash (pp. 54–57). But what further distinguishes Frey's artistic practice is his use of color. After he has cut the strips for a basket, he often uses Rit dyes to pigment them. Although he loves weaving with bold, bright colors—especially turquoise (pp. 84–85, 144–45)—he deploys these vibrant hues with great nuance.[6] Rarely does he create a basket entirely from dyed wood. His baskets

3. Theresa Secord, personal communication to the author, April 7, 2023.
4. Ibid. See the entry for *standard* in the glossary on p. 173.
5. Secord, personal communication, April 7, 2023.
6. Ibid.
7. Ibid.

incorporate significant quantities of undyed ash, which impart visual clarity to his weaves, while anchoring the lightest end of his color spectrum. This is key to his aesthetic. Because of the ways Passamaquoddy baskets are traditionally woven, Frey can add colors in vertical stripes, horizontal bands, and checkerboard patterns, as well as endless combinations therein; but it is also how he adds and combines colors that make his creations so recognizably his.

In his work, Frey continually explores different ways of layering colors. Sometimes he will weave the same color over itself (pp. 70–71, 152–55). This can create shadows that impart greater depth and intensity. When the color is dark, these portions of the basket may visually recede, allowing other features to become focal points. In contrast, when he weaves a light color over itself, the resulting visual effect often showcases the basket's woven structure (pp. 98–99). Frequently, however, Frey chooses to weave one color against another color or against undyed wood. When he works narrow strips of wood in this way, the colors take on a kind of gradient, creating a glittering mélange halfway between the two tones (pp. 78–79, 82–83). When he juxtaposes different colors using wider strips of wood, especially in close shades such as purple and wine, the basket almost becomes iridescent, like shot silk. But what is key to realize is that although Frey commits to many of the colors of his baskets from the moment he begins weaving them, their ultimate chromatic effect may not be fully visible until much later in the process of making each basket (pp. 118–19, 158–59). In his mind's eye, Frey has to anticipate how colors will react to each other and how they will be affected by his woven structures, as informed by his wealth of experience.

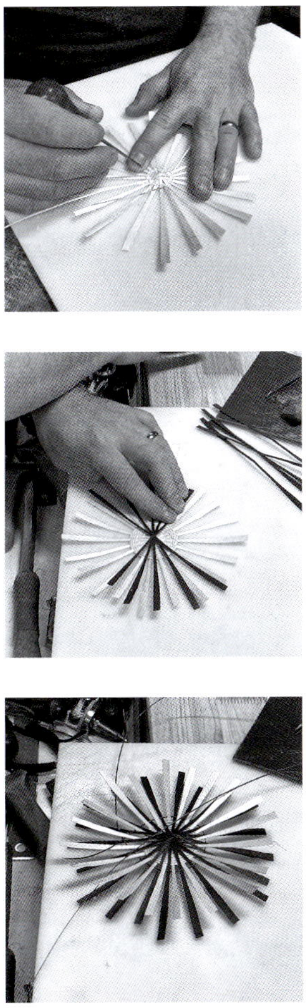

Figs 4a–c Frey starts a basket by adding the standards, 2022

Frey begins weaving by arraying the meticulously cut, tapered standards like spokes in a wheel (fig. 4a). Because he is right-handed, he lays them down in a clockwise direction. This becomes the bottom of the basket; indeed, all his baskets are woven from the bottom up. (Similarly, the lids are woven from the center to the rim.) To lock the spokes in place, he takes a filament of wood, called a weaver, and works it over and under the standards. The weaver must be wet, so that it is as flexible as possible. But as the standards radiate outward, they become too broadly spaced; so, as is traditional in this art form, Frey must introduce a second set of standards, layered on top of the first, each one filling gaps within the original cohort (fig. 4b). He bonds the two sets of standards together with another weaver as he had the first (fig. 4c). When this second set of standards is a different color, it can produce the vertical stripes characteristic of so many of Frey's creations (pp. 110–11, 152–55). In these instances, the weaver he introduces to bind the two sets of standards usually matches the second color, to create visual unity, and so that the new color does not seem to manifest from thin air. Depending on the size of the basket he is making, Frey could even add a third set of standards as the bottom grows in diameter—which is his entirely new innovation.[7]

As he binds the bottom of a basket together, a subtle trait develops that helps explain his art: from the outside, it may just look as if his baskets are composed of concentric circles or horizontal rows; in actuality, the wood is continually spiraling outward and upward. The place where one row stops and the next one begins, though invisible on the outside, is evident on the inside. Because of the even number of standards, Frey must skip over two in order to maintain the over-and-under weave. As a result, a long, slow spiral develops

Fig 5 The interior of a basket lid, 2022

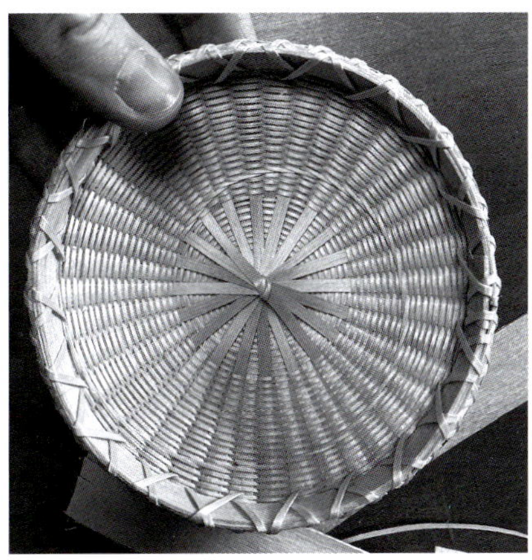

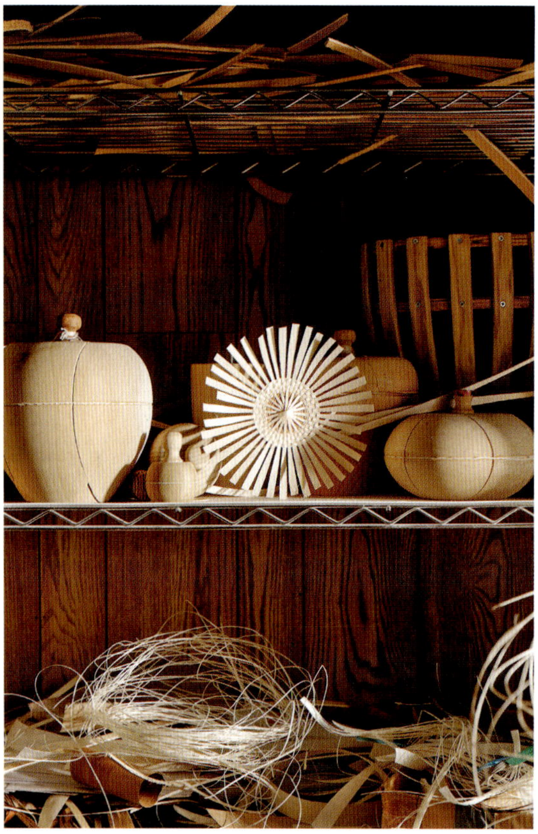

Fig 6 Basket molds, 2023

throughout the basket's interior that charts Frey's progress—as the inside of a lid makes visible (fig. 5). This contrast between interior and exterior is something Frey has explicitly explored in his art. Since around 2010, Frey has woven double-walled baskets that hide an entirely different woven structure inside them (pp. 160–61). These are his own invention and, according to Theresa Secord, were not previously seen in the two-hundred-year historical record of Wabanaki baskets in museum collections.[8]

Bound together, these many wooden standards become the basket's ribs; Frey's next feat is to give them dimension. To do so, he weaves his baskets over forms that are also made of wood. Frey possesses a huge collection of molds—all of which he has shaped and crafted by hand (fig. 6). For smaller creations, he carves the molds from poplar wood. He laminates planks together and uses a lathe to turn their graceful shapes. But in order for him to be able to remove the mold from inside a basket after he has woven its narrower neck, the mold cannot be solid. To navigate this step in the process, Frey creates puzzle molds, as his ancestors did, that are subdivided into several parts, each small enough to be extracted through the basket's mouth in a particular sequence (fig. 7). These molds allow him to produce the elegant forms that typify his work, yet they are also based in tradition. His low and round baskets—an established Passamaquoddy form—are called urchin baskets because they resemble the sea urchins long harvested by Passamaquoddy people along Maine's coast. For large baskets, however, such molds would be too cumbersome and heavy, and they would crush the woven bottoms. Thus, for his biggest pieces, Frey creates hollow rib molds—what essentially look like wooden barrels—that he weaves the baskets over. To date, Frey has created only four monumental baskets, including ones in the collections of the Denver Art Museum and the Art Institute of Chicago (pp. 84–85, 152–55). When his baskets are this large, Frey actually weaves them with the mold turned upside down because the long and heavy standards no longer stand on their own. This orientation allows the standards to hang with gravity (fig. 8). Because hollow rib molds still must be removed from the basket and cannot be disassembled, they can only guide the shape of the basket up to its widest point; Frey must shape the remainder of the basket freehand.

To begin weaving the sides, Frey wets the standards so they become pliable and then brings them up over the mold. He usually starts the sides with fine, undyed weavers, or perhaps a very simple color pattern, in order to create a margin that will visually frame the much more elaborate colors, complex patterns, and dynamic textures of the body of the basket. This subtle detail gives his compositions breathing room. As he begins to introduce his designs, he may work with only one weaver; however, in other instances, he may weave two simultaneously, what is called chase weaving, because one piece of wood chases the other.[9] These decisions lay the groundwork for the many forms of ornament that make his baskets "fancy."[10] But it is important to recognize that he

Fig 7 A seven-part basket mold, 2022
Fig 8 (opposite) Upside-down basket on mold, 2023

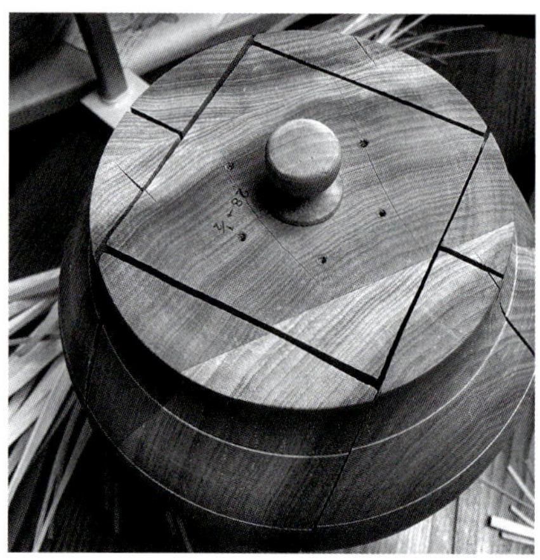

8. Ibid.
9. See the entry for *chase weaving* in the glossary on p. 172.
10. See the entry for *fancy basket* in the glossary on page 172.

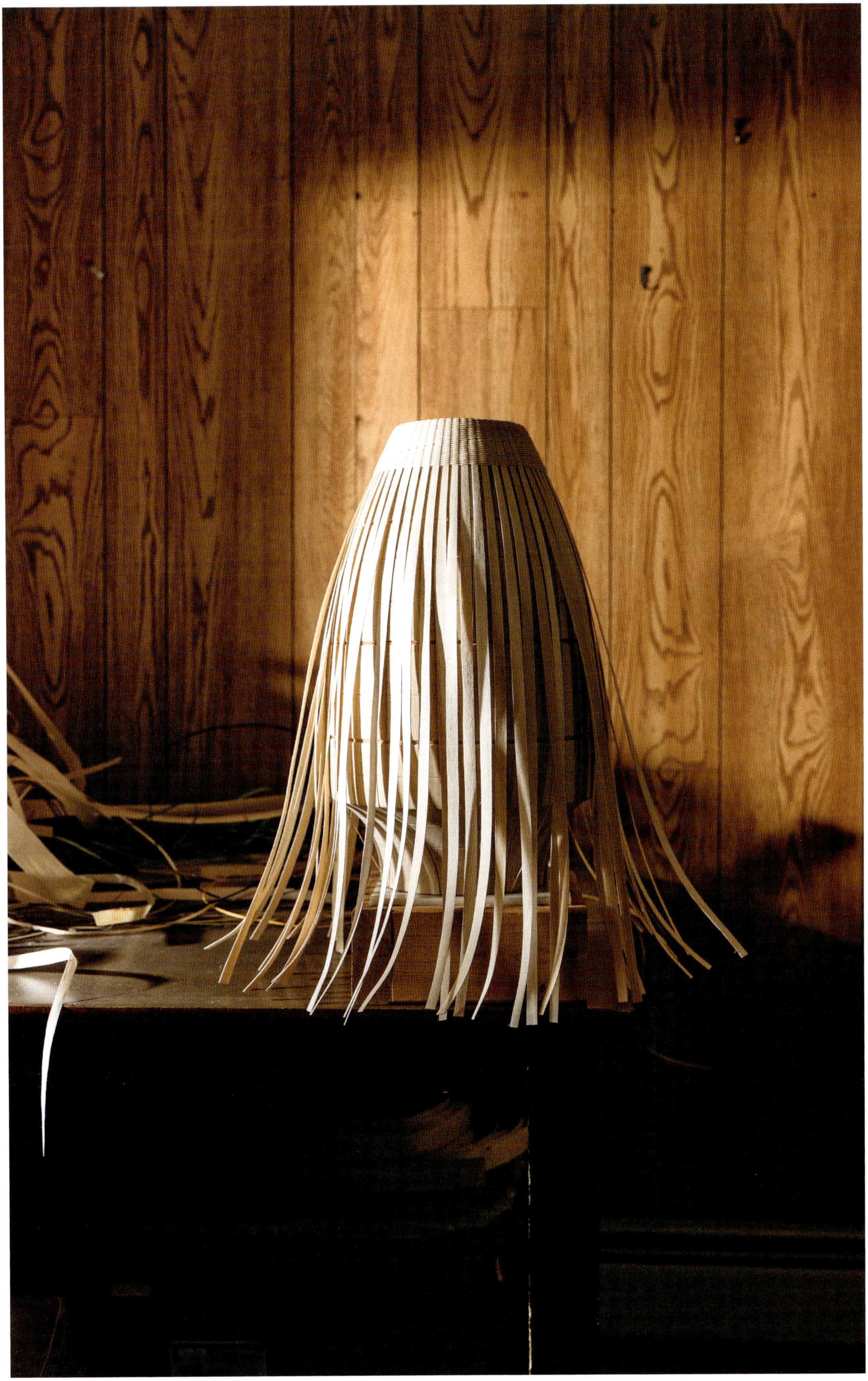

does not create the whole of the sides all at once or finish them during this stage. At this moment, he often weaves only a surface that, once the rest of the basket's form is complete, he subsequently embellishes with additional weavers and weaves. One of the most important considerations, at this point, is compacting the weave. Because the sides are the largest expanse of a basket, even minute spaces between the weavers would add up and result in a basket that is too loose and uneven. The seasons also play a role in Frey's quest for tight, hard weaves. When he makes a basket in the summer, the air is more humid, and his wood is more hydrated. During the winter, it is slightly desiccated, which means that when it later absorbs moisture, it expands, and the weave becomes even denser.

As Frey reaches the top of the basket, he again usually weaves a margin of narrow, undyed weavers, or in some cases a very simple color pattern. Like the band at the bottom, this handling of the neck accentuates and contains the more highly ornamented sides. This detail also visually draws attention to the unique treatment of the basket's rim or collar. Here, as is typical of Passamaquoddy baskets, Frey often introduces a new material—called sweetgrass, due to its sweet smell—which also grows across Maine's tidal landscape. He employs a long ash splint, called a binding or lashing, to anchor or bind the grass in place to the rim with overcast stitches. The basket in the collection of the Art Institute of Chicago features a binding that measures some eleven feet long due to the great circumference of its rim (pp. 152-55).

Baskets typically have only one opening at the top, but the sweetgrass rim has offered Frey a site for experimentation. Since as early as 2008, he has invented ways of creating many layered rims within a single basket (pp. 124-25). These multilevel baskets subvert the tradition of standards originating at the bottom and continuing up through the sides to the rim. In such works, it is hard to know which rim Frey formed from the original standards and which ones he grafted in. Because only one of the basket's rims is needed to support the lid, Frey has further interrogated the traditional forms of basketry by shaping the additional rims into diagonals, sometimes at angles to each other (pp. 122-23, 136-37). These multilevel baskets often visually blur the division between the body and the lid. When looking at the basket, it can be unclear just how much of it will lift off when the cover is raised. Since at least 2019, Frey has also used bark panels as well as shaped weavers to create ornamented collars around the necks of his baskets—another one of his inventions (pp. 86-87).[11] Their wavy and scalloped edges also visually confuse where the opening is. Because these collars descend from the rim, they look as if they might be an overhanging part of the lid. Around the same time, Frey also expanded on the concept of shaped bark overlays by encasing the entire basket in tailored birch-bark panels (pp. 76-77).

Birch bark, as a medium, has provided Frey yet another opportunity for innovation. In numerous baskets that he has made since 2015, he has incorporated birch-bark rondelles at the center of the lid as sites for quillwork, a long-standing art form in Maine and throughout North America.[12] This tedious and difficult-to-master art form was also originally taught to him by his mother.[13] Frey takes porcupine quills, each around two or three inches long; dyes them; and uses them to embroider images onto the wood. He painstakingly varies the width of the quill, the length of the stitch, and its orientation to give shape to the image—whether describing the arrangement of feathers in the wing of a cardinal (pp. 78-79) or the direction of the fur in the face of a mountain lion (fig. 9; pp. 84-85). The keratin of the quills reflects light and allows the images to gleam.

Only once a basket is structurally complete does Frey begin to add what will become its most conspicuous qualities. The sculptural surfaces of his baskets are all created through a variety of techniques that have long featured in Passamaquoddy fancy baskets, which

Fig 9 Partially completed quillwork on the lid of *Watchful Spirit*, 2022

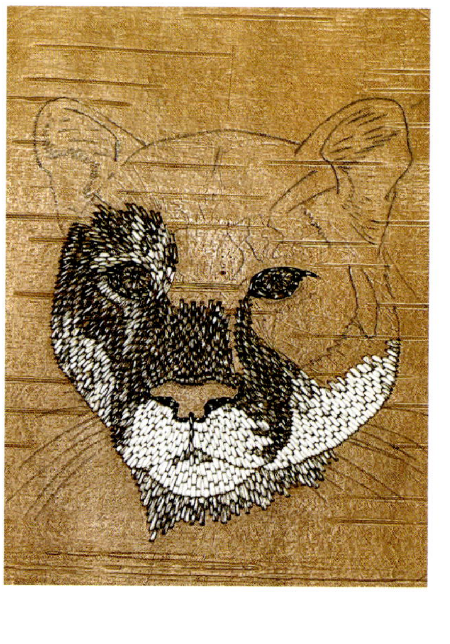

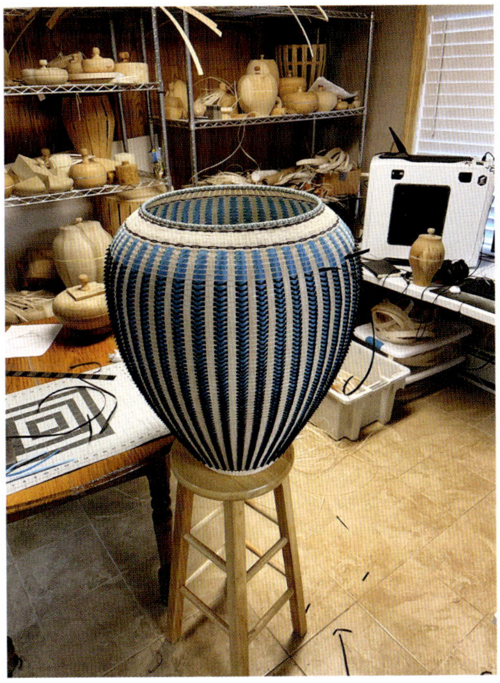

Fig 10 Making *Watchful Spirit*, 2022

Frey calls over-weaves. That is, he takes another weaver and works it back into the basket, over the original weaver, and manipulates the new one to create three-dimensional forms. Depending on how he twists the supplementary piece of wood, he can create curls or points (pp. 58-59). He prefers the latter because they are more difficult to make.[14] As he adds the over-weaves, both the texture and color of the basket wildly transform. For example, Frey wove his monumental basket in the Denver Art Museum with a smooth turquoise surface, then added black over-weaves throughout the body to create the points (fig. 10; pp. 84-85). Ultimately, the blue peeks through the spiky twists of black wood. In this basket, the points create dramatic columns, but in other baskets, the structure and spacing of the underlying weaves cause the points to be staggered in checkerboard patterns or diagonal lines (pp. 124-25). Frey also adorns his baskets with bands of Xs that are even more complex to make (pp. 128-29); as he inserts the over-weaver, he intertwines it with long braids of sweetgrass or ash. Although braided sweetgrass is a common feature of Passamaquoddy baskets, braided ash and cedar are yet another of Frey's inventions, which he has employed in his basketry since at least 2008.[15]

Some of Frey's most inventive baskets, created between 2014 and 2016, expand more dramatically on the concepts of over-weaves and overlays. In these works, Frey produces pointed ash splints of different sizes and shapes that emerge from or encase the exteriors of his baskets. In some, the effect is like an exoskeleton. A number are enclosed by ash splints interwoven at diagonals (pp. 134-35).

Finally, Frey makes the lids of his baskets in much the same way as the bodies—arraying the standards and weaving out from the center. As a result, both the interiors of the lids and baskets exhibit extraordinary radial symmetry—especially when held up to a source of light. The last thing he creates, the finishing touch, is usually the elaborately woven ring or finial that he affixes to the top of the lid. These rings were influenced by connections Frey made through the Maine Indian Basketmakers Alliance with male Hawaiian weavers, especially Mike Nahoopii, at the Smithsonian Folklife Festival in 2006.[16] Frey often weaves them with very fine chevrons or checkerboard patterns in the main colors of the basket. As he is quick to tell anyone handling his work, the ring is entirely decorative and should never be used to lift the lid. While imagining new techniques and woven forms might be Frey's favorite part of making baskets, he confesses that weaving the ring is perhaps his least favorite.[17] By this point in the process, Frey's mind is surely already eagerly plotting his next creation. Nonetheless, it is this meticulous attention to intricate details, right up to the very end, that makes Frey's baskets such satisfying and rewarding works to study and spend time with.

Basket by basket, Frey has continually expanded both his art and the potential for Passamaquoddy basketmaking. With virtuosic intensity, he has perpetually innovated new forms, techniques, and aesthetics, whether by the braiding of ash, the introduction of illustrated birch-bark panels, his juxtapositions of colors and textures, or his intricate quillwork images. Both the great joy and the challenge of writing about his art—for me as an author—are that, undoubtedly, this essay will become instantly out-of-date. Surely, as soon as Frey reads it, his creativity, ambition, and perfectionism will lead him to new ideas that will continue moving his artistic practice forward.

11. Secord, personal communication, April 7, 2023.
12. For a discussion of Native quillwork traditions, see Ruth Holmes Whitehead, *Micmac Quillwork* (Halifax, NS: Nimbus, 1991).
13. Secord, personal communication, April 7, 2023.
14. Ibid.
15. Ramey Mize, personal communication to the author, March 18, 2023.
16. Theresa Secord, personal communication, March 18, 2023.
17. Ibid.

Transforming Trees

Jeremy Frey and Materiality Beyond Expectations

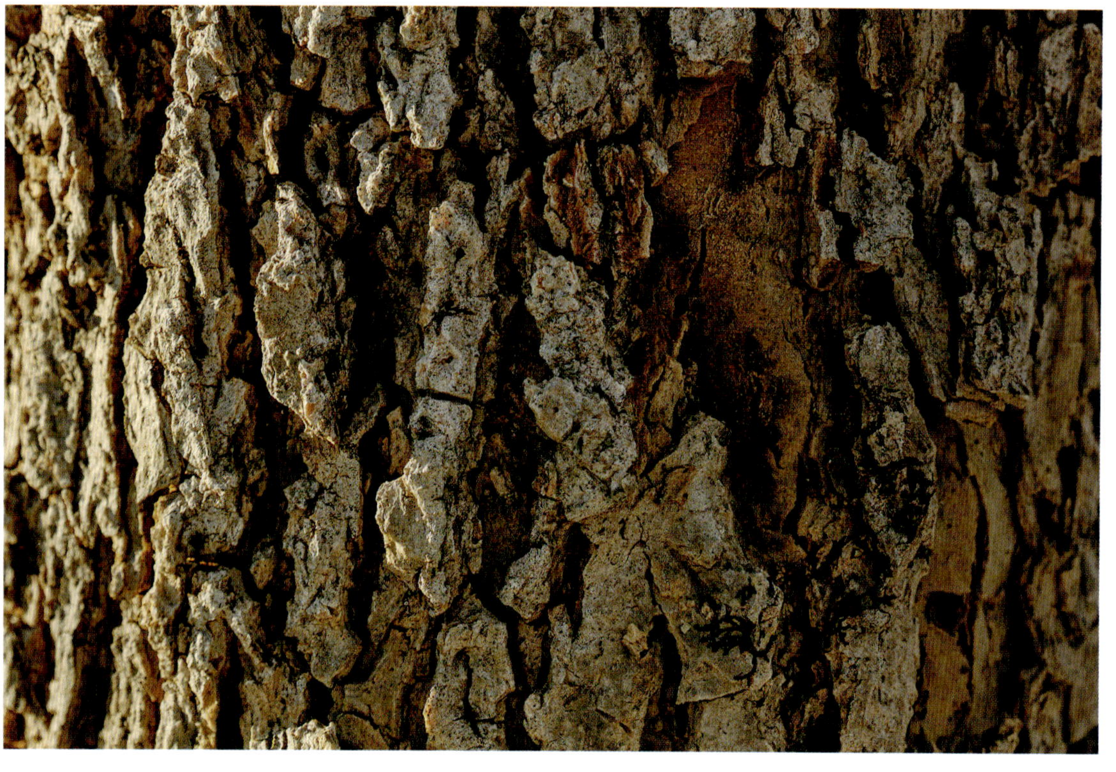

Dakota Hoska
(Oglála Lakȟóta Nation)

As I thought about this essay, that well-known dad joke kept popping into my head: "When is a door not a door? When it's ajar!" Cringeworthy, I know, but the mantra kept repeating as I wondered at the ability of artists, basket weavers, and specifically Jeremy Frey to see beyond the obvious nature of the materials they use to create artworks that seem impossible given the properties of their originating substrates. So, drawing this parallel to my dad joke, when is a tree not a tree? When it is an intricately woven basket made of finely measured ash splints in the hands of a skilled and dedicated artist like Jeremy Frey. The ability to imagine far past the immediate expectations of materiality is the marker of a great artist, and the focus of this essay (figs. 1 and 2).

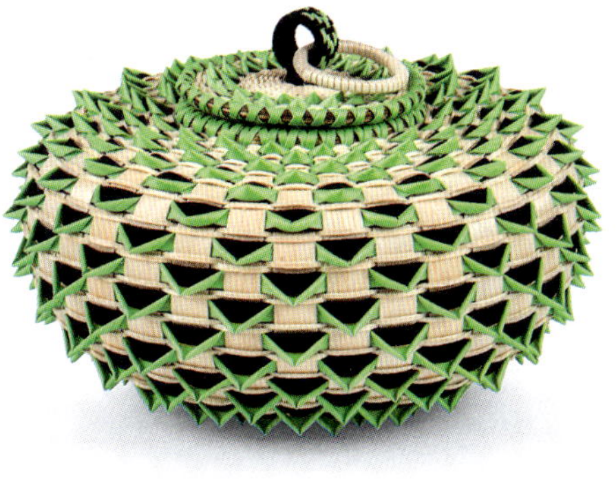

Opposite Bark of an ash tree, 2023
Fig 1 Jeremy Frey, *Green Point Urchin*, 2022, ash, sweetgrass, and dye, 4 × 6 × 6 inches. Collection of Dr. and Mrs. Ari and Lea Plosker

Frey joins a long list of Indigenous and non-Indigenous artists who can transform seemingly banal materials like trees, grass, mud, shoes, rocks, glass, baleen, and bamboo into items of incredible beauty. Artists like Frey look beyond the obvious. Through an intimate understanding of their materials, they create fine art constructions that are greater than the sum of their parts. Truman Lowe (Ho-Chunk, 1944–2019), Brian Jungen (Dane-zaa, born 1970), Don Johnston (Aleut Unangax̂, born 1962), Charles Loloma (Hopi, 1921–1991), Jeffrey Gibson (Choctaw/Cherokee, born 1972), and Christine Nofchissey McHorse (Diné, 1948–2021) are just a few examples of other artists who also come to mind when I contemplate this topic. I will examine three of them in conjunction with Jeremy Frey's work, but there are many, many others who, seemingly effortlessly, imagine a world beyond that which seems functionally possible given the properties of their chosen mediums. Each artist discussed here extends the materiality of their mediums into items that had not previously been imagined. And all remain grounded in originating work from their communities in one way or another. For Frey, that means building upon the Wabanaki basketmaking traditions, and it is this important grounding that provides the foundation for his innovative work.[1]

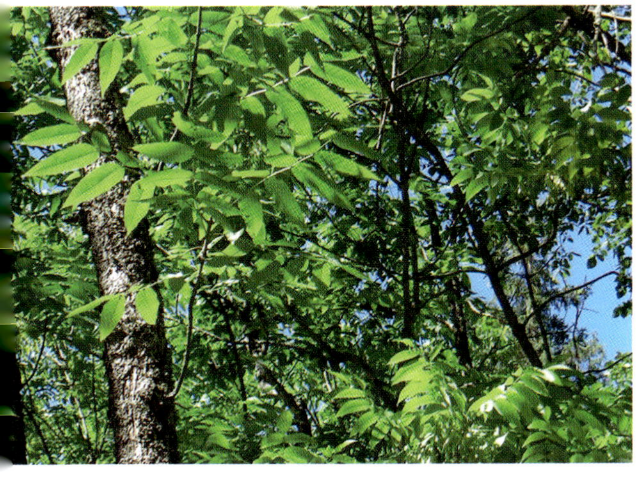

Fig 2 Black ash tree (*Fraxinus nigra*)

In some artistic circles, ideas of tradition are muttered about in ways that discredit ties to the historical or undermine the reality that all innovation stands on the shoulders of another's creation, insinuating that tradition is a barrier to innovation. A point to which I give a firm rebuttal. Helmut Federle (born 1944), a European abstractionist born in Switzerland, once stated that "one of the big problems is that art is always trying to invent something. It's this idea that the artist needs to be an inventor, or do something new. This is absolutely wrong."[2] Reflecting on Federle's statement, I applaud the way Frey and many other Native artists remain grounded by the traditional making and motifs of their communities. We also see excellent examples of this grounding in traditions found around the globe. For example, many contemporary Japanese bamboo artists spend years apprenticing under another artist, mastering the intricacies of splitting and weaving the bamboo in the signature styles of their mentors before they are considered ready to tackle their own creations. It can take another decade or even two before they feel capable of saying something original as an artist.[3] This kind of dedication to learning one's craft is akin to being a scholar or world traveler. The more you learn, the more you realize how little you know. As bamboo artist Abe Motoshi (born 1942) states about his weavings, "One can never master

1. Jeremy Frey is a member of the Passamaquoddy tribe of what is now called Maine. His people are part of a larger confederacy called the Wabanaki, and I will refer to both the Passamaquoddy and Wabanaki in this article because they have a shared history as it relates to basketmaking. For more information, see https://fourdirectionsmaine.org/about-four-directions/wabanaki-tribes/.
2. Carter Ratcliff and Paul Chaat Smith, *Kindred Spirits: Native American Influences on 20th Century Art* (New York: Peter Blum Edition, 2011), 16.
3. Robert T. Coffland, *Contemporary Japanese Bamboo Arts* (Chicago: Art Media Resources, 1999), 12.

everything about the art of bamboo, the more you learn, the harder it gets."[4] In my conversations with Jeremy Frey, he articulates the same dedication and an understanding that he may just now be coming into his own after all his years of making. He discusses how innovations and insights happen slowly and occur only through his continual work in and with his medium,[5] and he is quick to note that other weavers have the same experience, stating, "Baskets get better because each weaver finds their own micro-techniques in the weaving process; once you master the basics, you begin to find your own techniques within those techniques."[6]

Jeremy Frey was introduced to basketmaking when he was twenty-one years old, which is about twenty-three years ago at the writing of this essay. Like many of the bamboo artists I researched, he came from a weaving lineage on both his mother's and father's sides. It was his uncle Moose who first taught him the basics of harvesting and processing the brown ash that he uses to make his baskets. "It's a rinse-and-repeat process," Frey informs me, going on to say, "That repetition is important because it builds stamina."[7] But it was his mom, Gal Frey, who taught him his first weaving techniques for the "fancy baskets" he has come to be known for.[8]

Basketry came into Jeremy Frey's life at the right time. He was heading down the unforgiving road of drug use, Frey told me in a phone interview, adding that he's already lost most of the people he grew up with. Life in reservation communities can be difficult and filled with hopelessness for youth, as I witness on my own reservation. But Frey reminds me with a thankful note, "Basketry saved my life."[9] Looking for something to do with his hands, to keep his mind off using, Frey was introduced to basket weaving by his mom. He had an immediate feeling this was something he could be good at, and he had a drive to master weaving, which became a passion that replaced his addiction.[10] In some strange way, as Frey learned to transform his materials, they were also transforming him, from a troubled twentysomething who had never received positive affirmation for his behavior or academic achievements into a capable young artist who would eventually become one of the leaders in his field for his dedication to basket weaving and fineness of technique.

While Frey is quick to acknowledge the traditions and community members that his weaving rests upon, he may not think to explore his work in the company of artistic peers working in other mediums, and I believe that to date, scholars have failed to make this leap as well. In fact, Frey was only recently recruited by a gallery in New York, and he is one of the first weavers to transcend the label of "craft" in his work as he moves into broader artistic circles.[11] In the publication *Crafting America*, I read that the fact that an artwork can also be useful undermines its legitimacy in broader art markets, which often relegate it to being the result of a hobby and unworthy of a museum.[12] I think there is a real, unfortunate truth in this observation, and while I personally like to fight against this notion of "craft" as a separate category from that of fine art, that discussion will have to wait for another day. In this essay, I will instead examine other artistic heroes who have

4. Ibid., 36.
5. Jeremy Frey, virtual interview by author via Microsoft Teams, January 6, 2023.
6. Ibid.
7. Ibid.
8. Jeremy Frey, "Saved by Creativity," TEDxDirigo, accessed January 4, 2023, https://www.youtube.com/watch?v=W6RgGonpXOI. For additional information on how Wabanaki "fancy baskets" evolved, see "Tradition," Hudson Museum, University of Maine, accessed December 20, 2022, https://umaine.edu/hudsonmuseum/exhibits/online/tree/tradition/. See also Theresa Secord's discussion of fancy baskets on p. 9 in this volume.
9. Frey, interview.
10. Frey, "Saved by Creativity," TEDxDirigo.
11. I put the term "craft" in quotation marks because I personally disagree with this distinction in the arts, believing these monikers are based on Eurocentric definitions of artistic canons that Native arts get shoehorned into. I argue that items distinguished as craft to non-Native audiences are often forms of fine arts for Indigenous people. However, I do acknowledge that this terminology seems important at this moment in history and that being capable to move into a "fine art" classification from that of "craft" is significant for an Indigenous artist's career trajectory.
12. Glenn Adamson and Jen Padgett, *Crafting America: Artists and Objects, 1940 to Today* (Fayetteville: University of Arkansas Press, 2021), 81.

Fig 3 Bowhead whale

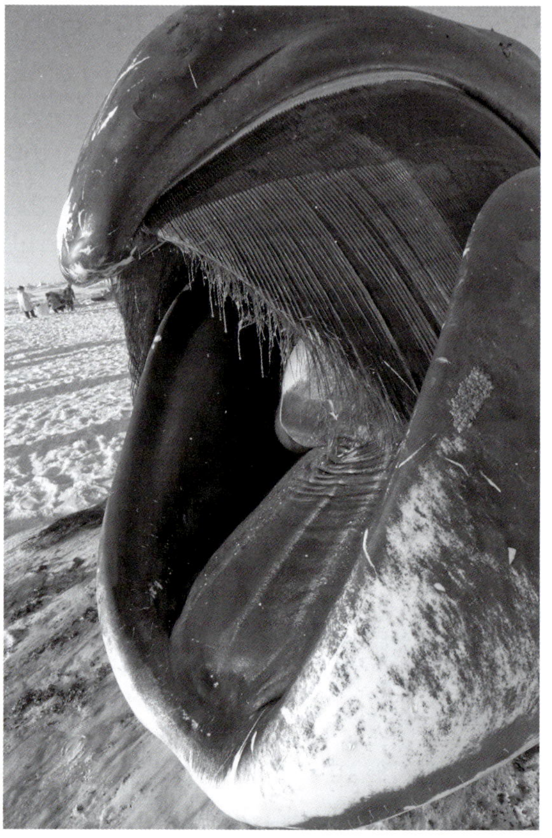

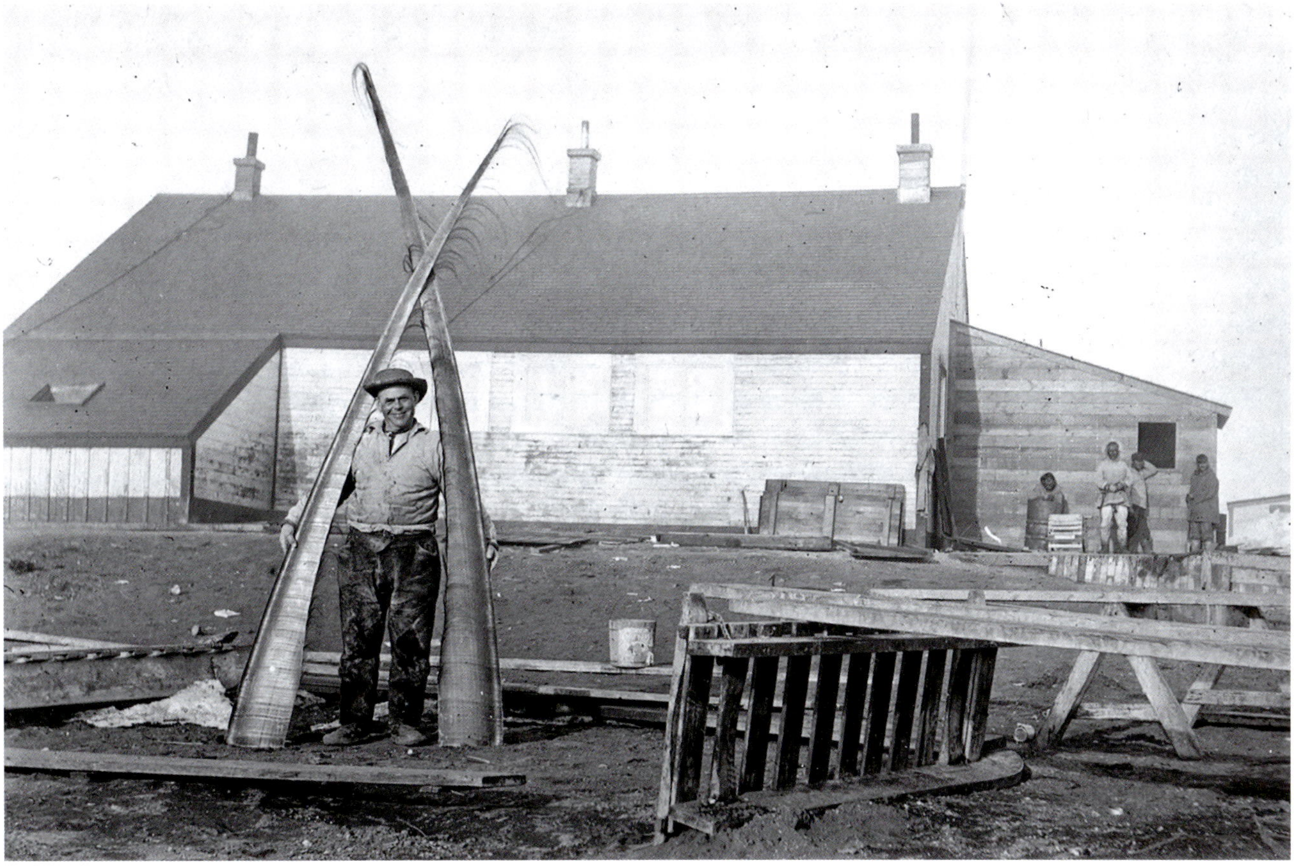

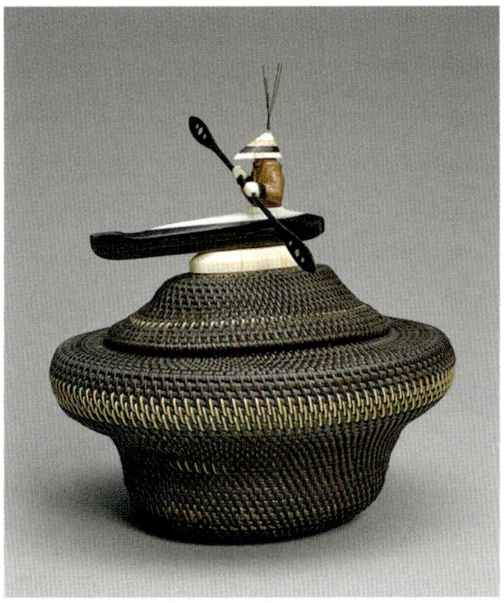

Fig 4 (top) *Charles D. Brower with baleen plates*, c. 1922, Denver Museum of Natural History, A. M. Bailey Archives, Cat. BA21-792
Fig 5 (bottom) Don Johnston (Aleut Unangax̂, born 1962), *Aiakuquing* (*Travel on the Sea*), 2017, baleen, whalebone, and ivory, 7¼ × 8⅛ × 8⅛ inches. Denver Art Museum: Gift of Loren G. Lipson, M.D., 2017.465

also transcended the "craft" moniker and who have, as Frey has done, pushed their mediums into new understandings of what's possible. Along the way, these artists have also come to redefine what can or should be considered "fine art."

Although the first example, a baleen basket, isn't perhaps the best illustration of a materiality moving into fine art, it is an excellent indication of what can result when artists push their materials beyond what people had previously imagined. Baleen is the keratinous substance harvested from the mouths of plankton-eating whales like the bowhead whale (fig. 3).[13] Inuit communities located in northern Alaska had many uses for this stiff substance (fig. 4). Like a tree, it could be split and sized for multiple purposes including buckets, ice scoops, bows, sled runners, fishing lines, and even boot insulation![14] It's hard to imagine this unforgiving substance being used inside a shoe without poking and irritating a tender foot, yet the Inuit people found uses for this material that truly boggle the mind. Europeans and Americans also hunted the bowhead whale for its oil and baleen, which was used in "whalebone" corsets, a misnomer applied to the baleen used in the "bones" or "boning" of Victorian corsets.

Perhaps it's not surprising that Indigenous people, living in some of the most unforgiving environments on earth, found uses for every part of the bowhead whale. However, the innovation of using this material in basket weaving was spurred by economic need and the opportunity to sell goods to burgeoning tourist markets.[15] Unfortunately, because of the focus on said tourist markets, connoisseurs disparaged these baskets as "modern" versus "authentic" historical artworks. This designation originally undermined their desirability in museums and among collectors. Thankfully, some of these somewhat petty distinctions (after all, aren't all artists selling to some kind of market?) are starting

13. Molly Lee, *Baleen Basketry of the North Alaskan Eskimo*, 2nd ed. (Seattle: University of Washington Press, 1998), 3.
14. Ibid., 7.
15. Ibid., ix.

to fall away as more and more people recognize the skill and artistry required to create these baskets and carve their ivory finials. In a basket by Don Johnston from the Denver Art Museum's collection, we clearly see how this contemporary artist, like many of his artistic ancestors, saw beyond the rigidity of his original materials to create a delicate item especially noted for its finesse and grace (fig. 5). As for the exploration of materiality by this artist, about two years ago I was privileged to receive a beautiful image from Johnston of a basket made of Argentium silver! Like Frey, this artist's innovation comes from his continual weaving in the style of the artists who have gone before him. Interestingly, Frey and Johnston were competitors in the past few years for the Best of Basketry award in the two largest juried Indian art markets, in Santa Fe and Phoenix. As Glenn Adamson notes in *Crafting America*, "To inherit the legacy of a craft is to make it one's own."[16]

The next artist to bring to your attention is Brian Jungen, whose unique creations utilizing sports shoes surprised and delighted viewers when he first introduced them in the 1990s.[17] Perhaps these early creations weren't as based in traditional ways of making as some of the others we'll discuss, but they were deeply based in prevalent expectations for Native art, which is certainly one obstacle that all Indigenous artists, including Jeremy Frey, are struggling against.

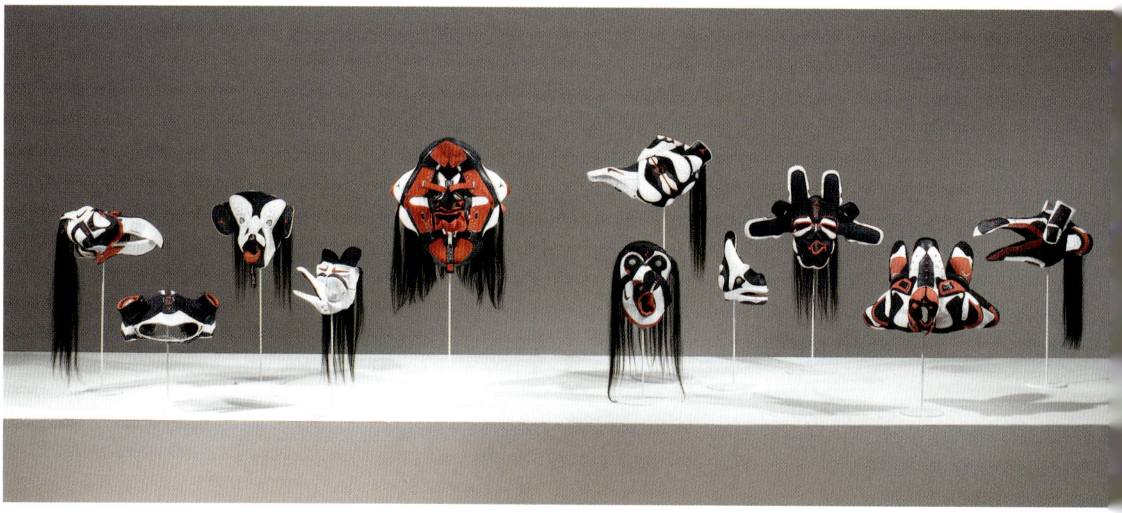

Fig 6 Brian Jungen (Dane-zaa, born 1970), *Prototypes for New Understanding*, 1998–2005, Nike Air Jordans and hair

Jungen originates from a ranching community in North Okanagan, British Columbia, Canada, but he went to art school in Vancouver, British Columbia. While there, he noticed how the motifs of coastal Native communities had really become signifiers for the entire province.[18] One day, on a visit to a Nike store, he saw Air Jordans displayed in vitrines, much like a piece of artwork might be. Something clicked. The commodification of those shoes reminded Jungen of the commodification of Northwest Coast Indigenous motifs.[19] These observations coalesced in the artist's mind, inspiring him to create mock Northwest Coast ceremonial masks out of Air Jordan tennis shoes. These innovative works captured viewers' imaginations through their humor, relatability, and innovation (fig. 6). Since those early days, Jungen has continued to experiment with commercial materials, creating unanticipated artistic structures that at once defy expectations for Native art yet are intimately tied to his relationship to his Dane-zaa heritage and Indigenous culture more broadly, as well as his own personal life experiences. Some of his more recent constructions include a kind of whale form generated out of everyday plastic lawn chairs and drum forms made of commercial chairs with hides stretched over their frames.[20]

16. Adamson, "Life," in Adamson and Padgett, *Crafting America*, 81.
17. "Brian Jungen in 'Vancouver' Preview," from episode in PBS series *Art in the Twenty-First Century*, Art21, July 29, 2016, accessed February 26, 2023, https://art21.org/watch/art-in-the-twenty-first-century/s8/brian-jungen-in-season-8-of-art21-art-in-the-twenty-first-century-2016-preview.
18. Note that Jungen himself does not originate from a coastal community but is instead Dane-zaa.
19. "Brian Jungen in 'Vancouver' Preview."
20. Examples of these works can be found online. For an example of the whale structure made out of plastic chairs, see https://catrionajeffries.com/index.php?p=artists/brian-jungen/works/brian-jungen-vienna-2003, or search for *Vienna* by Brian Jungen, created in 2003. For an example of Jungen's drum piece, see https://www.artsy.net/artwork/brian-jungen-fore-revolver-reverse, or search for *Fore Revolver Reverse* by Brian Jungen, created in 2011.

Frey, too, stands at the precipice of further innovation in his materiality, as he is potentially pushed into new directions by the unfortunate upcoming loss of the beloved and sacred brown ash trees in the Northeast area of the country. Perhaps as he moves into fine art galleries, his desire to expand upon his traditional learning will become a prevailing force. To quote again from Adamson, "Every living tradition must constantly reinvent itself in the unfolding present."[21]

I was eager to speak with Frey to hear how he planned to push his practice into ever-expanding and more experimental forms, feeling that he possessed the potential to move basket weaving into new heights of creativity. However, after our first conversation, I was somewhat disappointed by what I interpreted as Frey's unwillingness to do so. It was my discussion with his professional development mentor and longtime friend, Theresa Secord, that helped me better understand the way Frey has already been instituting innovation in his work and the reasons these things are not always apparent to non-weavers. She also helped me understand the things that have stood in the way of his being able to spread his artistic wings even further. According to Secord, Frey exhibited exceptional skill from the onset of his basketmaking career, so his ability to visualize and then execute new basket forms already began shortly after he started weaving. "No one here has really done what he has done with an ancient art form," Secord told me.[22] Frey began developing and making differently shaped mold forms, for instance, that no one else had used before and in unprecedented sizes. The basket that the Denver Art Museum recently acquired is an excellent example of his pushing baskets into new territories of scale (fig. 7; pp. 84–85). One of only two of this size (at the time of this essay's writing), this basket stands an impressive twenty-seven inches high, a scale that is hard to visualize from a picture alone. And the exceptional quillwork of a cougar on the lid of the basket reaffirms Frey's deep knowledge of his materials, as the cougar is composed using only the natural fiber colors of the porcupine quills.

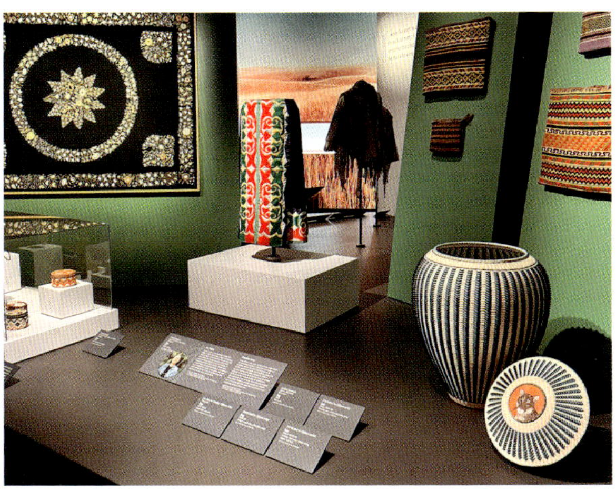

Fig 7 *Watchful Spirit* installed in the Denver Art Museum's permanent collection, 2023

These revelations of Frey's competencies aren't always immediately discernible to an untrained eye, or to people like me who aren't steeped in weaving methodologies or the cultural knowledge and intellectual property of Wabanaki basketry. It's different for someone like Adamson, who notes in the book *Crafting America* that experiencing the beauty of a basket happens all at once, including the way the artist brings age-old techniques into contemporary times.[23] While I agree with this assessment, I also believe that experiencing the basket in one look belies the amount of work required to create these complicated, and to some extent time-based, works, which can take years to finish. Adamson also notes, "At the upper echelons of skill, the manipulation of material comes to seem effortless."[24] This aptly describes Frey's work. Through his exceptional skill and perfectionism, baskets plié effortlessly atop museum risers in perfect balance, obscuring the proficiency required to create baskets that perform such a feat, thus allowing the objects to take all the credit for themselves.

Two other factors play directly into the ability of any Native artist, and more directly Jeremy Frey, to take greater risks in their work. As Secord pointed out to me, Frey was able to launch the baskets of his generation into the Indian markets, which is a tremendous coup. But artists who become successful at the markets must then be able to execute their visions quickly and concisely to maximize profitability.[25] Experimentation takes time and requires mistakes. It demands failure and rewards exasperation. A father of three simply cannot risk that kind of bravado, but Frey has recently overcome some of this necessity through his

21. Adamson, "What Is Craft?," in Adamson and Padgett, *Crafting America*, 60.
22. Theresa Secord, telephone interview by author, February 14, 2023.
23. Adamson, "The Pursuit of Happiness," in Adamson and Padgett, *Crafting America*, 168.
24. Adamson, "Liberty," in Adamson and Padgett, *Crafting America*, 129.
25. Secord, interview.

recognition in the wider art world. Secord feels confident that with some of the financial and time pressures lifted, Frey's creativity can only expand.[26]

As Adamson, once more, has stated in *Crafting America*, "For Native Americans who have experienced forced assimilation—attempts to eradicate their language, dress, and customs—craft represents an essential continuity with the past and an opportunity for self-invention."[27] How do Indigenous artists stay true to all the ancestral responsibilities they bring with them to their process yet define something completely new for themselves? Frey admits that he struggles with these seemingly opposing priorities. In a recent conversation, he admitted to me that he wants his baskets to be considered "art," but he also pointed out that he works within certain constraints because he also wants his works to remain *vessels*, grounded in that history but open to new directions.[28] Embracing this conflict—remaining grounded in tradition but wide open to change—is Jeremy Frey's guiding road map, which seems like a very complicated journey. He gently admonished me for my calls for more innovation by stating, "At one time or another, everything we did with baskets was contemporary. Someone came up with that new technique, that new direction."[29] In this statement, Frey reminded me that innovation *is* tradition for Native people, and he is well equipped to take his work into the next realm of excellence by staying true to his guiding principles.

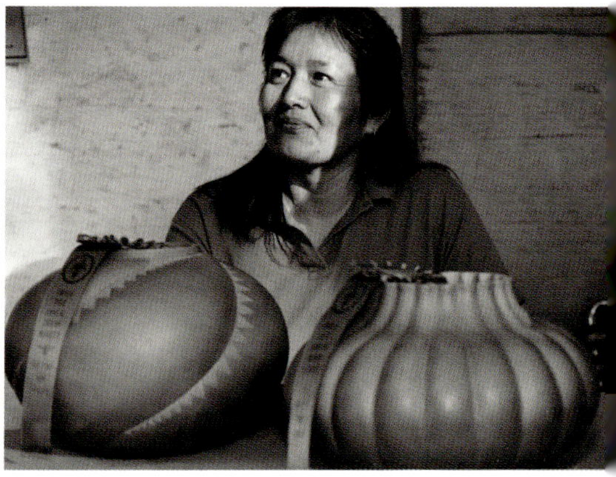

Fig 8 Chuck Rosenak, *Christine Nofchissey McHorse*, c. 1990. Archives of American Art, Smithsonian Institution, Chuck and Jan Rosenak research material, c. 1938–2008

Before closing, let me examine one last innovator in materiality, Christine Nofchissey McHorse (fig. 8). I wanted to bring her into this discussion because early in her career, her work was wholly and unapologetically grounded in the Taos tradition of coiled pot making. While she had originally explored Navajo (Diné) pot making (she herself was Diné), it was her husband's grandmother who taught her the traditional coiling method used by Puebloan people. McHorse became widely recognized as a renowned potter, and she won many awards creating works of art in this Puebloan style. However, as she progressed in her career, sculptural forms began to erupt from the traditions she had honored. The Smithsonian American Art Museum describes her later work this way: "McHorse's work has an elegance and sophistication that defy stereotypes about folk art and traditional Native American art."[30]

Fig 9 Christine Nofchissey McHorse (Diné, 1947–2021), *Spatial Concerto*, 2012, micaceous clay, 18¼ × 23 × 7½ inches. Collection of Bill and Christy Gautreaux

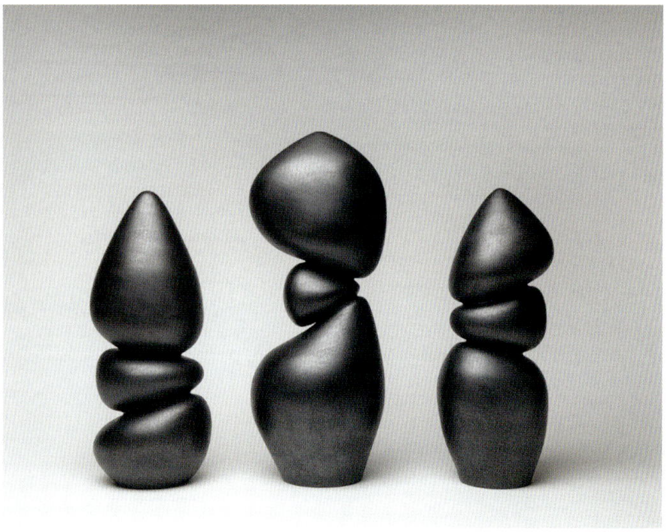

I first learned about McHorse when researching her for the traveling exhibition *Hearts of Our People: Native Women Artists* (2019–21), and her sculptural progressions thrilled me in their grace and elegance. Again, McHorse, like Frey, leaned into what had originally grounded her work, and it was that same commitment to structure and mastering of materials that allowed her to see beyond the original materiality, even in some cases abandoning that materiality to innovate into sculptural structures that spoke not only to her pottery background, but also to the delineation of space, the refractive nature of light, and the complexities of sculptural form (fig. 9). My deepest hope is for Jeremy Frey to explore and examine this kind of complexity in the new works he will create as he moves into this next stage of his career. He is perhaps the person best poised to launch basket weaving into this new interstitial space kicked wide open by his fellow Indigenous artists.

Jeremy Frey lives and breathes the heritage of the Wabanaki basket weaver every day. For centuries, the Wabanaki have produced baskets that shared in the daily rituals of life. These utilitarian companions went with the Passamaquoddy as they collected wood, stored items, prepared meals, welcomed babies, and marked a person's exit from this world.[31] Wabanaki baskets made from the splints of brown ash trees and adorned with sweetgrass rims became a means of economic and cultural survival during the nineteenth century as people faced starvation, deprivation, and removal from their ancestral lands.[32] Baskets also ushered the Wabanaki into the cash economy established through settler colonialism. The first unassuming utilitarian baskets, and later the more delicate fancy baskets (the style Frey creates), assisted the Wabanaki in resisting assimilation, maintaining tribal sovereignty, and preserving their self-determination in the face of unrelenting pressures from a dominant culture unconcerned with their continued existence.[33] That is a lot of responsibility placed on one vessel and the hands that made it.

Today, artists such as Jeremy Frey and Theresa Secord, among others, continue to take that charge to heart, promoting the Wabanaki traditions to a wider world that knows little if anything about their important histories. As Frey moves into a broader limelight, Theresa Secord reminds me that his ascent will only further the opportunities of all Wabanaki basket makers.[34]

In closing, I want to follow the theme of transformation, and seeing beyond the obvious, by examining the Wabanaki creation story. At the beginning of Theresa Secord's essay, there is a wonderful recounting of this narrative by a Passamaquoddy elder, Molly Sepsis. In it, Sepsis describes how Glooskap shot his arrow into the ash tree to create the Wabanaki. As we read Sepsis's account of this story, we come to understand two important things. First, the destinies of the Wabanaki people, basket makers, and Jeremy Frey are entwined with the ash tree from time immemorial. Second, Glooskap himself can serve as an inspiration to artists like Frey for seeing beyond the obvious nature of the materiality of a medium to create something much greater than the sum of its parts. In this way, Jeremy Frey has inherited a transformational legacy from his creator and his community. He sits at the summit of this history and joins his artistic peers in transforming his materials into something much greater than can originally be seen by the untrained eye. I look forward to this next journey in his career development, even as I revel in the beauty he has already accomplished through his uncompromising dedication to the basket art form.

26. Ibid.
27. Adamson, "Life," 81.
28. Frey, interview.
29. Ibid.
30. "Artist Christine McHorse," Smithsonian American Art Museum, accessed February 26, 2023, https://americanart.si.edu/artist/christine-mchorse-7467.
31. Bruce Bernstein, ed., *The Language of Native American Baskets: From the Weavers' View* (Washington, D.C.: National Museum of the American Indian, 2003), 9.
32. Deborah Gabriel Brooks, "Sweetgrass Basketry," accessed January 3, 2023, https://sweetgrass-basketry.org/about-us.
33. See Theresa Secord's explanation of basketmaking as a form of Wabanaki resistance and sovereignty on p. 13 of this volume.
34. Secord, interview.

Ash

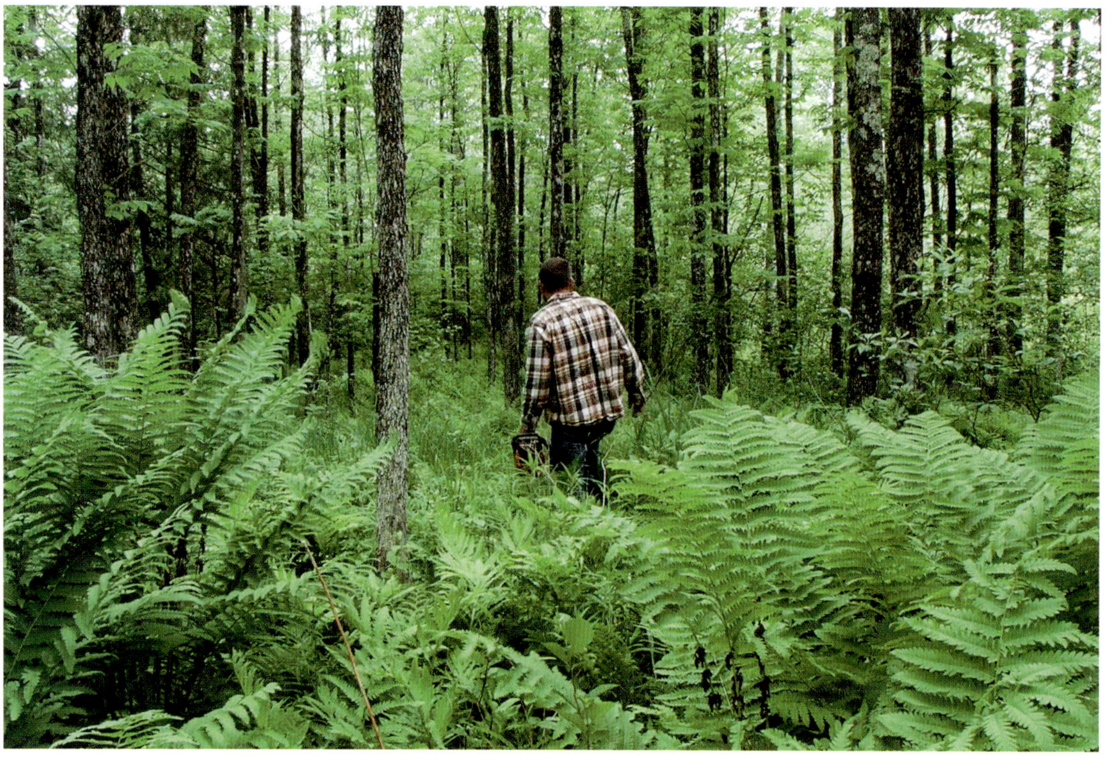

Jaime DeSimone

The video *Ash* is more than a story about a basket and its journey.[1] It is a complex narrative about the origin story of the Wabanaki people, about ancestral knowledge and place, about the act of creation, about life and loss, and about an artist coming into his own. No single plot takes center stage; rather, a confluence of ideas emerges, sparks curiosity, and lingers. Why the video unfolds in a seemingly chronological order of harvesting to destruction, no one interpretation is offered. This is Jeremy Frey's intention:

> Basketry is an art form that I can relate to in many ways. It is a part of my heritage, an art form that connects me to my relatives both living and past. For me to weave is a way of honoring my ancestors. However, it is also a way to honor future generations both through my teachings and through my personal carrying on of the art form. My work is always evolving; I try to create a newer and more elaborate version of my work each time I weave. I have refined the teaching of my mother beyond anything I would have considered possible.[2]

Opposite Jeremy Frey, "Frey Entering Ash Forest," *Ash*, 2023. Film still. Cinematographer: Joshua Reiman

One might argue that the video *Ash* is also beyond what Frey would have considered possible. At the Southwestern Association for Indian Arts (SWAIA) Santa Fe Indian Market of 2021, Frey and I first discussed the possibility of this new direction in his work; a project that would relate to his ancestral traditions yet in a new medium: video. In that moment, we agreed the new work would not be a basket, yet rather a "non-basket." (I will return to his use of the term "non-basket" later in this essay.) This concept had been on his mind for many years. Like many artists, Frey operates with a pragmatic sensibility; he is forward-thinking, practical, and deliberate at every juncture of his professional practice, especially the release of his first video, which would represent a completely new terrain for his artistic pursuits. So I challenged him to consider it as a continuation of his practice, running parallel to basketry yet framed as contemporary art, further blurring the lines of art historical categorization. *What if we mounted an exhibition and your new video was its finale?* We mutually agreed and spent the next few months brainstorming ideas (for both the exhibition and the video), interviewing filmmakers and collaborators, and testing the plot with other curators, collectors, and thought partners.

Commissioned by the Portland Museum of Art on the occasion of this exhibition, *Ash* is the first video work by Frey. Over the course of two years (2022–23), it was filmed in various locations throughout the Land of the Dawn, from undisclosed forests to his studio outside Bangor, Maine, where hours of B-roll and audio were captured and recorded to be distilled into a final video of approximately ten minutes. Frey collaborated with Portland-based filmmaker Joshua Reiman, whose sense of cinematography, unique vantage points, and emphasis on immersive sound realized Frey's vision. Frey's preference was to be both visible and invisible in the frames; this important play on discernibility is a constant reminder to the viewer that Frey is only one of many Passamaquoddy Knowledge Keepers[3] of basketry. He does not claim to be the singular voice of his community or cultural traditions, yet rather part of a community that upholds and advances them in the present day. Thus, Frey insistently crafts a story in which the brown ash tree and the resulting basket are the video's lead protagonists.

Ash begins with a man who carries a chainsaw as he walks into a densely populated lush forest (opposite). His body immediately becomes immersed, almost camouflaged, among the high ferns as he continues deep into the woods. The further he enters, the more his body dwarfs in scale. Hints of life and wind, such as rustling leaves and chirping birds, are abundant as a psithurism (the sound

1. Jeremy Frey in conversation with the author, November 27, 2022.
2. Jeremy Frey quoted in artist profile at Abbe Museum's website, https://www.abbemuseum.org/attending-artists-profiles/jeremy-frey.
3. The term "Knowledge Keeper," or "Traditional Knowledge Keeper," refers to someone who has been taught by an Elder or a senior Knowledge Keeper within their community. This person holds traditional knowledge and teachings; each has been taught how to care for these teachings and when it is, and is not, appropriate to share this knowledge with others. For this definition and others, see "Elders, Knowledge Keepers, and Cultural Advisors," Queen's University, https://www.queensu.ca/indigenous/ways-knowing/elders-knowledge-keepers-and-cultural-advisors.

of the wind whispering through the trees) overtakes our senses. The natural environment is suddenly disrupted by the visceral sound of the chainsaw. Its screeching intensifies as the throttle increases in power. Its blade cuts through the trunk. Frey's body is barely visible at the tree's base, like a boulder or rock from which it grew, only a blur of plaid flannel reminding us of his presence. Then the ash tree falls into the ferns, stumbling on its way, but its descent appears delicate, almost natural, and inevitable. The stump, which remains connected to the earth, is inspected by the forester (fig. 1). Frey reemerges with the fallen log on his shoulders, grunting as he steadies its weight and carries it out of the forest. The freshly cut log is balanced over his shoulders in great contrast to the vertical, living trees that surround Frey as he exits the forest. Each harvested log must be hand-carried out of the woods.

From forest to studio, the process of pounding ash starts. The viewer, who is now at eye level with the log, recognizes how Frey uses the back of his axe to chip the bark off (fig. 2). Chip, chip, chip, the artist works to splinter the log's outer surface onto the ground with a light touch. The log is rotated, the steps repeated. The process is methodical and time-consuming. The sounds of the axe hitting the log change from light to heavier thumps as his pounding efforts intensify. A rhythmic interplay between body and log continues. The log remains naked on the ground.

Then Frey gently splits and peels each layer of the ash's growth rings into long strips, pulling them from one edge of the log to the other. The strips, about a few inches wide, appear agile, following Frey's command to release themselves from their previous existence. We witness the ash, from solid form to malleable material, in a state of great transition. With each removal, the log's diameter decreases. Through a variety of ways, Frey processes and prepares each strip into more refined strands that will be used for weaving the basket. He carefully stacks the strands into bundles, tying them with a loose piece of ash (fig. 3).

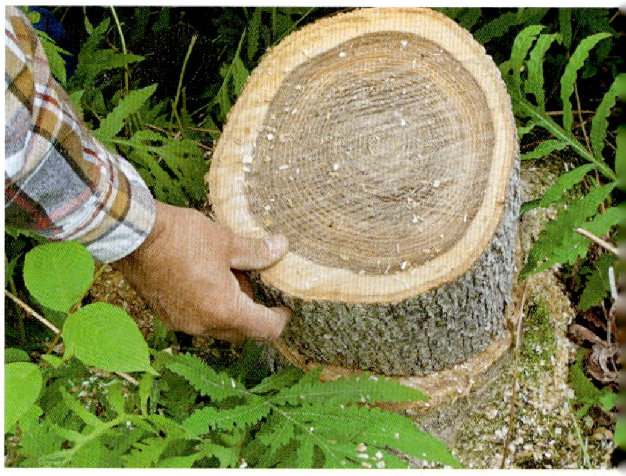

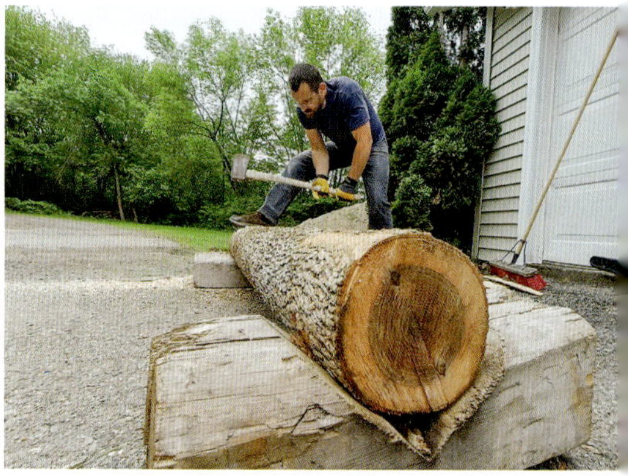

Fig 1 (top) Jeremy Frey, "Tree Stump," *Ash*, 2023. Film still. Cinematographer: Joshua Reiman
Fig 2 (bottom) Jeremy Frey, "Frey Pounding Ash," *Ash*, 2023. Film still. Cinematographer: Joshua Reiman

Scrape, scrape, scrape. The blade of Frey's knife runs along a fine piece of ash as he gets ready to weave. Here, again, the basket comes into being, with Frey as a secondary object. We observe his hands wrapping and tightening the strands of ash into place over the mold, an armature on which the woven form is constructed (fig. 4). The rhythm and pace of his respectful handling of material remain consistent throughout the video. The monotonous sounds of weaving recall the whispering of winds in the forest or the pounding of ash. A familiar cadence recurs as the next stage of the basket's being comes into existence.

The narrative arc of *Ash* creates a sincere investment on the part of the viewer. We become committed to the process, the material, and the final basket. We observe the magnitude of Frey's effort to accomplish just one object. While *Ash* could have ended with the deeply satisfying creation of a basket, it does not. Its climax is its finale: its slow, unfathomable burning (fig. 5). The culmination of every ounce of labor destroyed. Crackling. Burning. Flickering. Blazing. Mesmerizing. Smoldering. Gone. What once was is now lost forever.

Ash is not a demonstration video of Frey's process. It is a work of art born out of the Wabanaki creation story. Glooskap is a Wabanaki culture hero with supernatural powers, who is central to many legends.[4] In Wabanaki creation myths, Glooskap fires an arrow into a brown ash tree, and out of the tree come

4. There are many variant forms and spellings of Glooskap's name, including Gluskabe, Glooscap, Gluskabi, Kluscap, Kloskomba, and Gluskab.

the people.[5] In Frey's case, when pounded with the back of an axe, the tree splits apart between each growth ring, producing splints to make baskets. Frey, who is well versed in this creation story, respectfully addresses it, re-creating it as part of his process and incorporating it into the video's narrative.

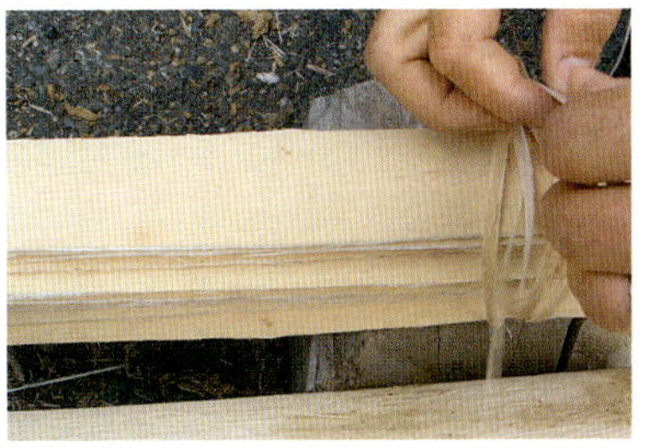

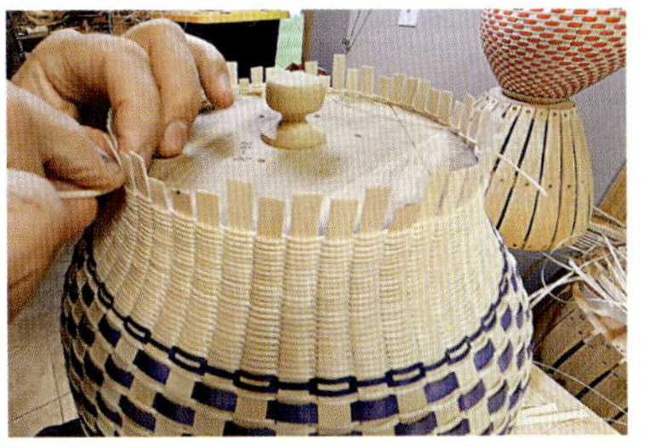

Fig 3 (top) Jeremy Frey, "Split Tree and Tie into Bundles," *Ash*, 2023. Film still. Cinematographer: Joshua Reiman
Fig 4 (bottom) Jeremy Frey, "Making Dawnland," *Ash*, 2023. Film still. Cinematographer: Joshua Reiman

Penobscot artist, author, and basket maker Jennifer Neptune writes about the tradition of ash splint basketry, stating: "In one Passamaquoddy creation story, Wabanaki people are born from the ash tree. This tree is favored over all others for the strength and flexibility of its splints."[6] In *Ash*, Frey is now on record pounding ash; a process that echoes Neptune's statement about ash's material properties while also commenting on the artist's physical endurance. The viewer's senses become overstimulated with the repetitive sound—thud, thud, thud—as the harvesting process unfolds in the frame. Frey's uncle Moose passed on the knowledge related to selecting, harvesting, pounding, and splitting the ash wood (and sweetgrass) necessary to weave his handmade baskets. By visualizing this activity, the artist celebrates his uncle's legacy through his absence. Thus, *Ash* may be interpreted as encompassing universal, personal, and familial stories.

Place and history are also critical, yet understated, narratives in *Ash*. The opening frame, the brown ash forest, is representative of many wooded areas throughout what is now called Maine. According to the Passamaquoddy Tribe at Motahkomikuk (Indian Township) website, "Land has always been the Native people's most valuable possession."[7] The Wabanaki rely on the brown ash (also commonly known as black ash, or *Fraxinus nigra*, a species of ash native to much of eastern Canada and the northeastern United States) both spiritually and economically as a way of life. According to Neptune, "many Native Americans in the Northeast turned to the trade and sale of splint basketry as a means of survival early in the eighteenth century."[8] In Frey's video, the forest, the ash tree, the resulting log, and the supplies all reference the complicated histories of Indigenous peoples and land sovereignty in the United States. Yet the artist is neither overtly political nor apolitical. He is conscious of the complex histories that have transpired since Wabanaki contact with settlers and his communities' forced removal from their ancestral land. *Ash* is not necessarily part of the current "Land Back" call-to-action movement to restore governance and stewardship of the land for a sustainable future and return of equity to a stolen territory. But, as Frey says, "If it encourages a Land Back action or corrective retelling of my peoples' history, great."[9]

Weaving, art, and survival are words synonymous with how Frey began his practice. Theresa Secord's essay in this publication on the artist's trajectory explains the importance of the Maine Indian Basketmakers Alliance (MIBA) on his early career when he came of age in his twenties. At that time, few men wove the smaller, more artistic style of ash baskets, called "fancy baskets"; instead, men wove the larger utility or work baskets for use in hunting, fishing, gathering, and ceremony.[10] Frey is now the most renowned basket maker of the Wabanaki Confederacy, some may argue even the United States. However, he does not take this acclaim for granted and acknowledges that his practice may have an expiration date due to the impact of climate change on biodiversity.

Today, Maine's ash forests are endangered by the emerald ash borer, a parasitic beetle. It was first detected in Maine in 2018, after killing ash trees across the United States, a number of years prior to estimations. Frey is cognizant of this ongoing threat to his chosen material. *Ash* may be viewed as a valentine or memoir about it. Aware of the ash tree's mortality, he constantly strives to find

5. There are variations to the legend of Glooskap, as each tribe of the Wabanaki adapted the legend to its own region. However, within each tale, the creator Glooskap is consistently portrayed as "kind, benevolent, a warrior against evil and the possessor of magical powers." See Stanley T. Spicer and Teresa MacPhee, *Glooscap Legends* (Hantsport, NS: Lancelot Press, 1991), n.p.
6. Jennifer Sapiel Neptune, title essay in *Spirit of the Basket Tree: Wabanaki Ash Splint Baskets from Maine*, exh. cat. (Hanover, NH: Hood Museum of Art, Dartmouth College, 2008), 5, https://hoodmuseum.dartmouth.edu/sites/hoodmuseum.prod/files/hoodmuseum/publications/spirit_of_the_basket_tree_final.pdf.
7. Passamaquoddy Tribe at Indian Township, "Culture & History," https://www.passamaquoddy.com/?page_id=24.
8. See Neptune in *Spirit of the Basket Tree*, 5, and the same essay for more information on Wabanaki history as it relates to land, the American Revolution, and the Treaty of Paris in 1783.
9. Jeremy Frey in conversation with the author, January 15, 2023.
10. Maribel Alvarez, "Weaving Survival and Art: Maine Indian Basketmakers Alliance," ArtChangeUS: Arts in a Changing America, https://artsinachangingamerica.org/weaving-survival-memory-and-art-maine-indian-basketmakers-alliance-from-the-archives-of-artography/.

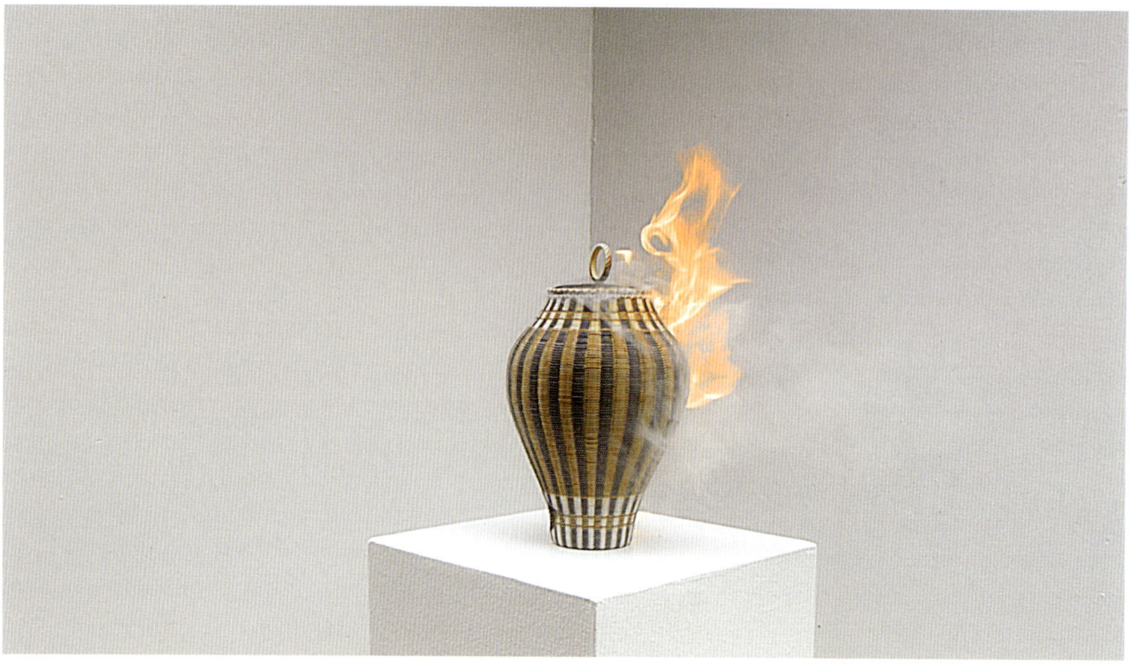

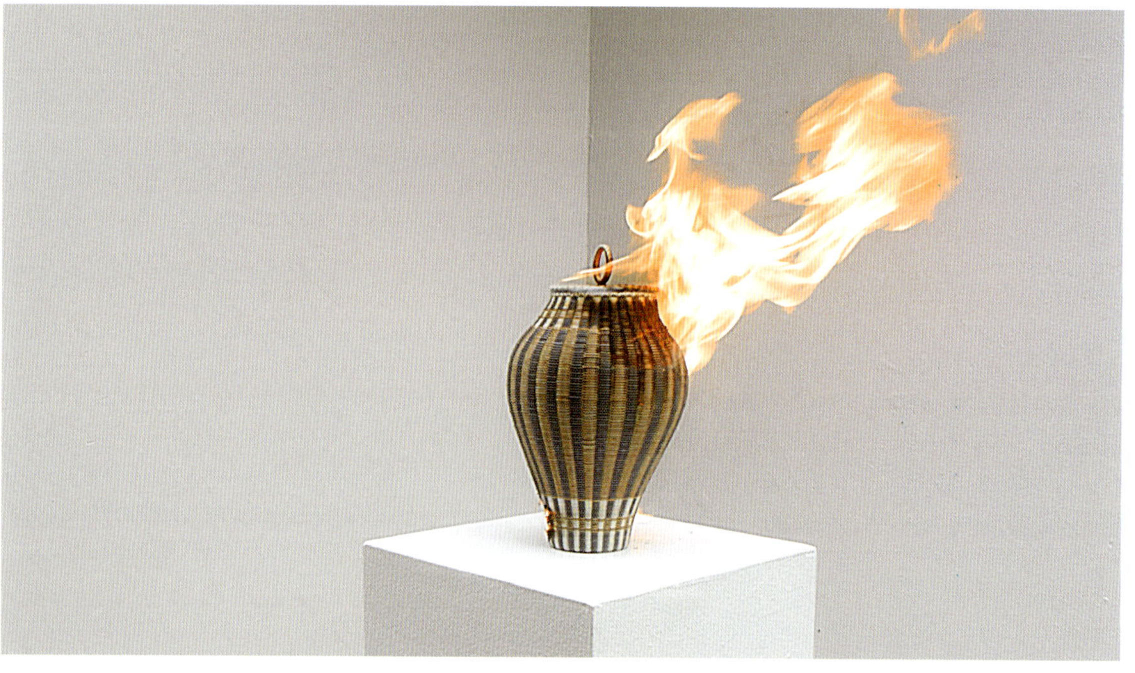

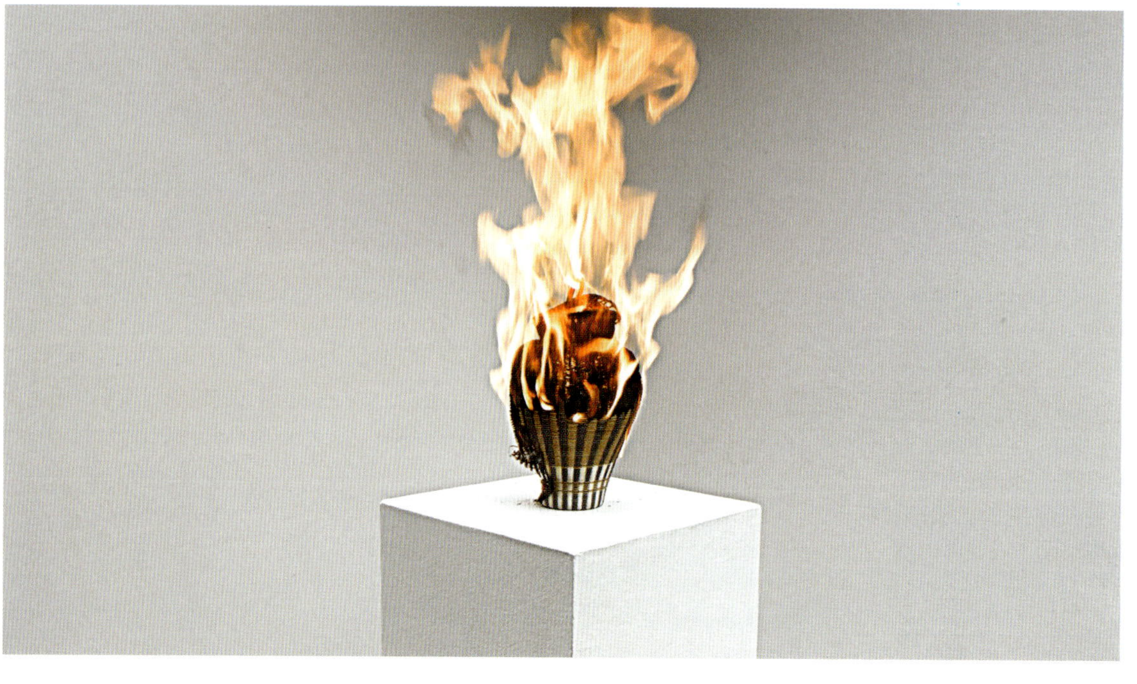

new ways to preserve his chosen material, whether it means trying to harvest it in bulk or experimenting with freezing it. This video is his first work in a new direction that upholds these traditional practices in another medium.

Is *Ash* a "non-basket" work? Let's clarify Frey's aspirations and initial meaning of the use of this term. I believe he meant a work of art that was not a physical object categorized as a basket, vessel, or three-dimensional sculpture. To date, his artistic output has been dedicated primarily to mastering and advancing traditional techniques of weaving and quillwork on fancy baskets. Frey's exploration into video or new media aligns with the practice of many Native artists, including Kent Monkman (Cree, born 1965), Nicholas Galanin (Tlingit and Unangax̂, born 1979), and Jeffrey Gibson (Choctaw/Cherokee, born 1972), among others, who, at a critical moment of self-recognition, identified new possibilities to amplify and expand narratives. Witnessing Frey in this moment of self-awareness was extraordinary. In *Ash*, he repurposes his primary artistic practice—basketry and weaving—into the subject in a manner that is empathetic, powerful, and educational. The basket as a protagonist is a guise for a larger commentary about people, land, and survival on Turtle Island (a Native name for North America). In his words, "My practice turns an ancient, traditional form into a contemporary piece of art."[11] *Ash* continues this trajectory.

Fig 5 Jeremy Frey, "Burning Basket," *Ash*, 2023. Film stills. Cinematographer: Joshua Reiman

The ongoing excitement and philosophical conversations about Frey's aspirations to position his artistic practice—Native versus non-Native, traditional art versus contemporary art, or maybe both—were some of the most thought-provoking and encouraging conversations of this project's life span. Questions about such categorizations (should they matter outside of museology) remain unanswered. Until then, we must watch and ruminate on *Ash* to enhance our understanding of his work and Wabanaki history, past, present, and future. Jeremy Frey should be applauded for *Ash*; it marks a significant moment in his career about intersectionality and self-determination that can be pinpointed to an exact moment in his history.

11. Jeremy Frey, acceptance speech at Southwestern Association for Indian Arts (SWAIA) Santa Fe Indian Market "Best in Basketry" Award for the basket *Dawnland*, August 19, 2022.

Jeremy Frey
Full Circle

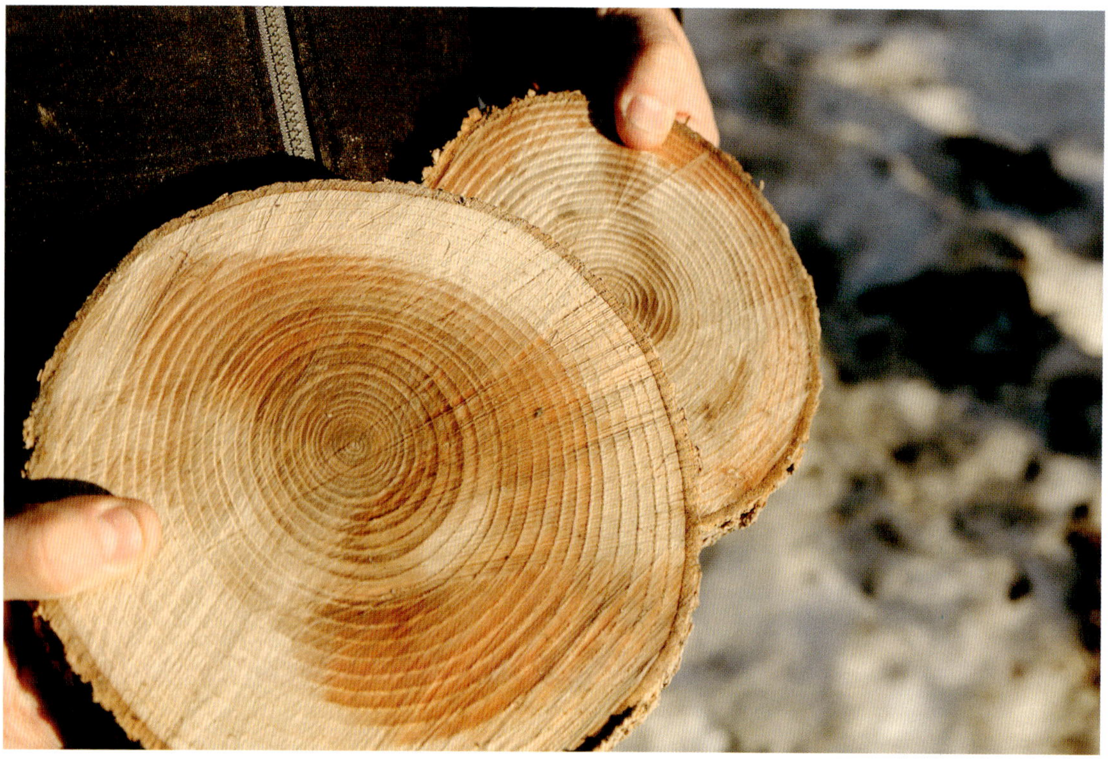

Ramey Mize

When you pound ash trees apart, you go back in time.
—Jeremy Frey[1]

When Frey described his process this way, I had to press him further—basket-making as time travel? Patiently, he explained further: his baskets' core material does not come from arbitrary cuts of wood, but rather the growth rings of the ash tree itself. He emphasized that the creation of a basket is decidedly different from the process of wood veneer, wherein thin layers of wood are derived from a tree trunk by slicing lengthwise *through* the growth rings. Frey and other Wabanaki basket makers instead work to disaggregate the concentric rings whose layers add up to the life of a tree (opposite). As my fellow authors have helped to explain throughout this volume, ring separation is achieved through pounding, a step in the work's production that involves hammering every inch of the ash log, often with the blunt end of an axe.[2] The application of such force loosens the rings, which Frey then peels apart into individual strips and further hones into differently sized splints, from thick "ribs" that provide the vertical armature of his pieces to slim, threadlike pieces that inflect his work with fine detail (fig. 1). Depending on the thickness of a given strip and the extent to which it is refined, certain parts of a basket may be composed from one year of the tree's growth, or five, or ten. In this way, Frey's baskets are a study in time.

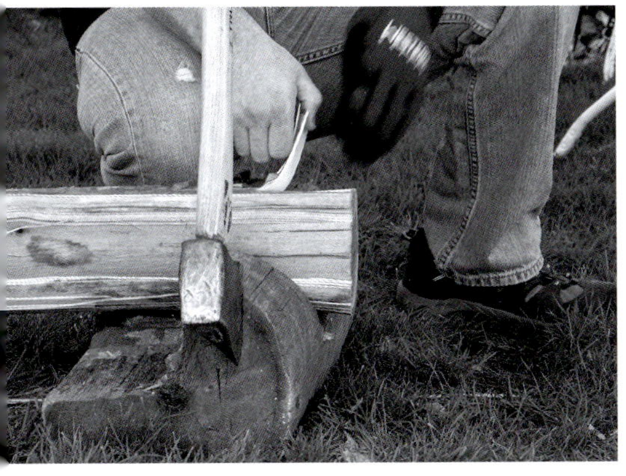

Opposite Ash tree rings, 2023
Fig 1 (above) Jeremy Frey peeling growth rings apart into strips after pounding. Heard Museum Guild Indian Fair and Market, 2015

I am interested in how time manifests in Frey's work across registers as layered as his wood medium. Another layer beyond the timescale of the tree's life is the protracted period necessary to harvest, prepare, and ultimately produce a single basket. Audiences are often astonished to discover that it can take many months for the artist to complete one work. Indeed, *Watchful Spirit*, which Frey created for the Denver Art Museum, was the culmination of over six months of concentrated effort (pp. 84-85). A third timescale may be perceived in the more than two decades that Frey has worked, advancing his practice to increasingly complex levels. He does so while remaining mindful of the deeper roots of Passamaquoddy community history that ground his art form as a whole—a fourth layer of time. With this concluding essay, I hope to briefly trace these temporal arcs and intersections, attending to the ways Frey's baskets channel the past, present, and future.

Tree Time

Ash is flexible, supple, and represents a connection to the earth. It is the traditional material, and it is a sacred tree. It's the embodiment of our physical history in Maine—there's an emotional connection that goes deep. —Jeremy Frey[3]

The centrality of ash to both Frey's art and broader Wabanaki culture cannot be overstated. As he explains above, ash lends itself exceptionally well to basketry, so much so that it is often referred to as the "basket tree."[4] Indeed, Frey is quick to point out: "In many ways, it is otherwise useless—not even good for firewood."[5] Found in bogs and swamps or along streams, this tree species grows best in nutrient-dense, moist soil, reaching heights of sixty to seventy feet and a diameter of eight to twenty-four inches.[6] Branches cluster toward the top rather

1. Interview with the artist, November 2, 2022.
2. See the essays by Theresa Secord, Jaime DeSimone, and Andrew James Hamilton in this volume, pp. 8-29, 38-43.
3. Interview with the artist, November 2, 2022.
4. Kathleen Mundell, *North by Northeast: Wabanaki, Akwesasne Mohawk, and Tuscarora Traditional Arts* (Gardiner, ME: Tilbury House, 2008), 34.
5. Interview with the artist, November 9, 2022.
6. Jennifer S. Neptune and Lisa K. Neuman, "Basketry of the Wabanaki Indians," in *Encyclopaedia of the History of Science, Technology, and Medicine in Non-Western Cultures*, ed. Helaine Selin, 3rd ed. (Berlin and New York: Springer Reference, 2016), 856.

than the lower trunk, and the bark is distinctly corky and spongy in texture.

Theresa Secord has memorably described ash as "the silk of the basket woods" for its lithe growth rings, flexible and sinewy due to the water frequently found at its feet.[7] The rings chart the trunk's growth and tell a story, keeping time for the tree as the years unfold. Trees like ash must increase the size of their xylem, the plant tissue that transfers water and nutrients from the roots to the stems and leaves.[8] They do so by adding new tissue between the existing xylem and the bark, a portion called the cambium layer.[9] Cambium cells are "perpetually embryonic," dividing again and again to widen the trunk.[10] In temperate climates, this process occurs with a seasonal cadence that witnesses new growth bursting forth during the lushness of spring and a dormant winter period following the dropping leaves in fall.[11] When a given year experiences balanced amounts of rain and sun, healthy wide rings form; if there is a drought year, the space between the rings narrows. This ring pattern offers a window into the tree's past, and its contours and widths help determine whether it is viable as a "basket tree" or not. Frey adapts his own life and work schedule to tree time; as the new rings begin to form in early spring, you can be sure he will be making his way through the deep northern Maine woods in search of promising ash.

7. Quoted in ibid., 861. See also Jennifer Neptune and Kathleen Mundell, *Wiwənikan . . . the beauty we carry* (Waterville, ME: Colby College Museum of Art, 2019), 25. White ash (*Fraxinus americana*), by contrast, is dry and coarse, and is instead purposed for axe and hammer handles or baseball bats—"anyplace where a good strong straight piece of wood was needed." Stephanie Francis and Scott Francis, eds., *Baskets of the Dawnland People*, with assistance by Donald Soctomah (Old Town: Maine Indian Basketmakers Alliance, 2008), 2.
8. R. L. Phipps and J. McGowan, *Tree Rings: Timekeepers of the Past* (Denver: U.S. Department of the Interior, U.S. Geological Survey, 1993), 4.
9. Marcus J. Thomson, "Dendrochronology and Sclerochronology," in *Encyclopedia of Ecology*, 2nd ed. (New York: Elsevier Science, 2019).
10. Robin Wall Kimmerer, *Braiding Sweetgrass: Indigenous Wisdom, Scientific Knowledge, and the Teachings of Plants* (Minneapolis: Milkweed, 2013), 144.
11. Ibid.; Phipps and McGowan, *Tree Rings*, 6.
12. Interview with the artist, November 9, 2022.

Harvest Time

Everything I do in basketmaking, I harvest and process myself. I have to specialize in all these things and know the materials intimately. Harvesting each component of my work helps me to better understand each piece. Every [ash] log I have has its own personality. . . . For example, one particular log could specifically lend itself to the making of basket ribs. —Jeremy Frey[12]

Following visual cues learned over time and through repetition, Frey finds the ash tree specimens most suitable for his art (fig. 2). It could be something as subtle as a specific slope of ground above a stream that catches his eye, or the color and texture of certain bark. Once that's identified, Frey cuts and hauls the ash log from the forest for pounding. After the rings have been stripped (always from the top of the tree, where the wood is looser), Frey isolates the outer rings for his weaving, because this more flexible sapwood is ideal for fine basket weaving. The light color of these rings also absorbs dye better than the darker and typically less pliable internal heartwood. Frey's uncle Moose, like many generations before him, imparted this harvesting knowledge, instilling in the artist a keen observation of his natural environment. As Frey described it to me, the principle of "use what's around you" is a distinctly

Fig 2 Jeremy Frey in an ash stand, 2023

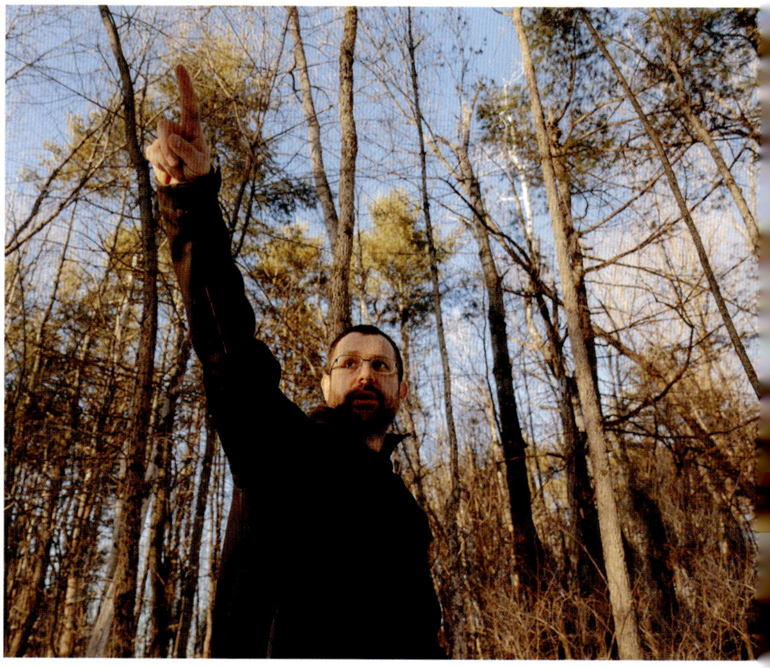

Native philosophy and one he pursues with determination and well-earned pride.[13]

Harvest season expands well beyond spring. In Frey's words, "No matter how busy you are, you have to keep harvesting."[14] As part of his constant search to push the limits of his art form, Frey frequently incorporates a dynamic array of natural materials in his baskets beyond ash. A more traditional addition is sweetgrass, which Frey and others gather from ocean-hugging marshes in summer. This species of sweetgrass, *Hierochloe odorata*, is one of eight found in northern Europe and North America.[15] When picked, it is a vivid green and emits the sweet, vanilla-like fragrance behind its name. Even when braided and woven into a basket, the plant's summery scent can fill a room (fig. 3). Sweetgrass has been described as "part of Passamaquoddy poetry repeated through countless generations," and it frequently features in Wabanaki basketry, Frey's included.[16]

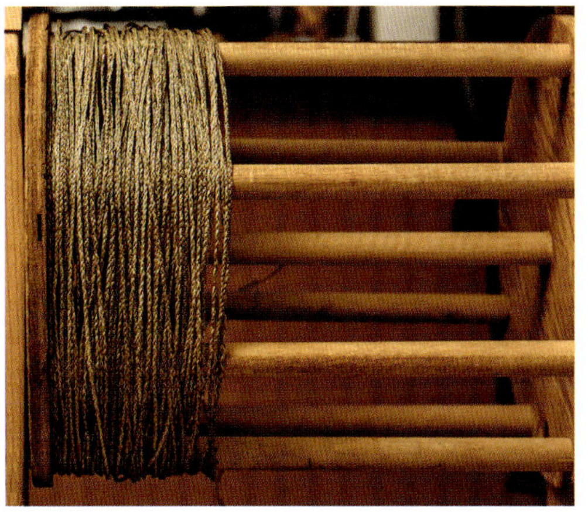

Fig 3 Braided sweetgrass, 2023

Frey also looks in less conventional places for harvesting, including the sides of roads and highways. There he finds the remains of porcupines that have met an untimely end after straying too close to traffic. Their glistening quills provide another medium with which the artist has gained exceptional dexterity, following in the footsteps of many Wabanaki (and other Indigenous) artists before him who used these needles to embellish boxes, baskets, and other forms. Initially inspired by his mother, Gal Frey, he continued to experiment in incorporating quills into his baskets with the purpose of adding diversity to his catalogue of work. Quills must be softened and sterilized in boiling water before use; they are easier to extract from the porcupine in summer when the animal has shed its fur. Frey pokes holes in a birch-bark ground and deftly inserts their slender forms through the wood, building them one by one into a composition.

Quills come in a variety of colors: black, white, brown, and orange. Frey either dyes these quills—one color per needle—or works with their natural coloring, depending on his design. Indeed, as Frey tells me, quill tone and texture are naturally suited to the representation of fur and feathers, and it is largely for this reason that he utilizes them to create striking animal portraits across his basket lids. Loons feature frequently as emblematic symbols of Maine woods and waters (pp. 66-69, 80-81). They also carry a certain nostalgia for Frey, who heard their songs and calls while growing up near Lewey Lake at Indian Township. Likewise, the cardinal atop *Color in Winter* references a family of cardinals that live near his current home in Eddington, Maine; this basket is a tribute to the ways in which their feathers brighten an otherwise monochrome winter landscape (pp. 78-79).

These quilled animals are arresting and have become a signature element of Frey's work—they have a certain vitality that Frey attributes to his method of beginning first with the eyes. In his view, "Good quillwork has to have life in its eye."[17] Recently, baskets such as *Observer* (2022) incorporate quillwork in more geometric patterns across areas of the basket beyond the lid (pp. 86-87). In this case, the complex neck of the piece serves as the quill canvas, but again, the needles form a semblance of eyes (the origin of the work's name), carrying forth Frey's associations of this material with a kind of gleaming life force. Here he also expresses a distinctly Wabanaki worldview regarding the natural world through depictions of animals, which often feature in family clans.

Other materials such as birch bark, cedar, and spruce root find central roles in Frey's work. Though birch bark is an essential medium in Wabanaki arts such

13. Ibid.
14. Ibid.
15. Francis and Francis, *Baskets of the Dawnland People*, 17.
16. Ibid., 18.
17. Interview with the artist, November 9, 2022.

as canoes, boxes, and wigwams, it is less common in ash basketry. Beyond serving as a ground for quillwork, birch bark provides another design element in Frey's ever-changing practice, as Andrew James Hamilton discusses in his essay in this volume.[18] Late winter or early spring ushers in the appropriate time to harvest cedar from cedar bogs; Frey began incorporating braided cedar by following the same pattern as with sweetgrass or ash (pp. 112-13).

Frey's decision to utilize cedar was partly out of an interest in innovation and the visual effects of its warm brown color, but it was also due to the existential threat that the emerald ash borer poses to ash stands across North America. An invasive species of beetle from Asia, the insect was discovered first in 2002 in Michigan, likely arriving via a shipping pallet. This insect kills all ash species by laying its eggs on the bark of the tree; the larvae that hatch bore through the trunk, feeding on the inner bark and leaving S-shaped grooves that eventually destroy the tree from the inside out.[19] The emerald ash borer expanded its territory exponentially due to the transport of infected firewood and other wood products and has already decimated millions of trees in the eastern United States. Wabanaki people, in concert with Akwesasne Mohawk and Great Lakes tribes, have led the defense of ash trees in the region by working with foresters and entomologists from the University of Maine, the Maine Forest Service, and the U.S. Forest Service, encouraging seed saving and slowing the spread of infected wood.[20] For Frey's part, he has expressed: "I'm trying to work with the material of the ash tree as best as I possibly can in order to respect what's left of it. It's almost like I have a responsibility to these trees. And for every tree I harvest to make a basket, I harvest another one and store it."[21] This mindset—of responsibility, reciprocity, and care—reflects his efforts to extend the tree's life as long as possible, both for the ash itself and for future generations.

Old and New Growth

Every piece is a part of the whole.
—Jeremy Frey[22]

In April 2023, Frey debuted the basket *Navigating Tradition* (figs. 4a and 4b). This work serves as another symbolic encapsulation of time: the past two decades of his art practice as well as his connection to the much longer history of Wabanaki ash basketry. Featured in Karma gallery's inaugural presentation of the artist's work, this piece also commemorates an extraordinary and historically significant moment: the first solo exhibition of a Wabanaki artist in a fine art gallery in New York (figs. 5a and 5b).

Importantly, *Navigating Tradition* showcases one of the many unique forms and techniques that Frey has developed over time: the double-walled basket. This type of vessel is intricately layered, incorporating a "basket-within-a-basket"—one basket nestled within another, or two baskets in one.[23] The outside basket is composed of undyed ash, harvested from different sections of the brown ash tree that provides the vital material for all Frey's work. Here one can discern a rich tonal and textural interplay between the ash tree's rougher external bark and the smoother, lighter internal wood. The darker color that characterizes the external bark is the index of where the tree's bark has been bruised from pounding and shows an actual smoky ash stain (made with water mixed with ashes from the wood stove) that Frey painted on the log to help trace

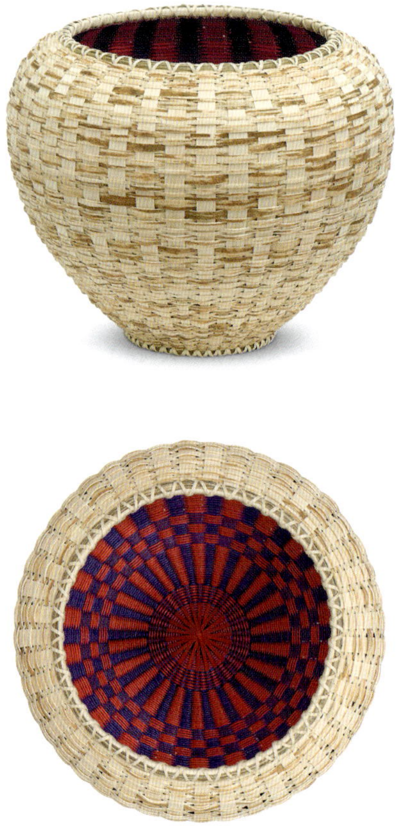

Figs 4a and 4b Jeremy Frey, *Navigating Tradition* (two views, detail on bottom), 2023, ash, sweetgrass, and dye, 6¾ × 9½ × 9½ inches. Portland Museum of Art, Maine. Museum purchase with exchange funds from the gift of Joseph and Ruth Sataloff, 2023.35

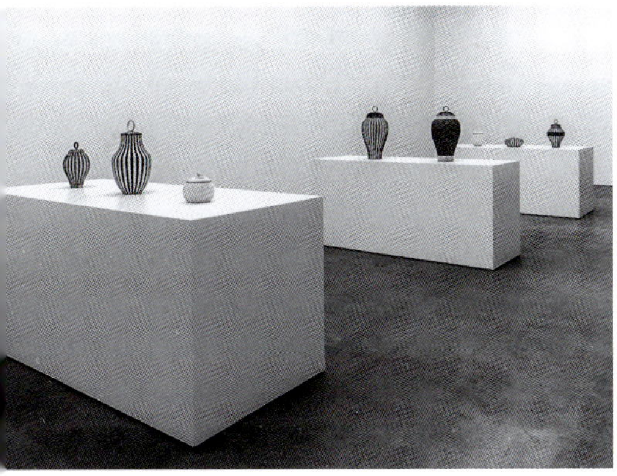

Fig 5a and 5b (above and overleaf) *Jeremy Frey: Out of the Woods*, 2023, Karma, New York, installation view

where his axe blows had fallen. *Navigating Tradition* marks the artist's first incorporation of this part of the wood—one that bears the signs of the tree's remarkable transformation from log to vessel, raw matter to art.

Also immediately apparent are the horizontal splints encircling the exterior basket that have been cut at varying widths, alternating in size across the dense weave. This size disparity is, of course, intentional and all the more striking for the fact that Frey is known and celebrated for his profoundly precise and uniform weavings. Frey adopted these differently sized, textured weavers in order to visually signal the early roots of Wabanaki basketry, which was both tool and aesthetic expression. In this context, art is not divorced from function—the two are not mutually exclusive. Before the imposition of a settler cash-based economy, Wabanaki artists produced baskets for a variety of purposes, including hunting, food preparation, and travel, and they continue to do so today. These objects have since been designated by artists and scholars as "utility baskets," indicating their function. They are often distinguished by thicker, rougher ash splints, incorporated into forms without as much fine-tuning as is evident in the later, more elaborate works known as "fancy baskets," which feature delicate designs and colors in a dazzling array of forms. Frey is better known for his work in this latter "fancy" artistic format, but he also descends from utility basket makers, including his uncle Moose. With this work he pays homage to that lineage, as well as the deeper foundations of Wabanaki baskets, which were put to everyday use.

The colorful interior basket thus gestures to the artist's signature fine weave forms. Indeed, few artists have pushed basketry to more intricate levels than Frey, who has developed increasingly complex, award-winning designs throughout his creative trajectory. The vivid red-purple color scheme also speaks to the artist's distinct style, one that explores bold combinations of synthetic dyes. Even so, Frey rarely abandons all evidence of the natural, undyed ash—a pale blond, very light hue that is further accentuated when incorporated as a visual element in his vibrant palettes.

This contrast is evident in *Navigating Tradition*, and the overall combination—of weavings, textures, and color—allows the artist to meditate on the suspension of past and present, old and new, that his practice has always endeavored to uphold. *Navigating Tradition* offers a "full circle" moment, inviting viewers to reflect on the art form's rich past as well as its remarkable evolution in the hands of one of the medium's foremost innovators, who shows us that tradition is, in essence, ever-changing.

18. See pp. 22–29.
19. Neptune and Neuman, "Basketry of the Wabanaki Indians," 859.
20. For more on this invasive species, its environmental and cultural consequences, and steps that Wabanaki people have taken to mitigate these effects, see Keller Leet-Otley, Grace Neumiller, and Tommaso Wagner, "Brown Ash Endangerment and Indigenous Solutions," *The Lantern*, June 2019, https://web.colby.edu/thelantern/2019/06/11/brown-ash-endangerment-and-indigenous-solutions/. As these authors clarify, however, even these protective measures are challenging to ensure, as the emerald ash borer is exceedingly difficult to eradicate following infestation of a particular area.
21. Ibid.
22. Interview with the artist, November 9, 2022.
23. See the essay by Andrew James Hamilton in this volume, which also discusses the double-walled basket, pp. 22–29.

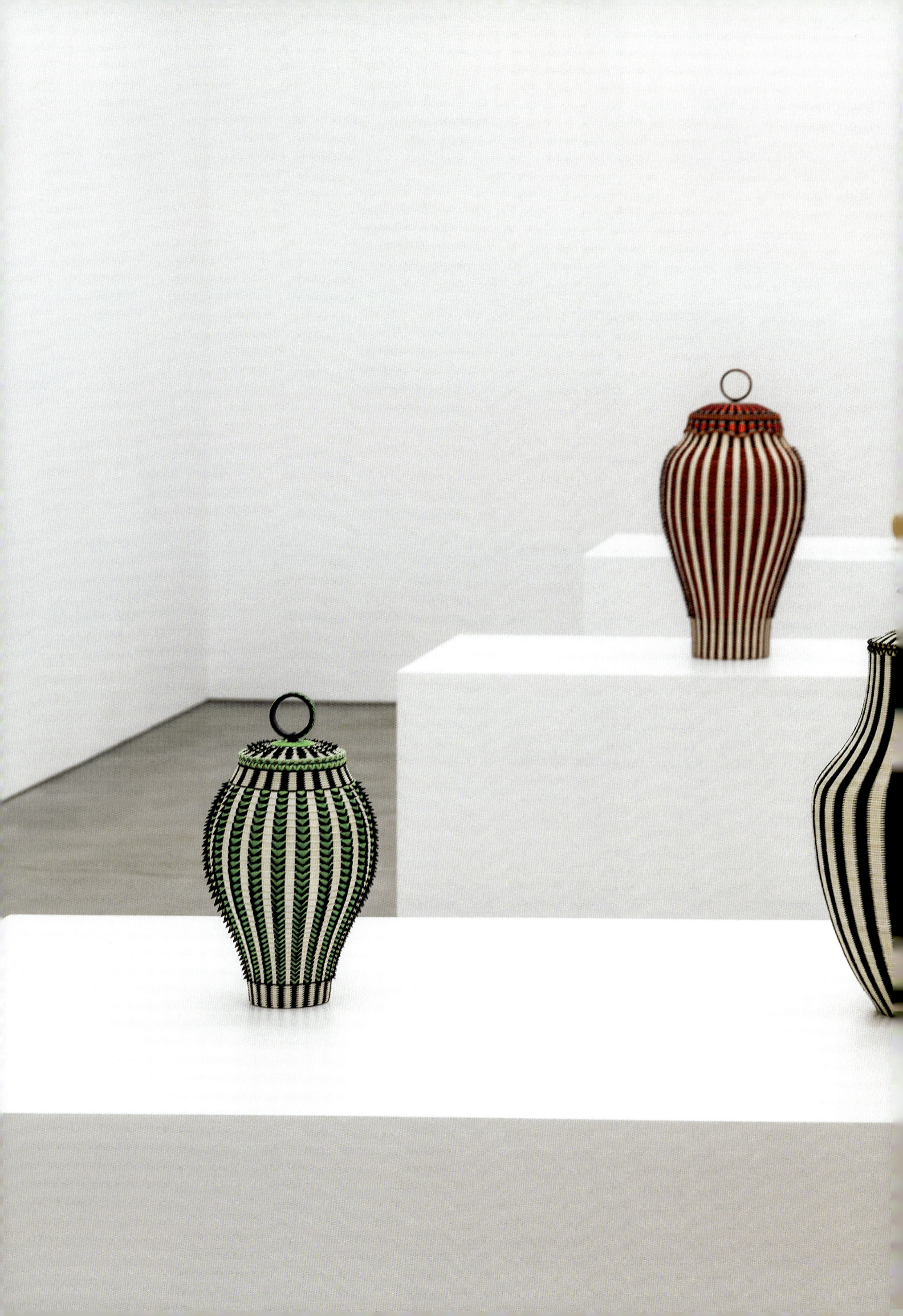

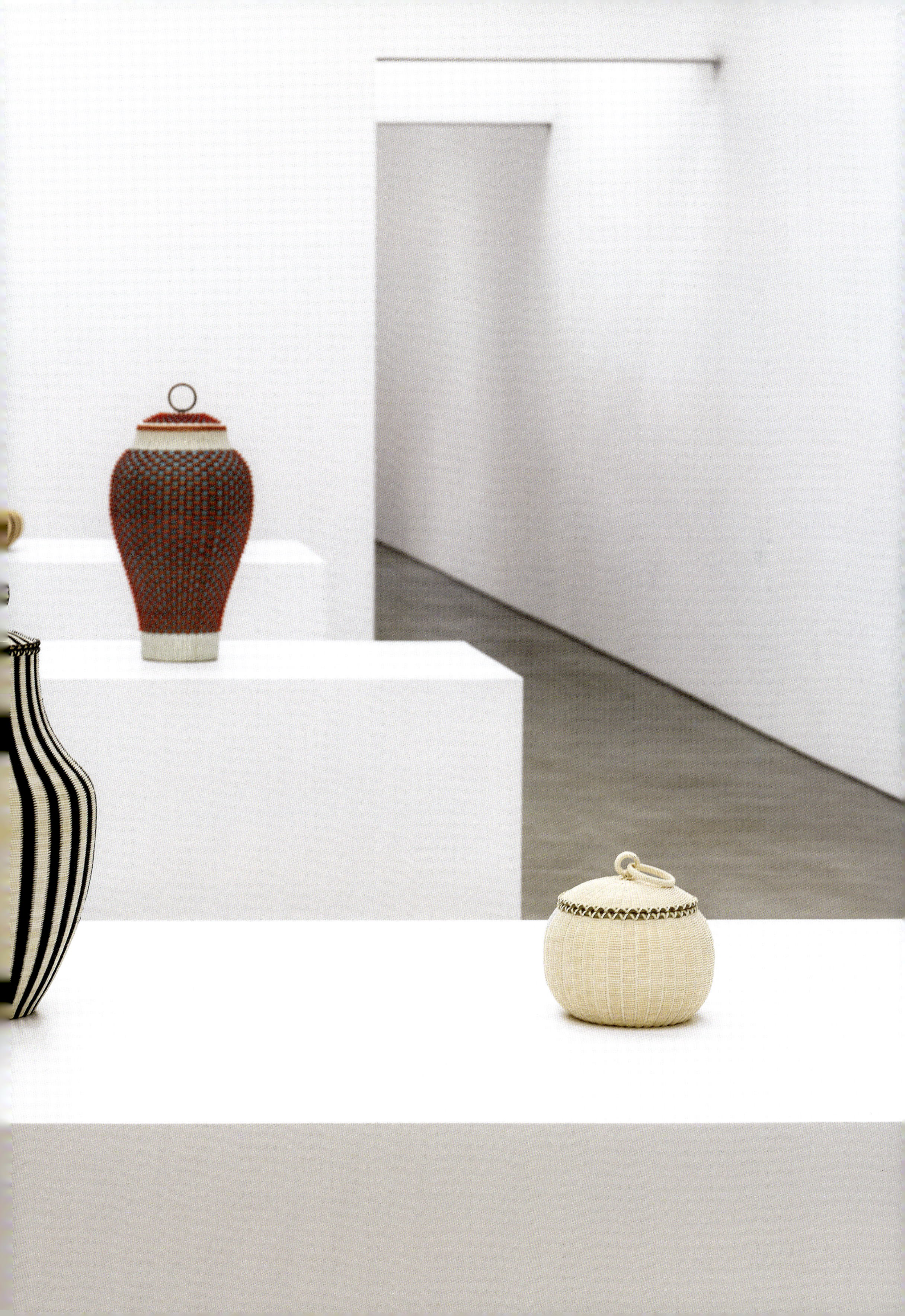

Early Point
and
Fine Weave Baskets

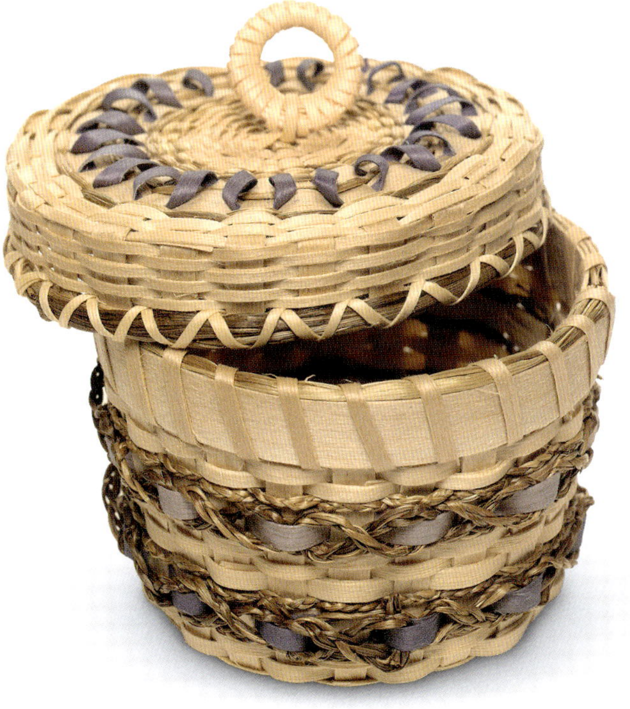

Basket with Cover, 2003

Ash and sweetgrass
3⅛ × 2¾ × 2¾ inches
National Museum of the American Indian, Smithsonian Institution, Washington, D.C., 261581.000

54

Basket with Cover, 2003

Ash, sweetgrass, and porcupine quill on birch bark
12¼ × 8¼ × 8 ¼ inches
National Museum of the American Indian, Smithsonian
Institution, Washington, D.C., 261580.000

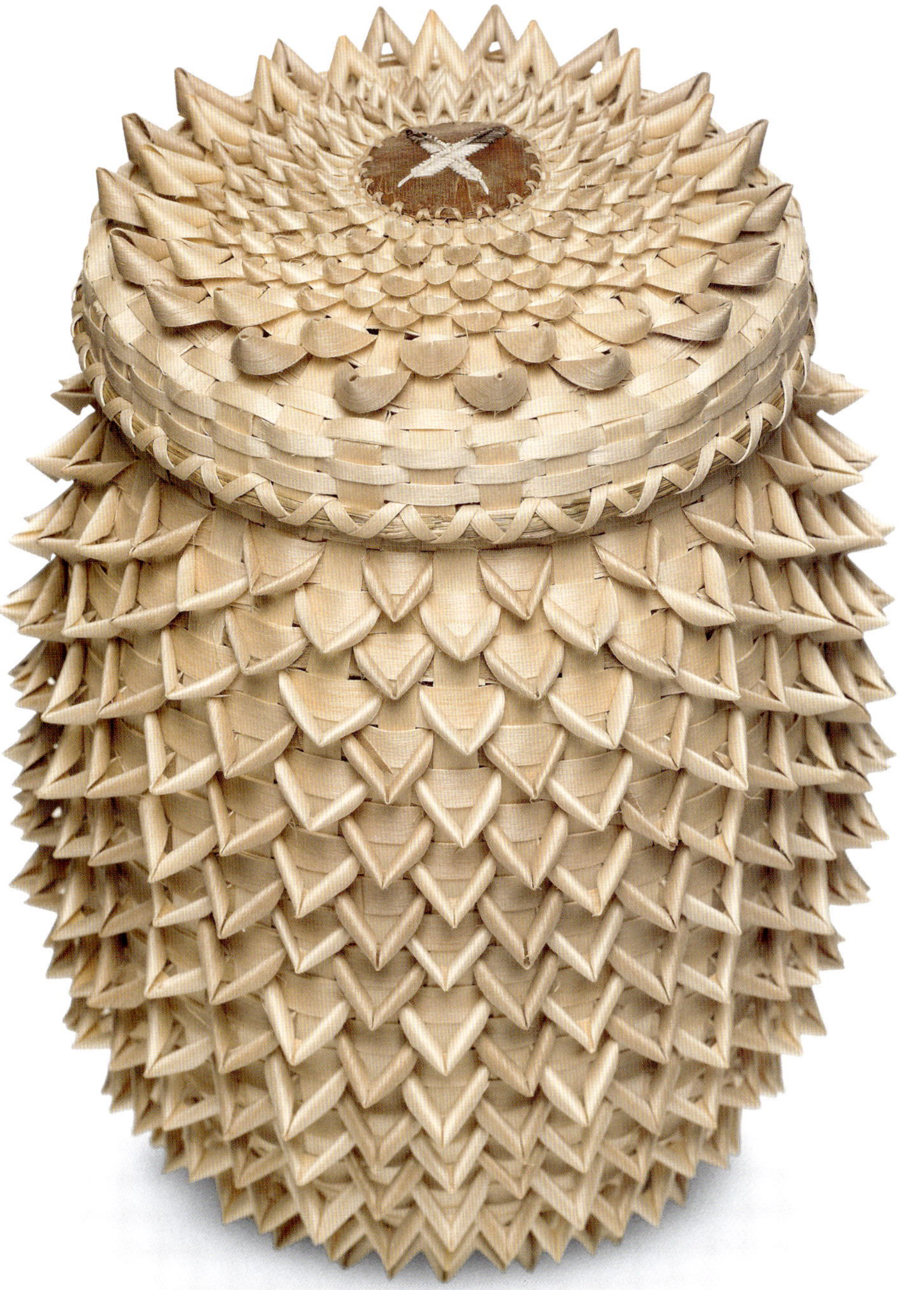

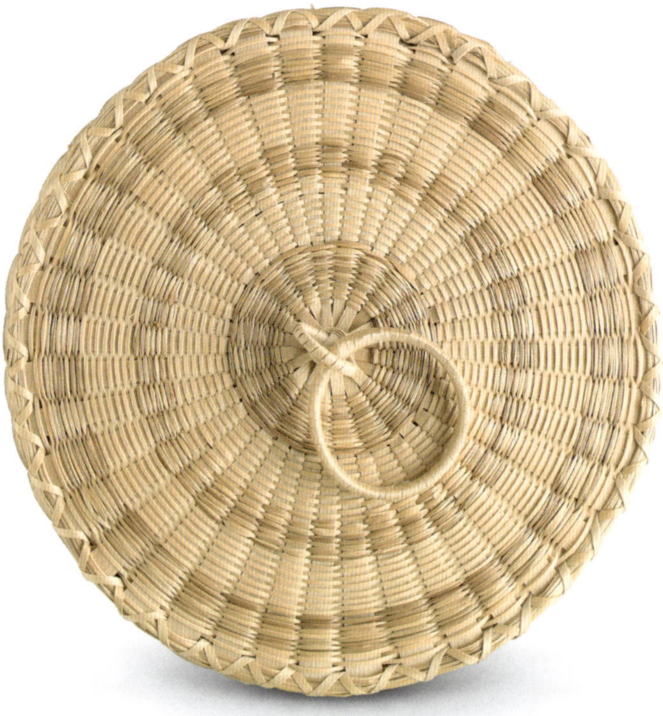

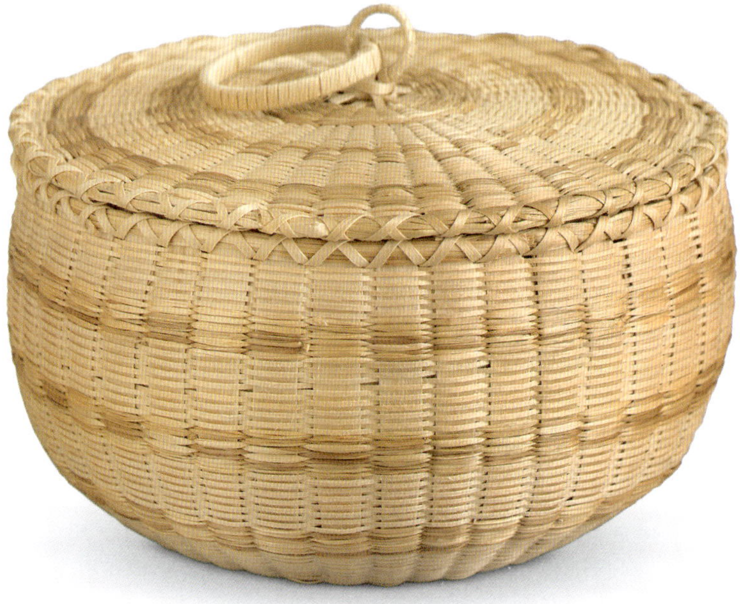

First Fine Weave, 2003

Ash and sweetgrass
3½ × 6 × 6 inches
Collection of Gal Frey

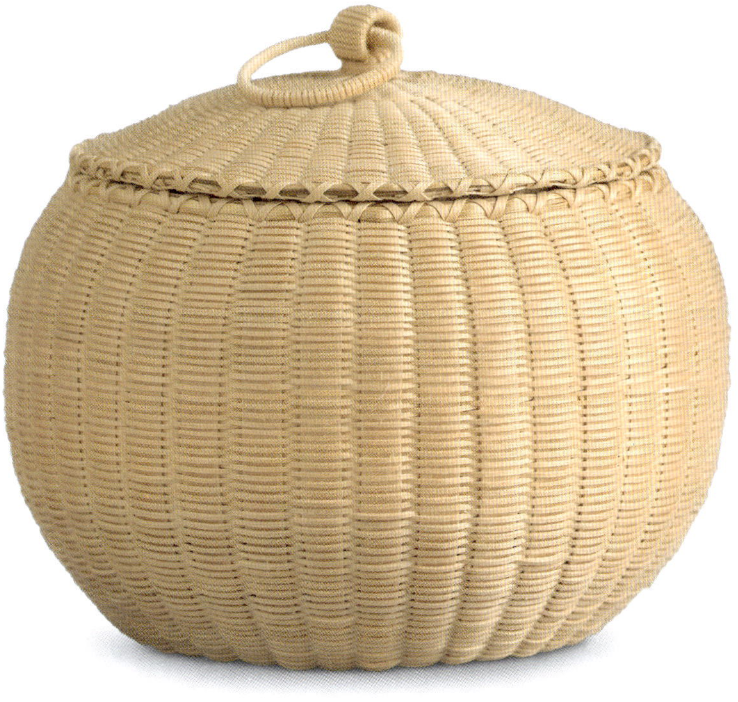

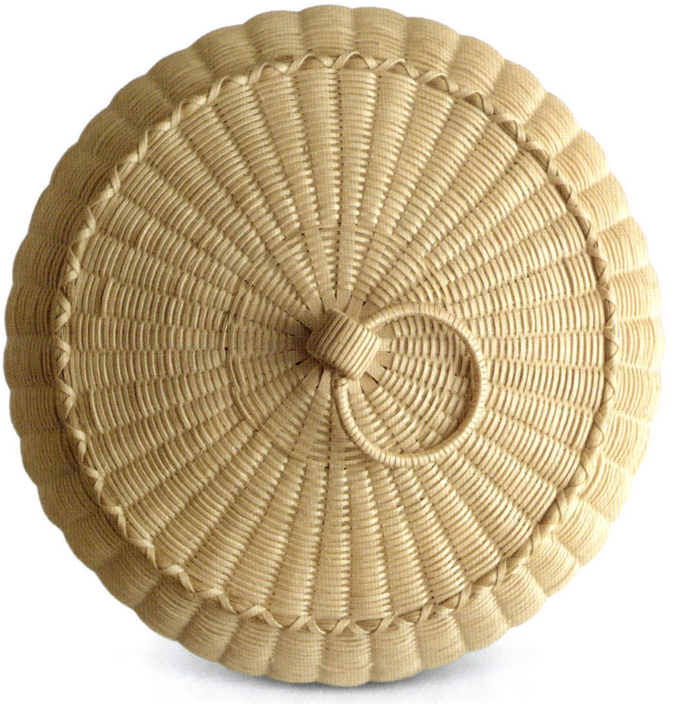

Fine Weave, 2008

Ash and sweetgrass
5½ × 6 × 6 inches
Collection of Gal Frey

Shooting Star, 2008

Ash, sweetgrass, and dye
6 × 7½ × 7½ inches
Portland Museum of Art, ME . Museum purchase with support from the Peggy and Harold Osher Acquisition Fund, 2022.30a,b

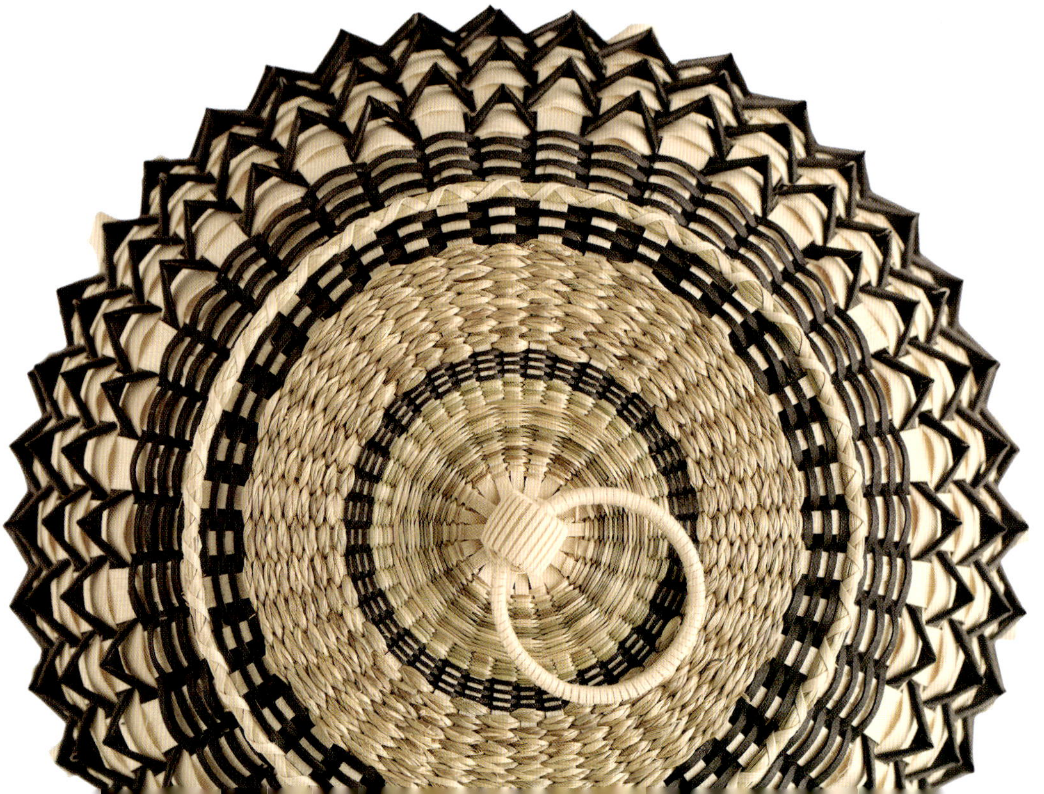

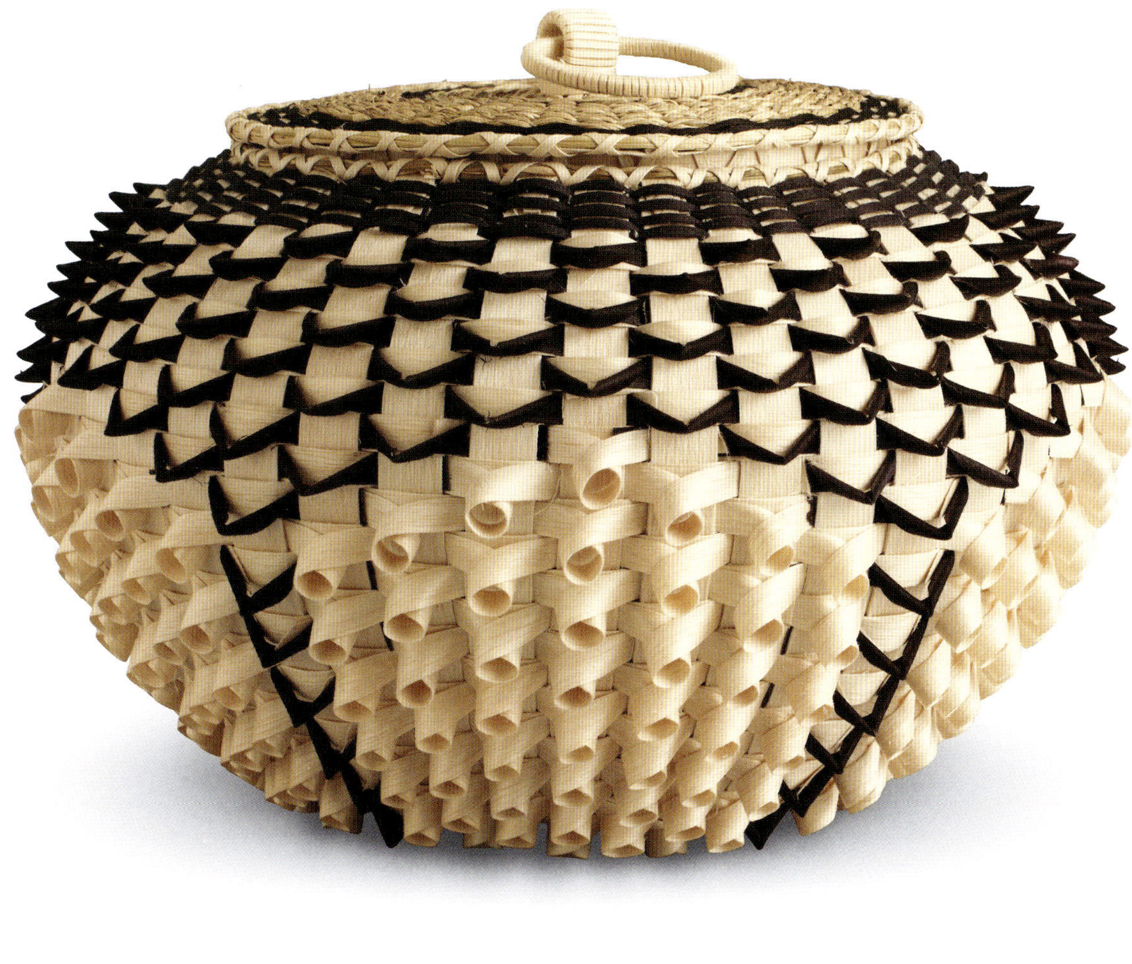

Basket within Basket, 2012

Ash, sweetgrass, and dye
9 × 13 × 13 inches
Collection of Dr. and Mrs. Ari and Lea Plosker

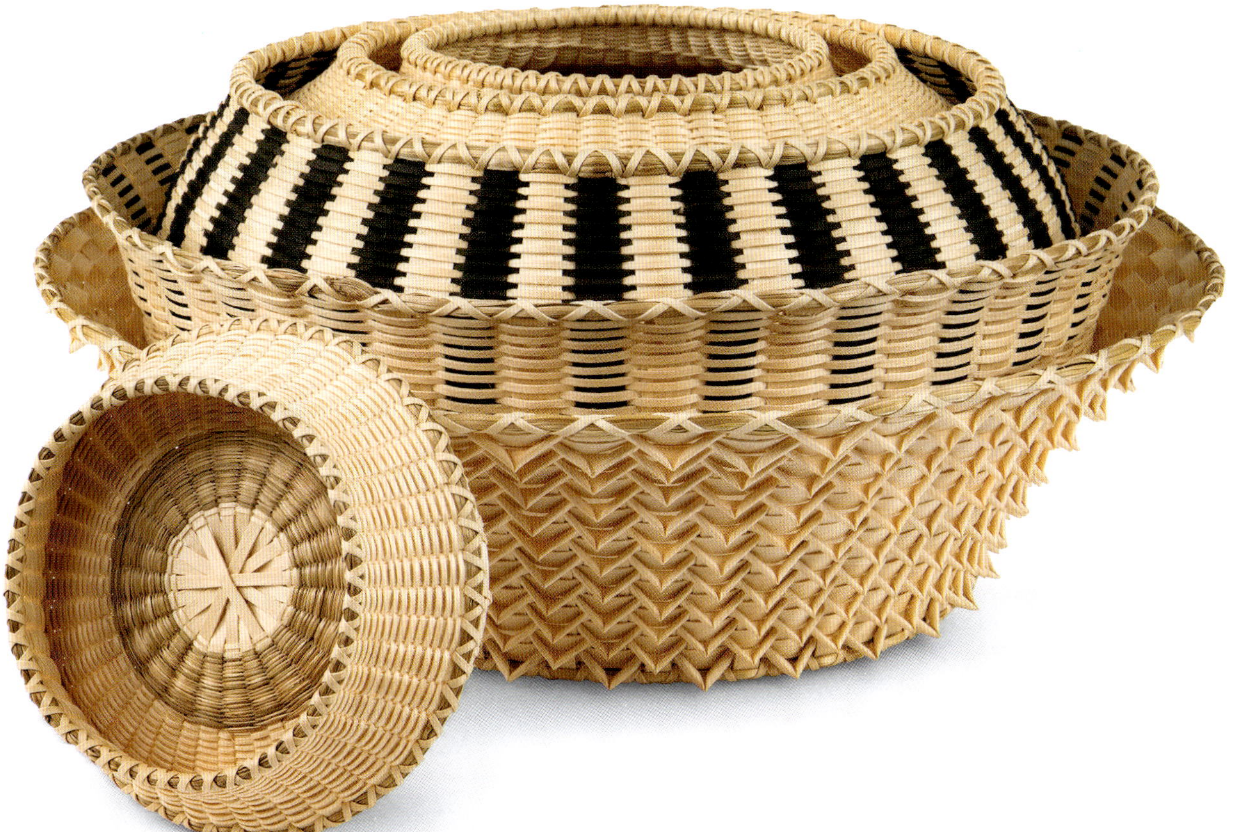

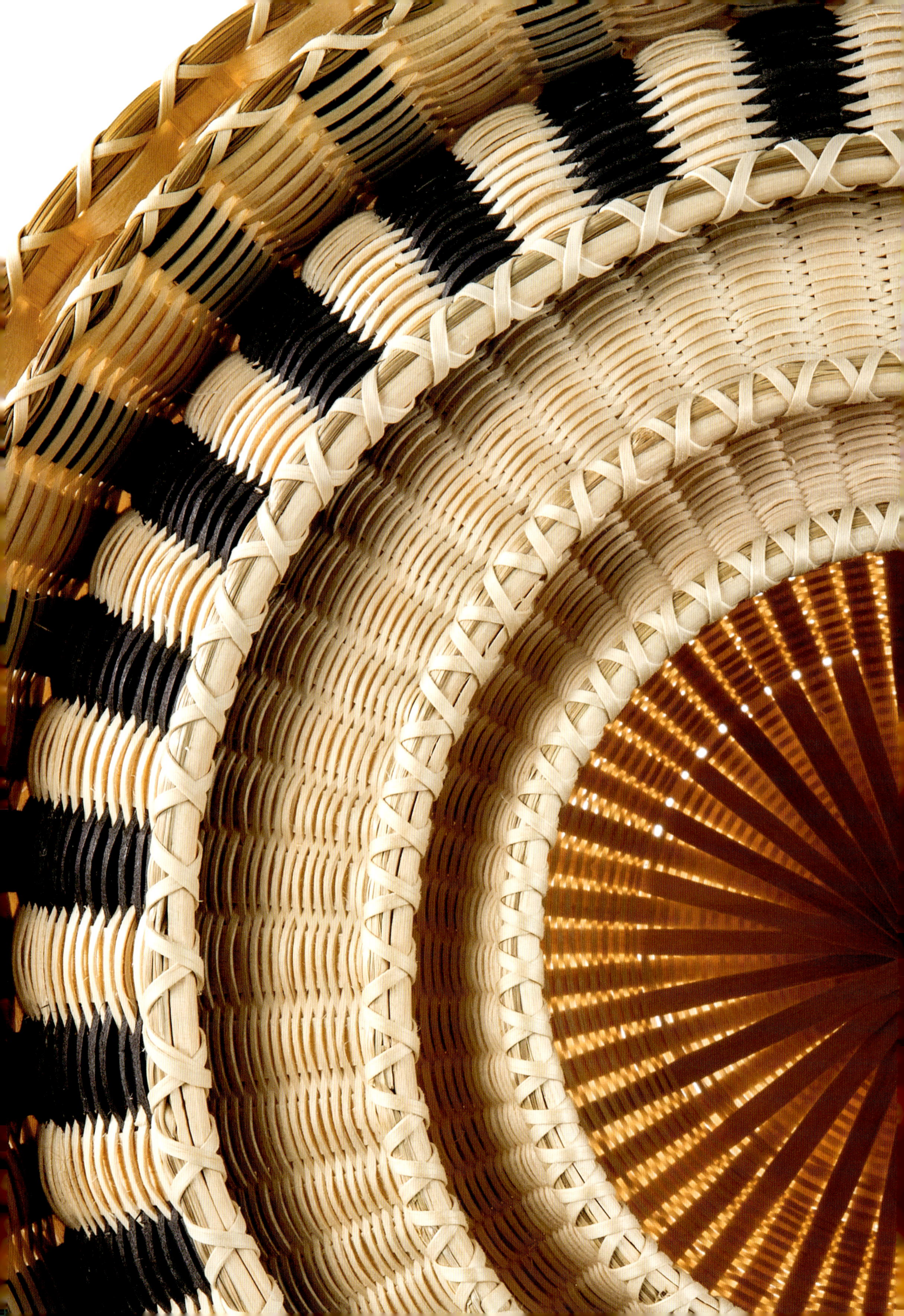

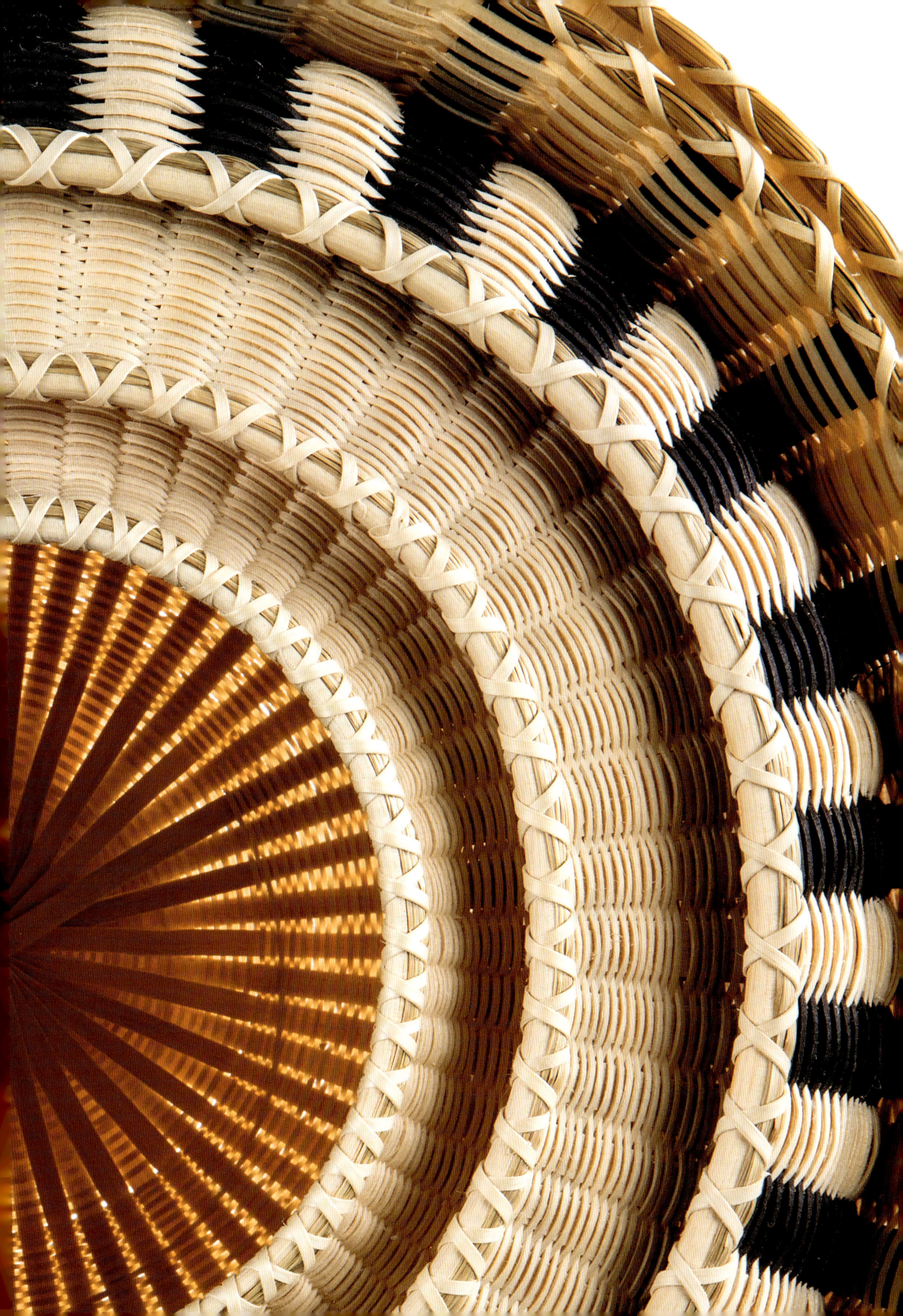

Fine Weave, 2016

Ash and sweetgrass
6 × 5 × 5 inches
Collection of Dr. and Mrs. Ari and Lea Plosker

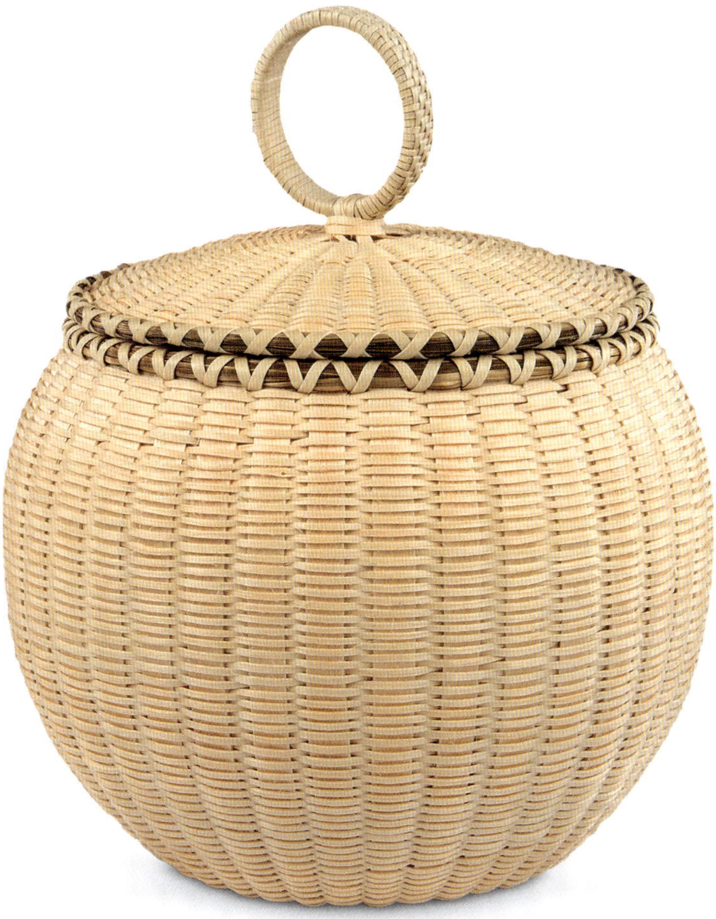

Porcupine Quillwork Baskets

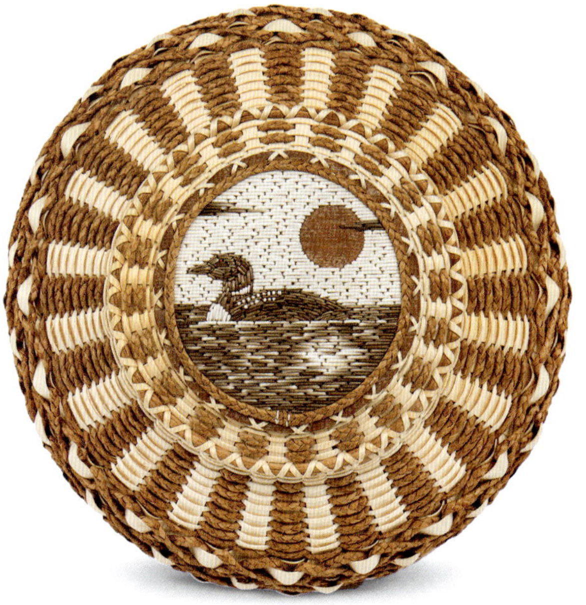

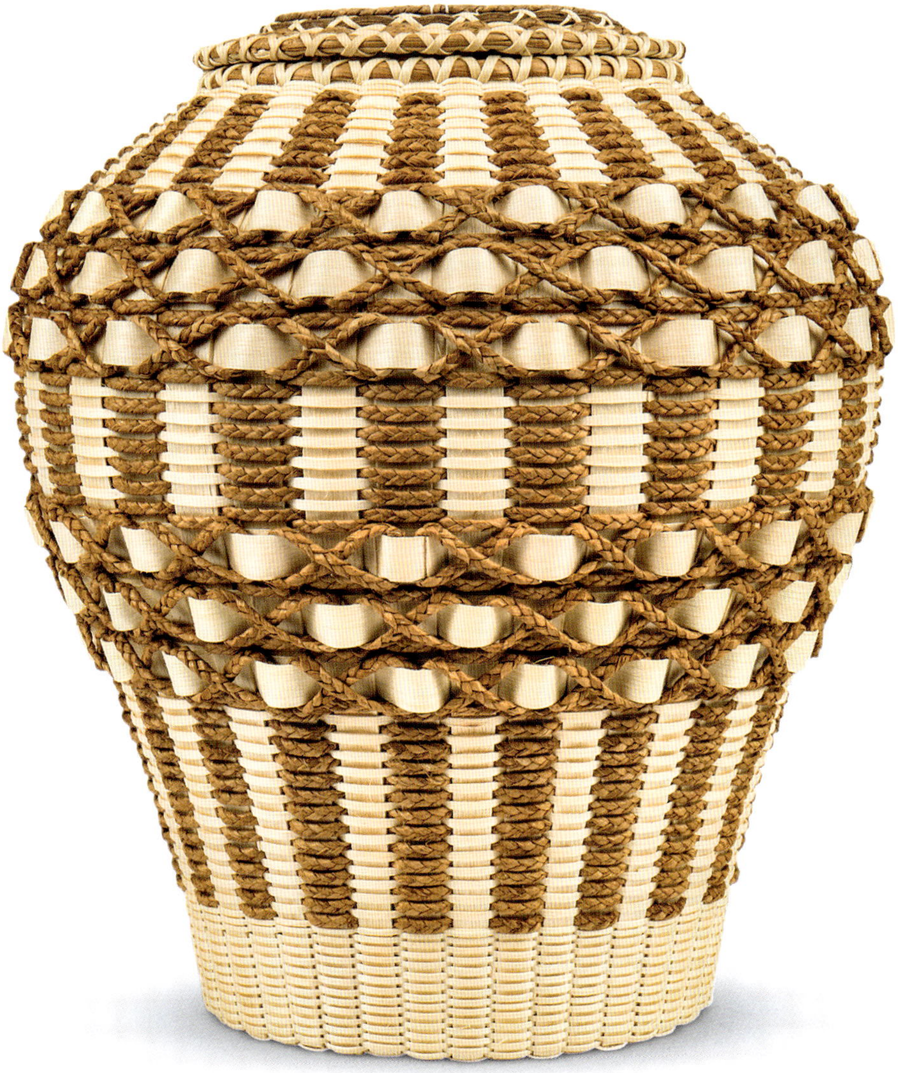

Cedar Loon Moon, 2011

Ash, braided cedar bark, sweetgrass, and porcupine quill on birch bark
9 × 8 × 8 inches
Collection of Dr. and Mrs. Ari and Lea Plosker

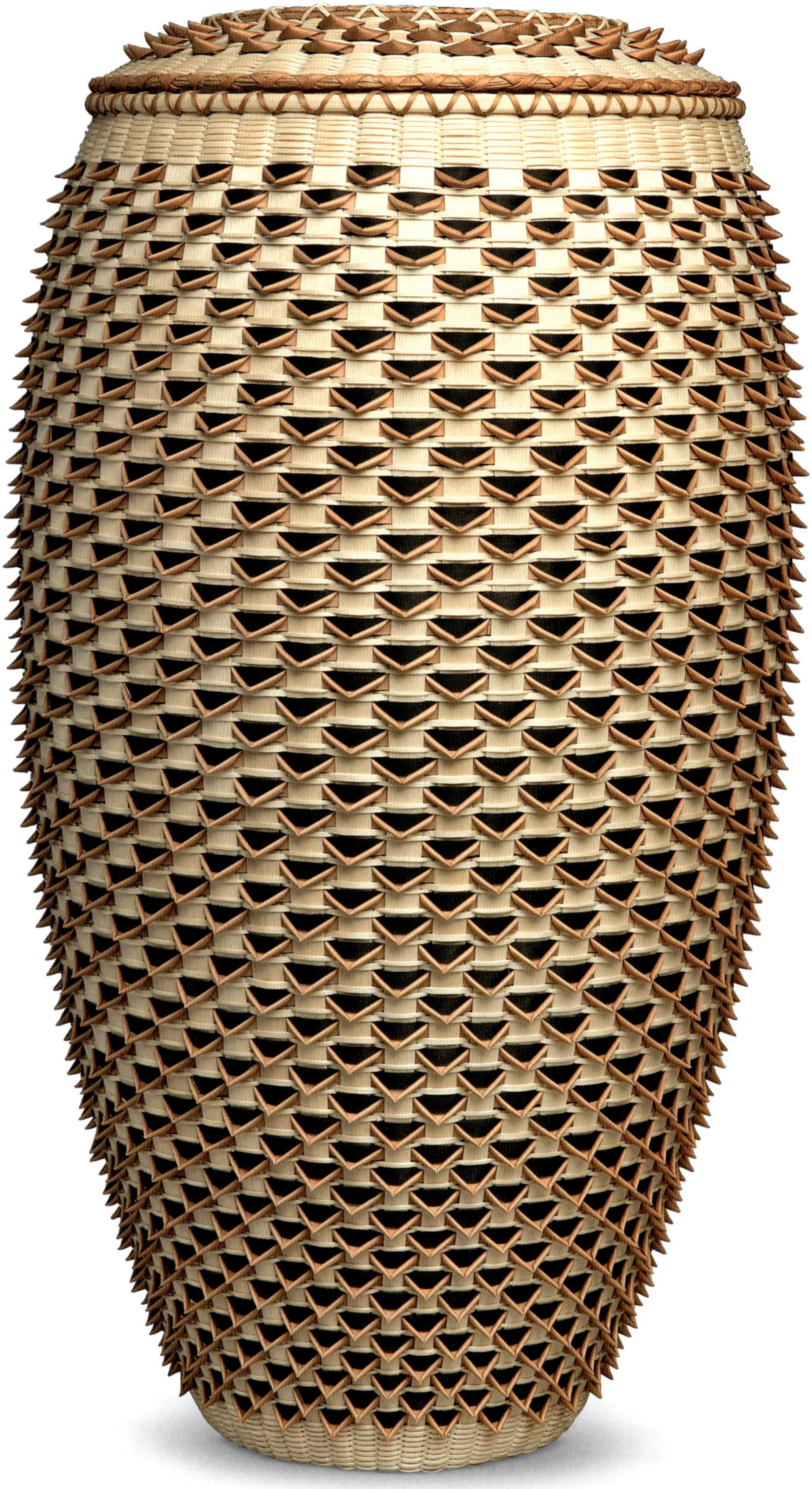

Loon, 2015

Ash, cedar bark, porcupine quill on birch bark, and dye
19 × 10 × 10 inches
Collection of Dr. Marc and Lynn Appelbaum, New Mexico

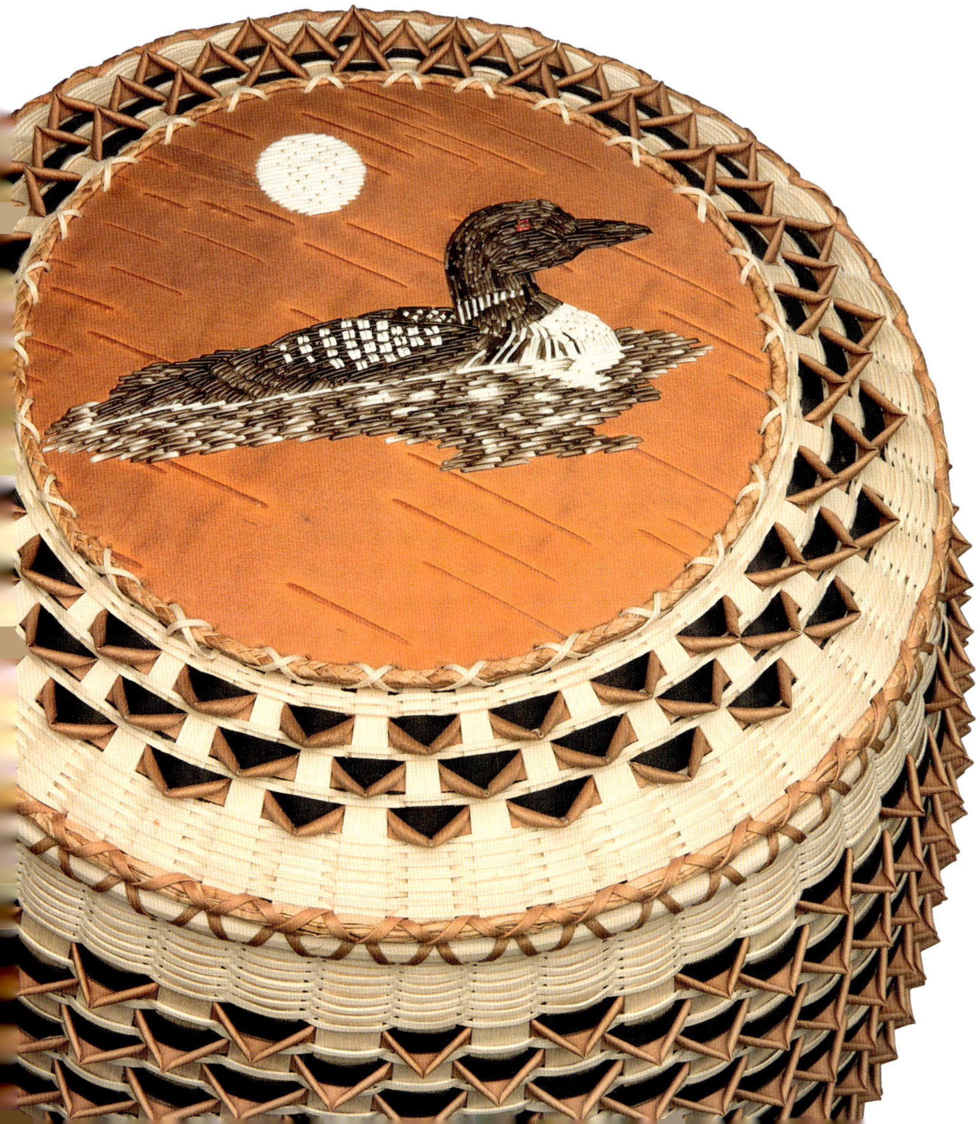

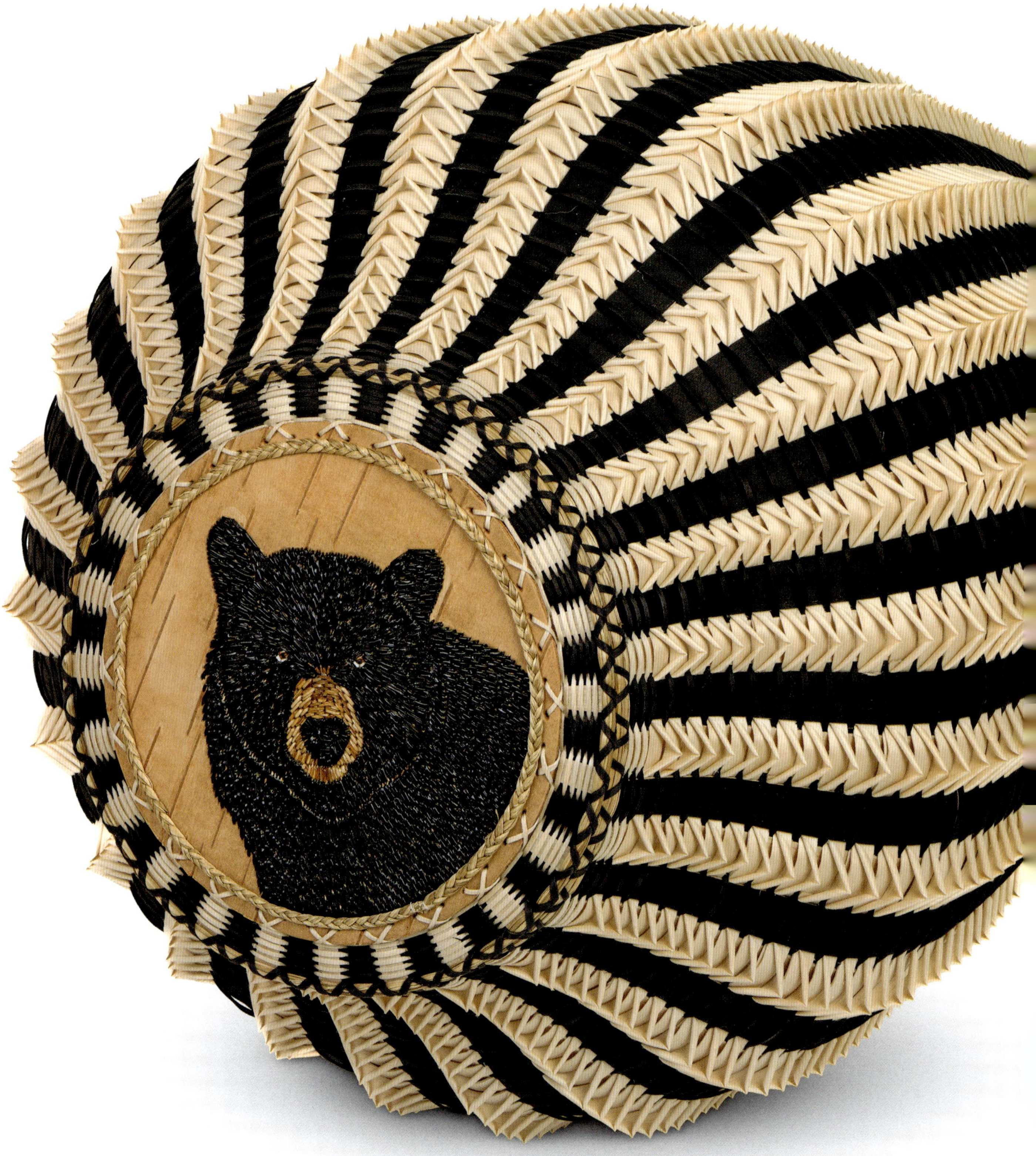

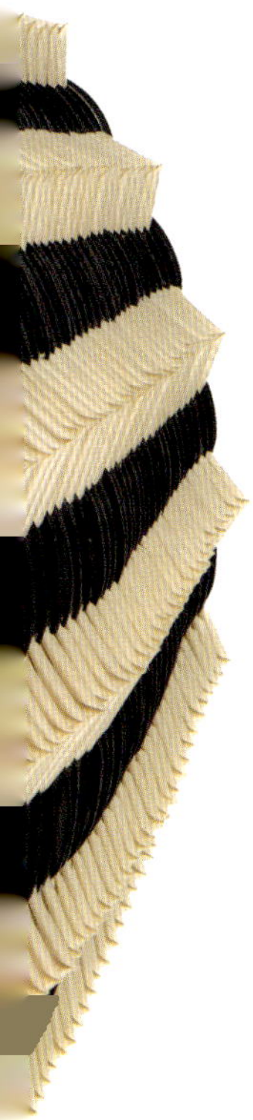

Muwin (Bear), 2017

Ash, sweetgrass, porcupine quill on birch bark, and dye
13 × 7 × 7 inches
The Buker Collections

Cubs, 2018

Ash, sweetgrass, porcupine quill on birch bark, and dye
19 × 10½ × 10½ inches
The Buker Collections

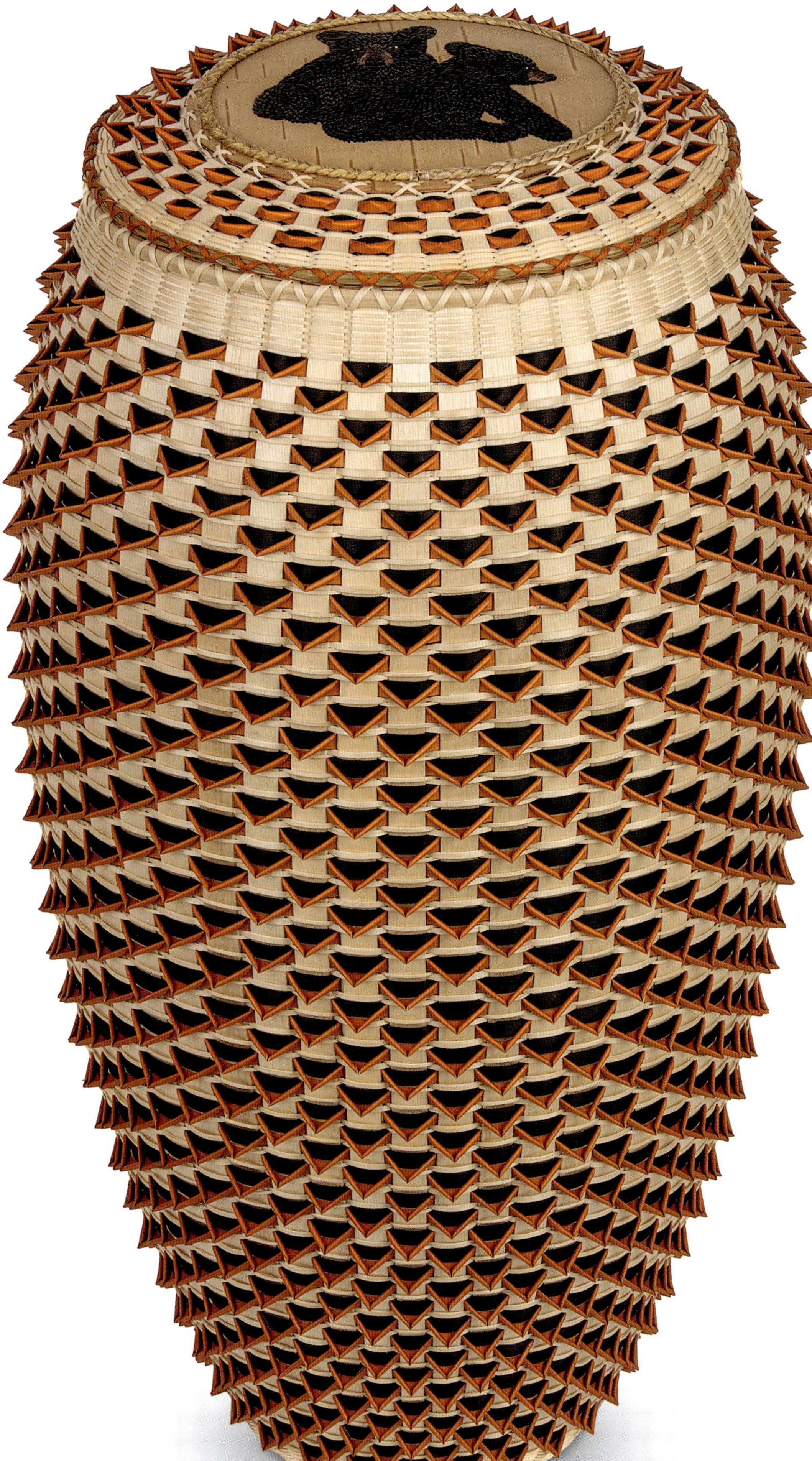

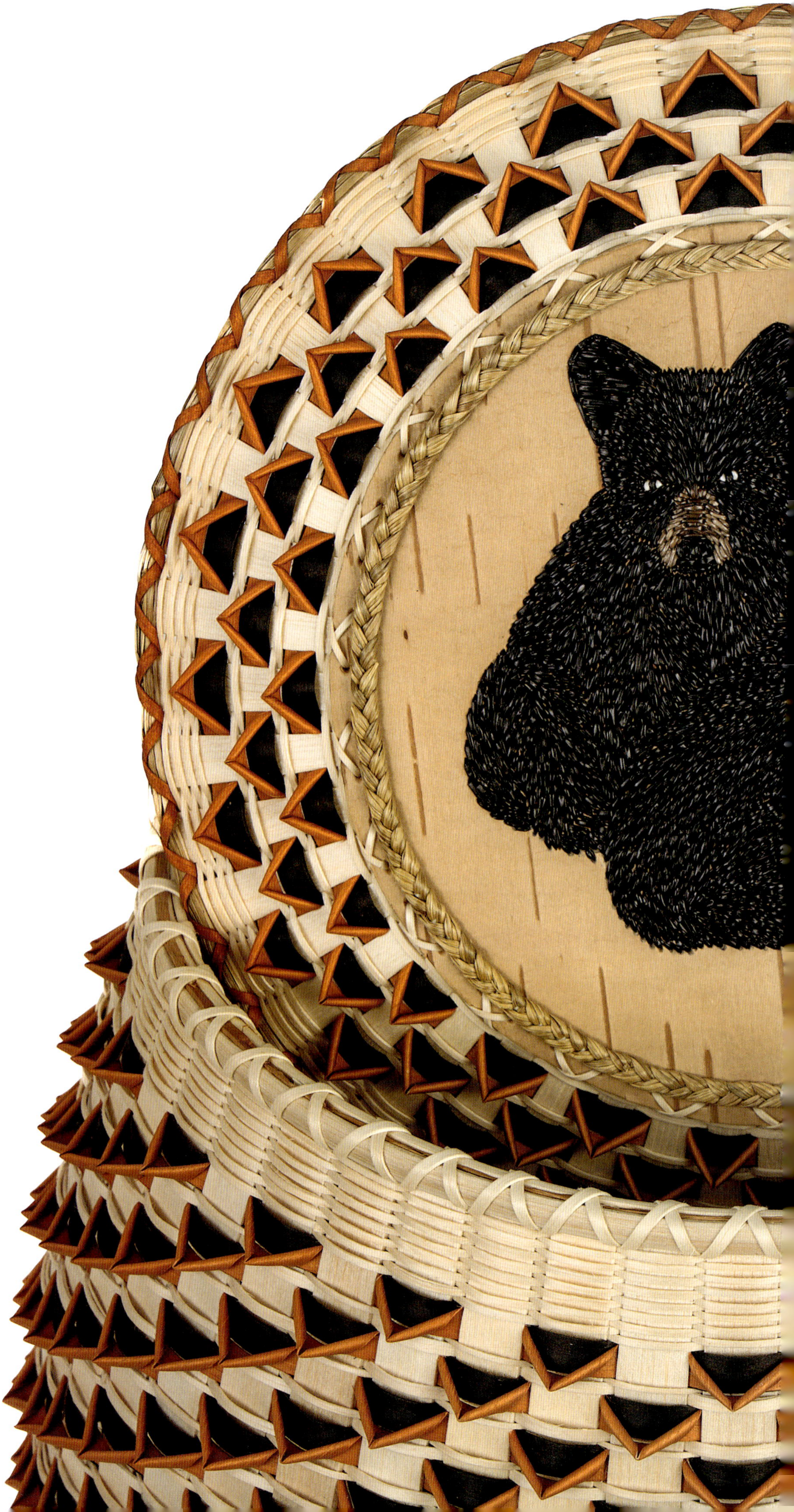

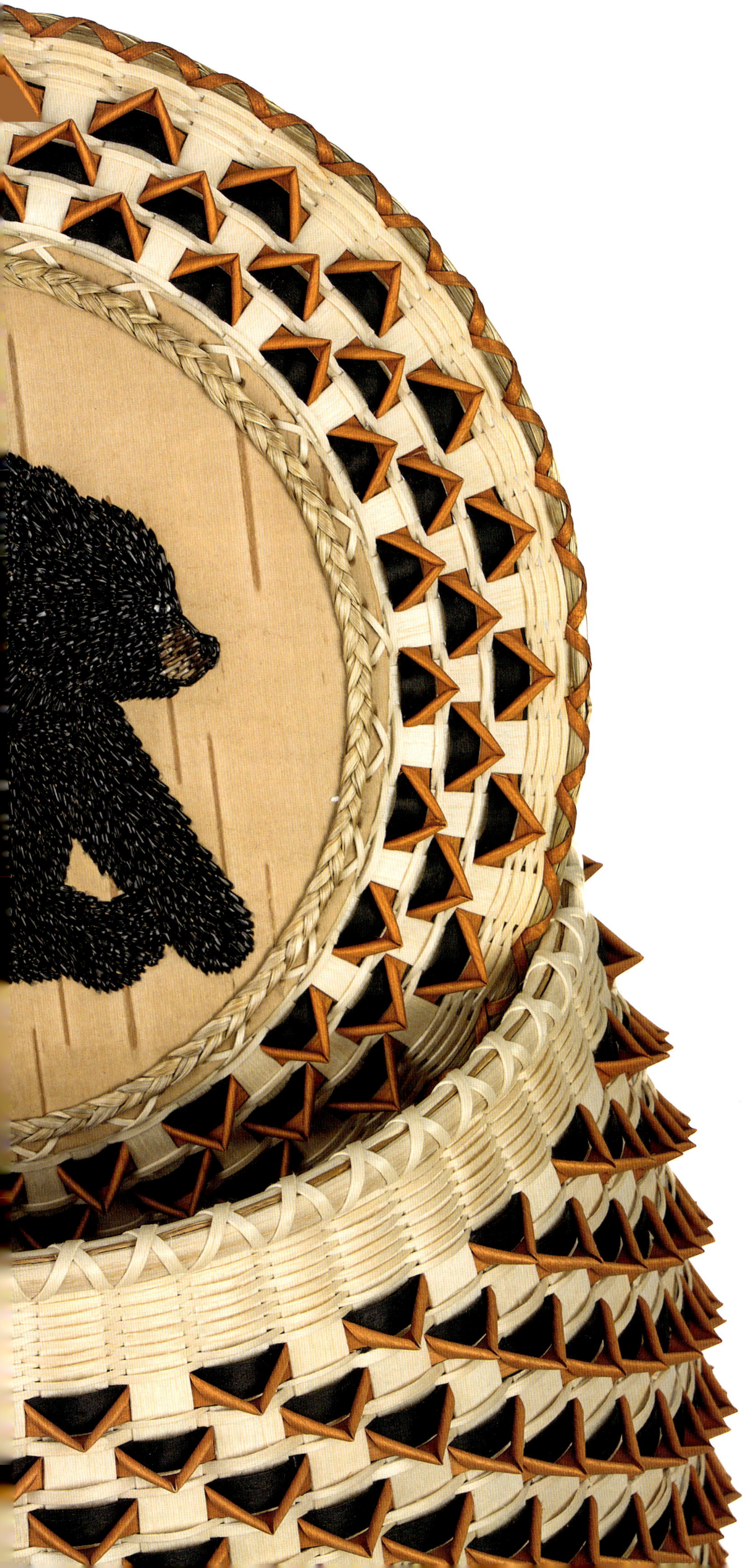

Cihpolakon (Eagle), 2019

Ash, cedar bark, birch bark, porcupine quill on birch bark, and dye
10 × 7½ × 7½ inches
Collection of Carole Katz

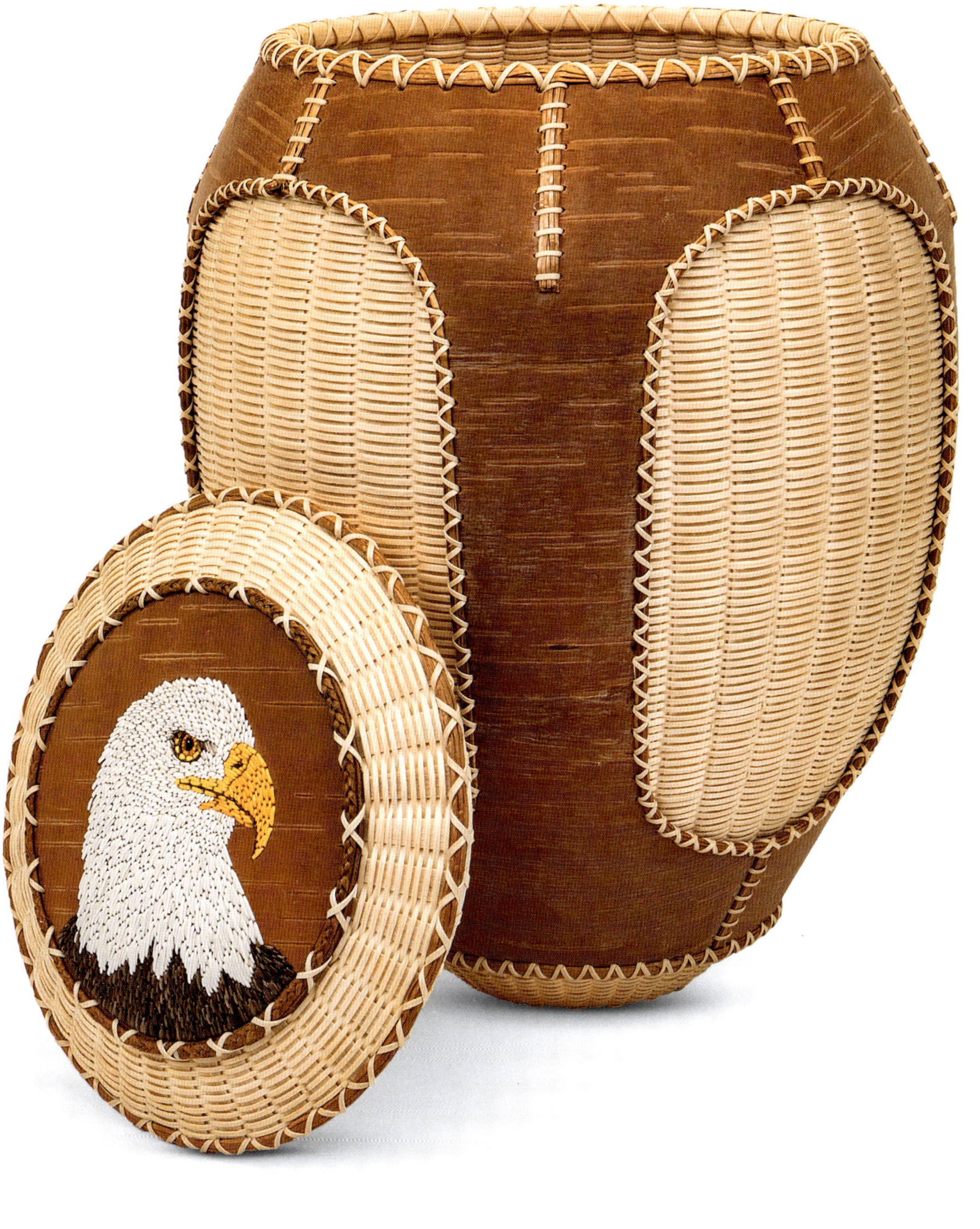

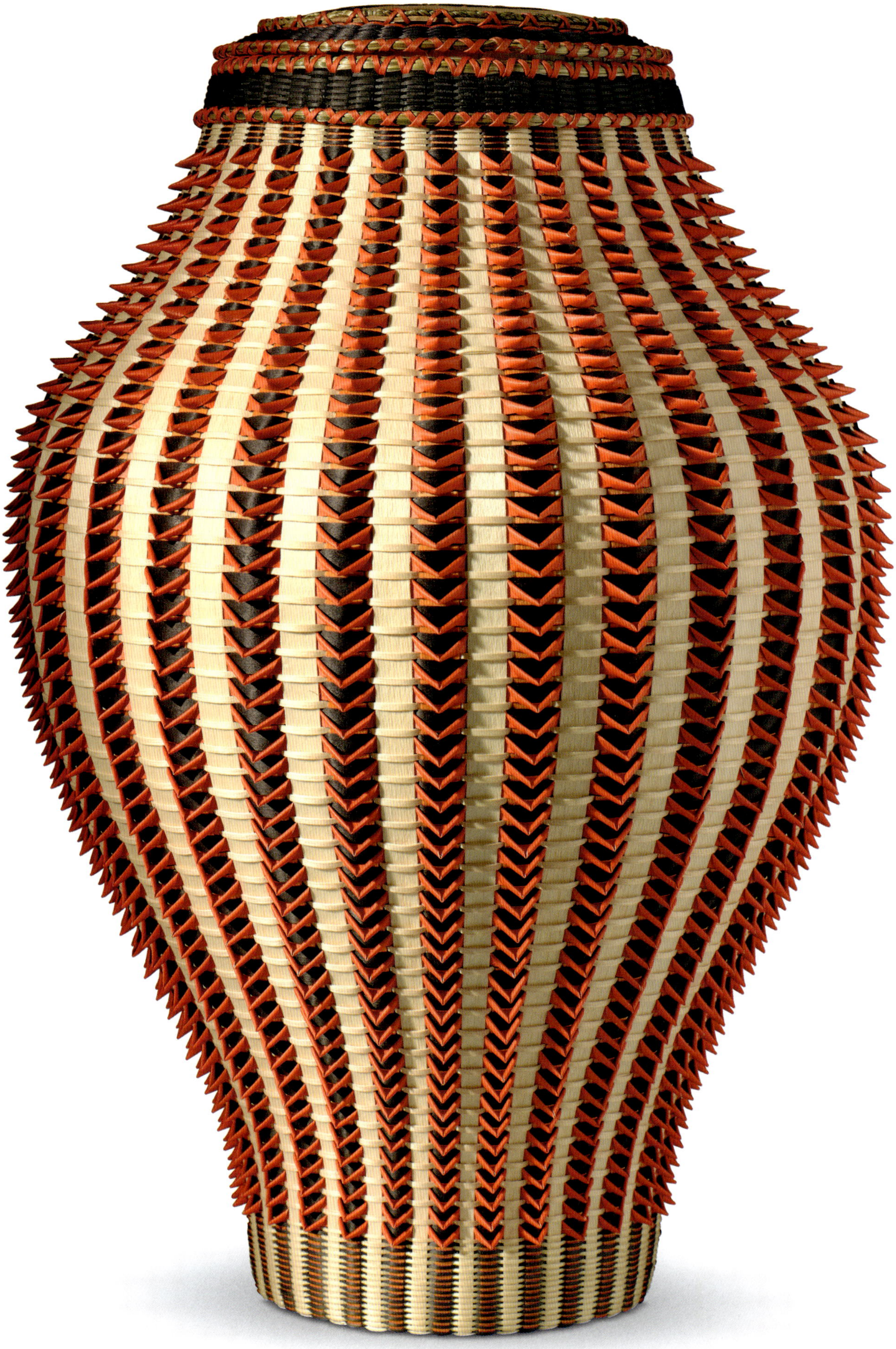

Color in Winter, 2019

Ash, sweetgrass, porcupine quill on birch bark, and dye
16 × 12 × 12 inches
Colby College Museum of Art, Museum purchase from the Bruce C. Drouin '74 and Janet L. Hansen '75 Maine Art Endowed Fund and Friends of Art, 2019.026

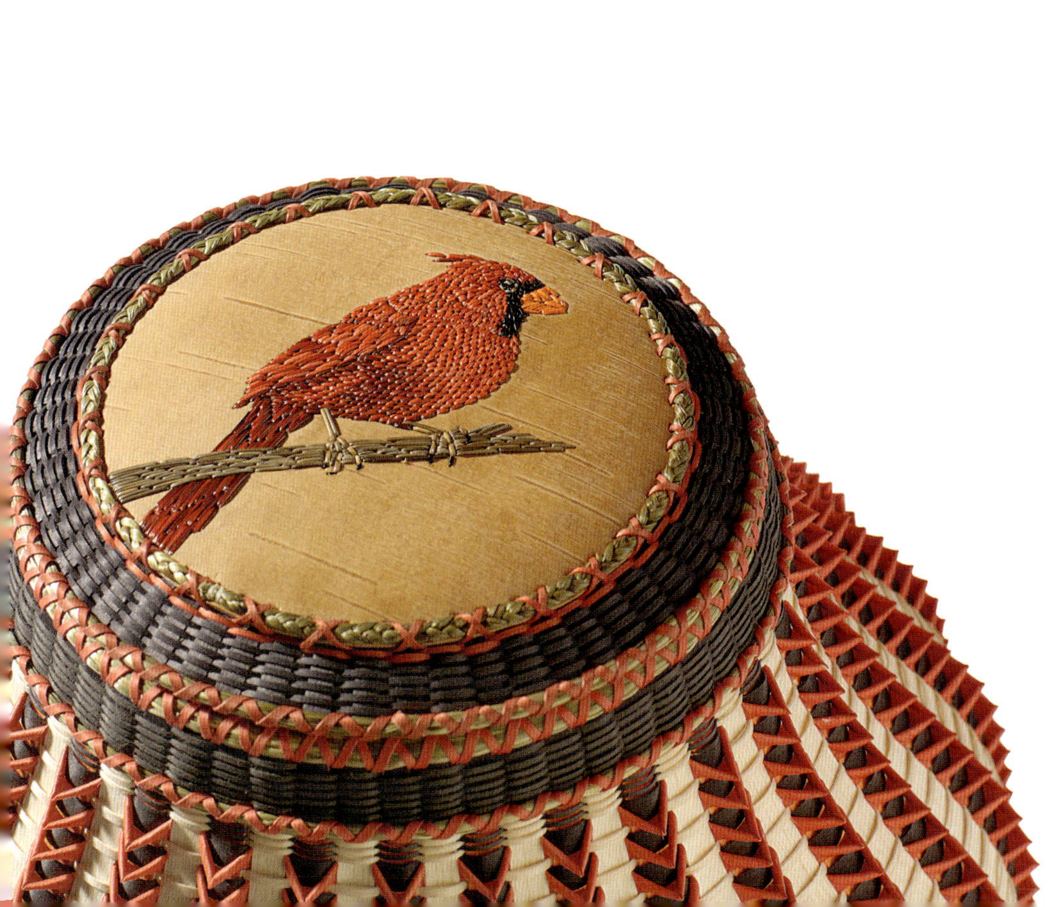

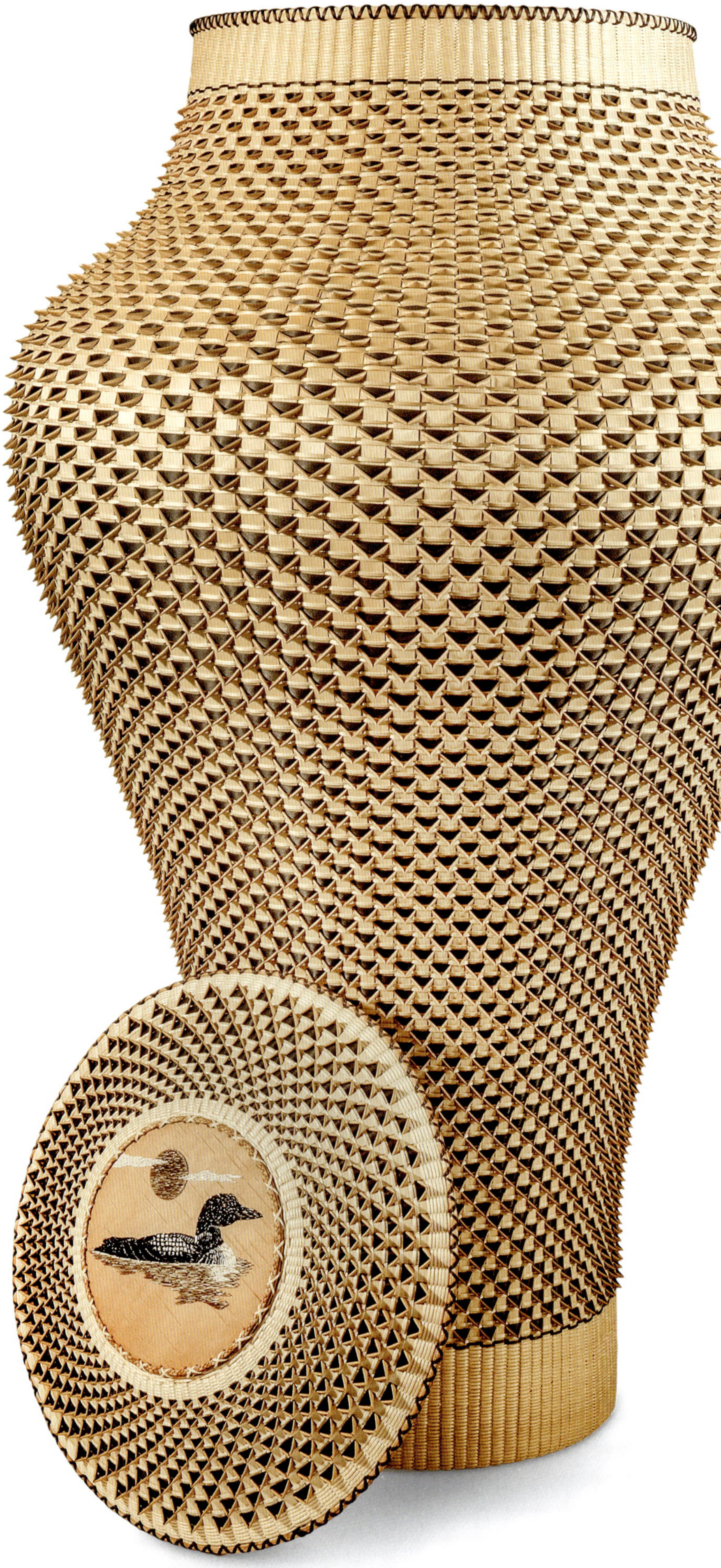

Loon, 2020

Ash, cedar bark, porcupine quill on birch bark, and dye
36 × 23 × 23 inches
Private collection of Catherine Stiefel, California

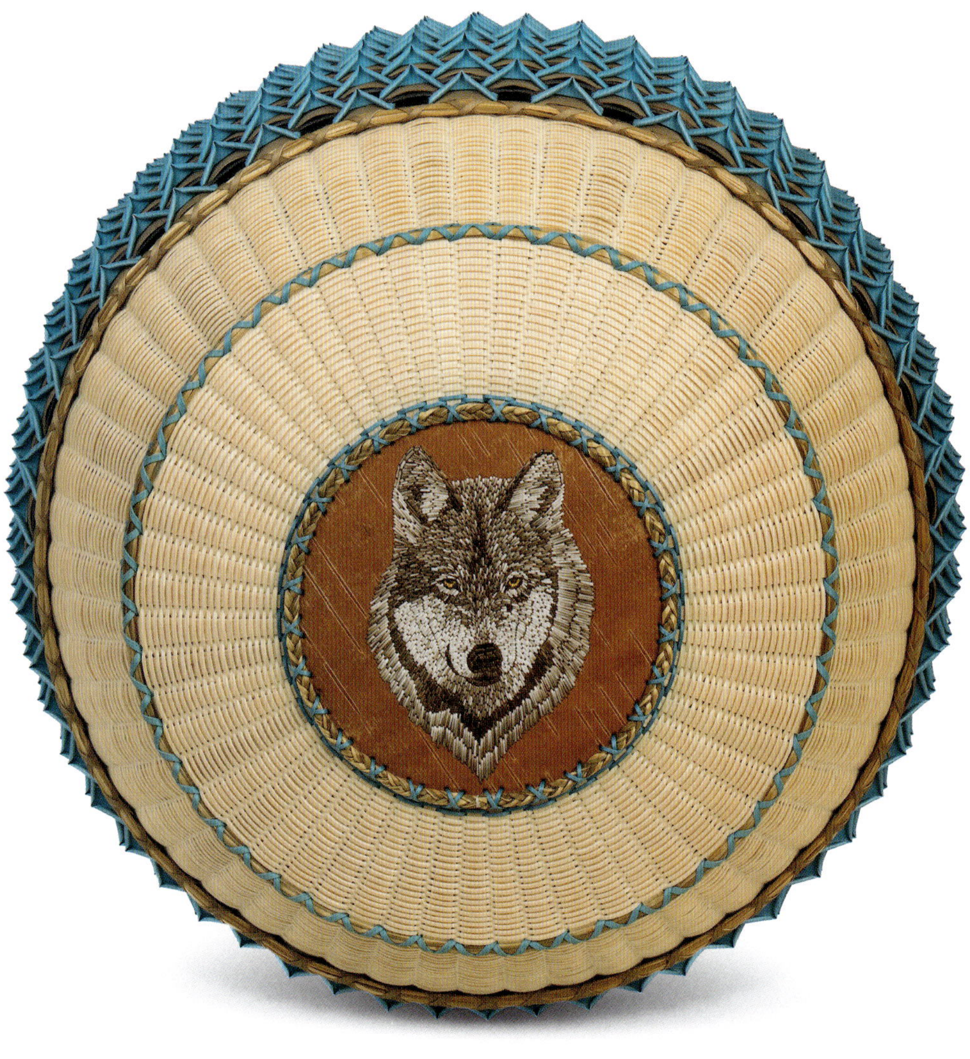

Malsom (Wolf), 2021

Ash, sweetgrass, porcupine quill on birch bark, and dye
16 × 10 × 10 inches
The Buker Collections

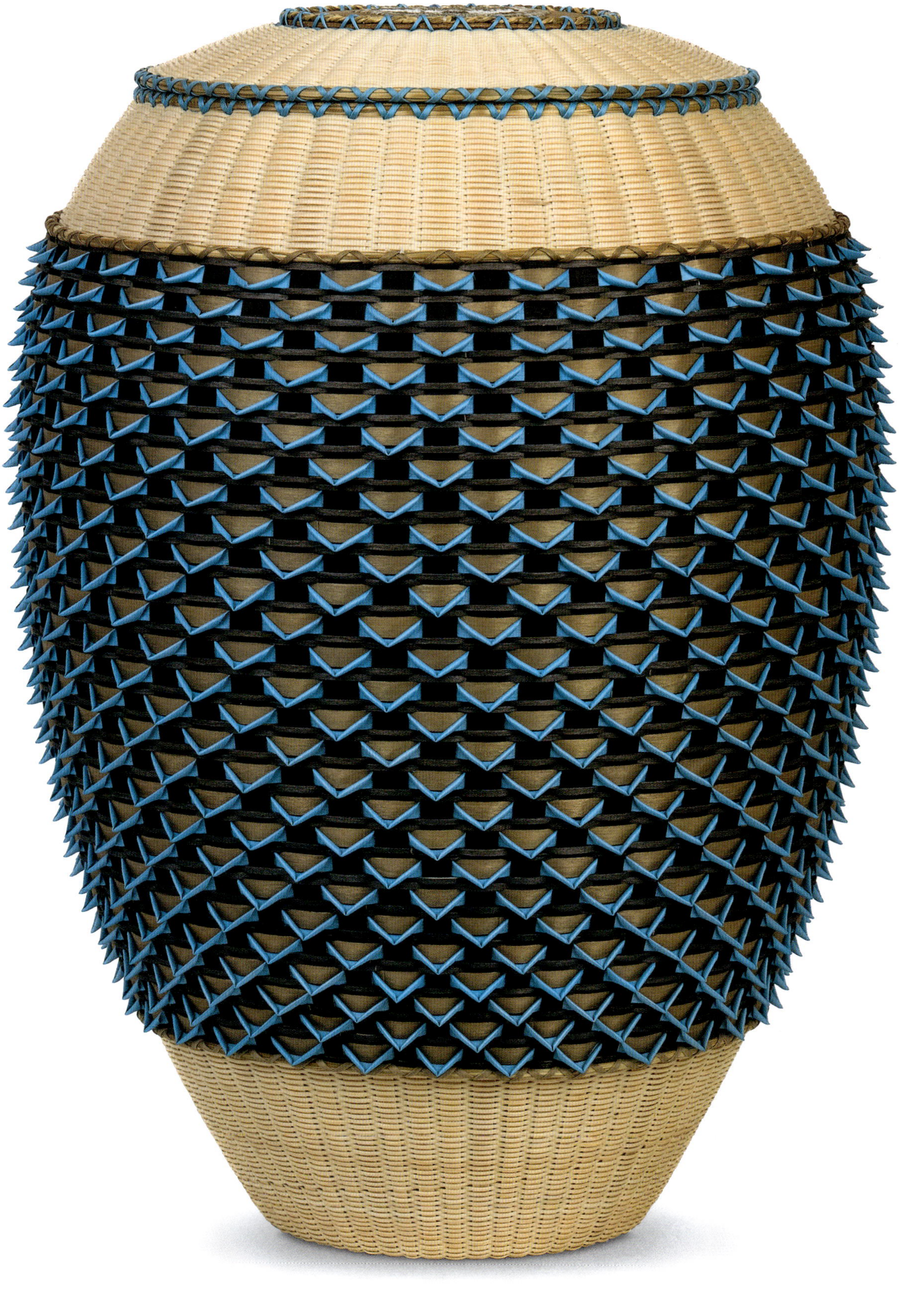

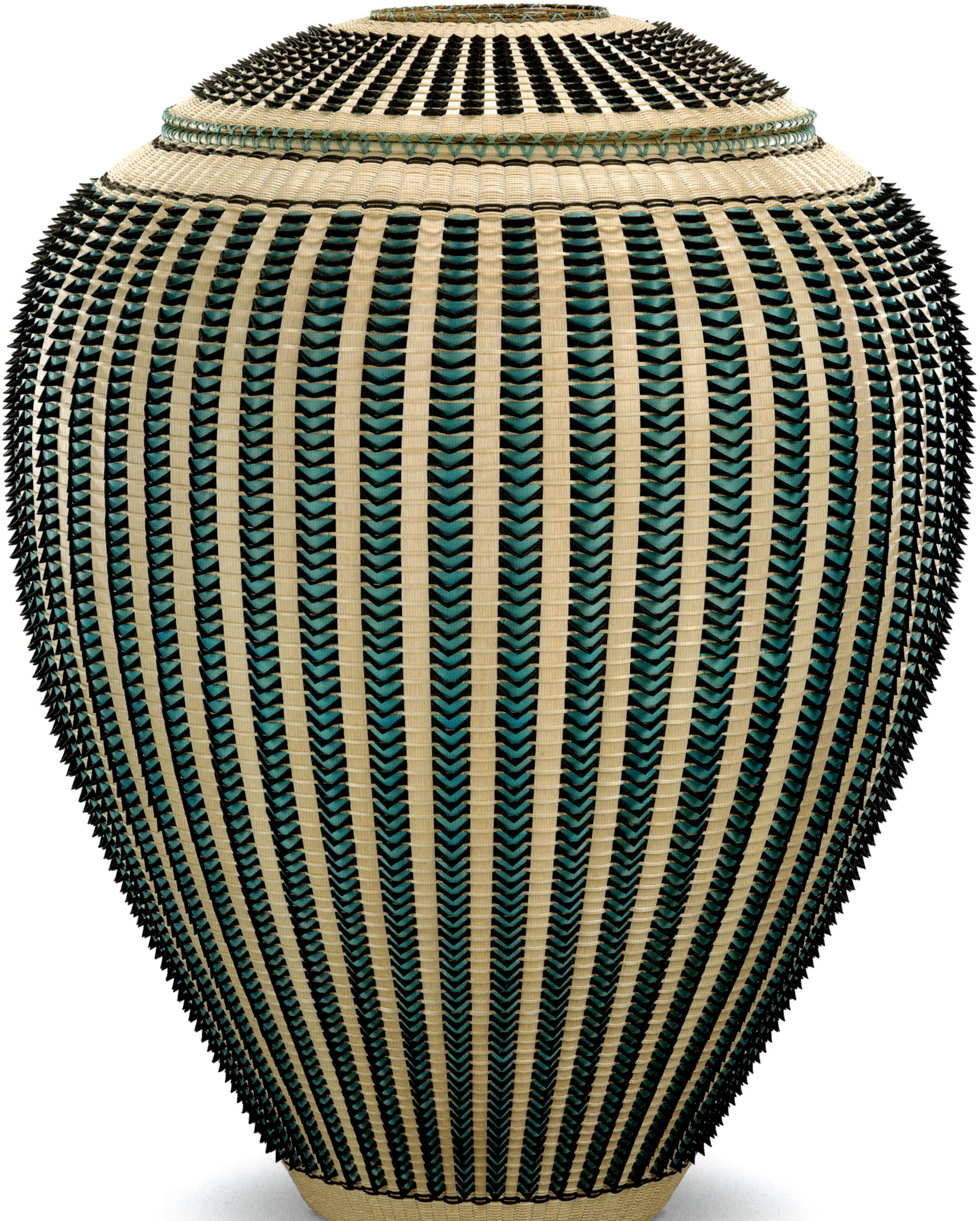

Watchful Spirit, 2022

Ash, sweetgrass, porcupine quill on birch bark, and dye
27⅜ × 22¼ × 22¼ inches
Denver Art Museum: Purchased with the Nancy Blomberg
Acquisitions Fund for Native American Art, 2022.51A-B

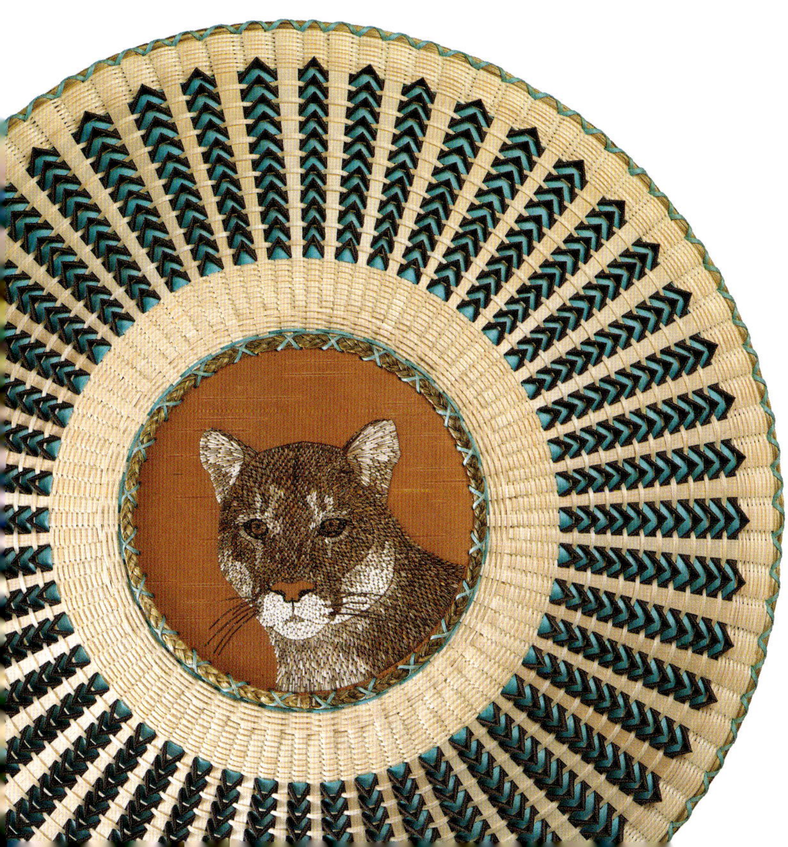

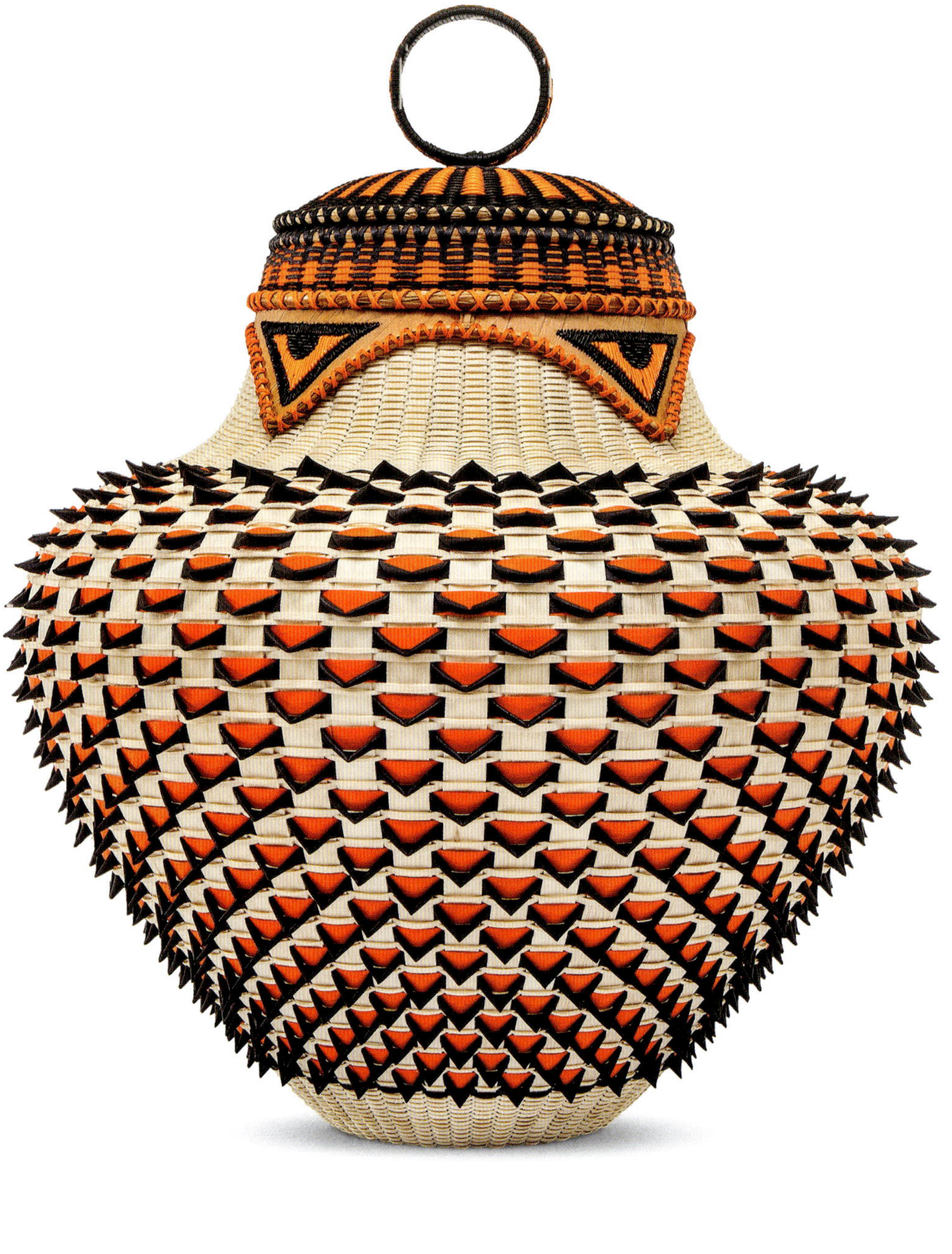

Observer, 2022

Ash, sweetgrass, porcupine quill on birch bark, and dye
13½ × 10½ × 10½ inches
Collection of Carole Katz

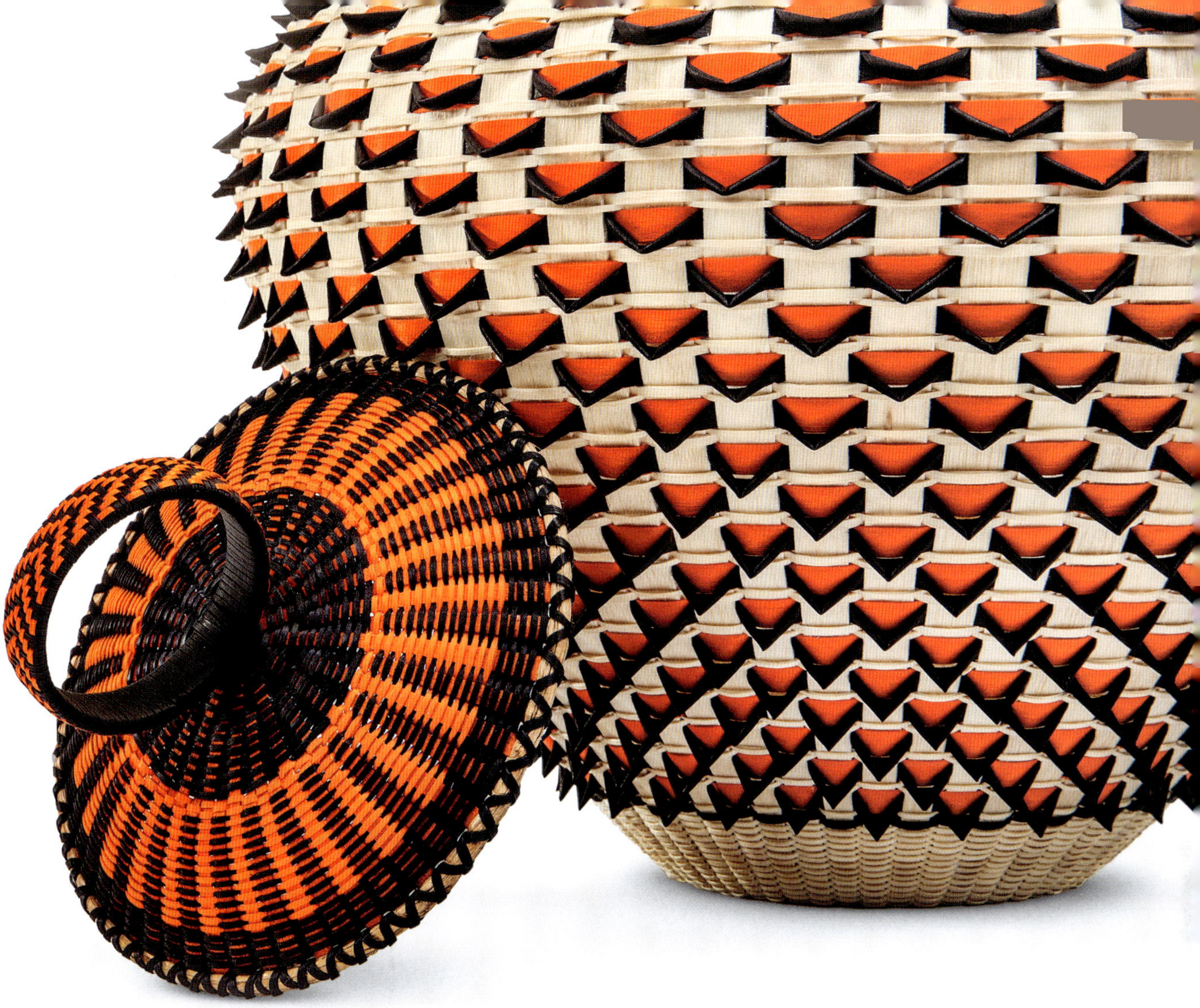

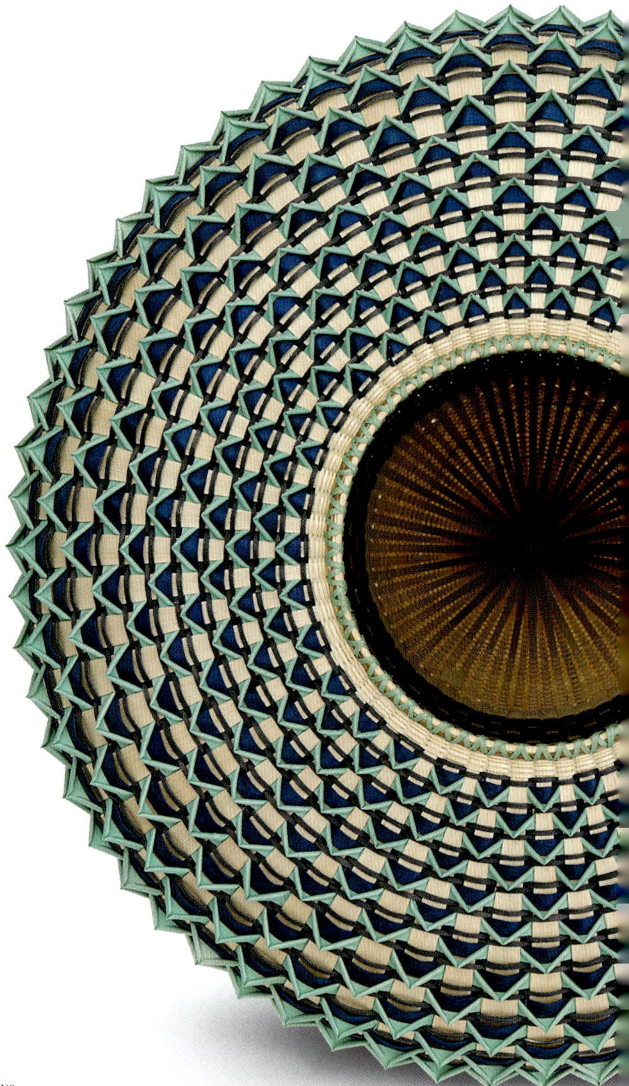

First Light, 2023

Ash, sweetgrass, porcupine quill on birch bark, and dye
$11\frac{1}{4} \times 16\frac{1}{2} \times 6$ inches
Farnsworth Art Museum, Rockland, ME. Museum purchase,
Lynne Drexler Acquisition Fund, 2023.10

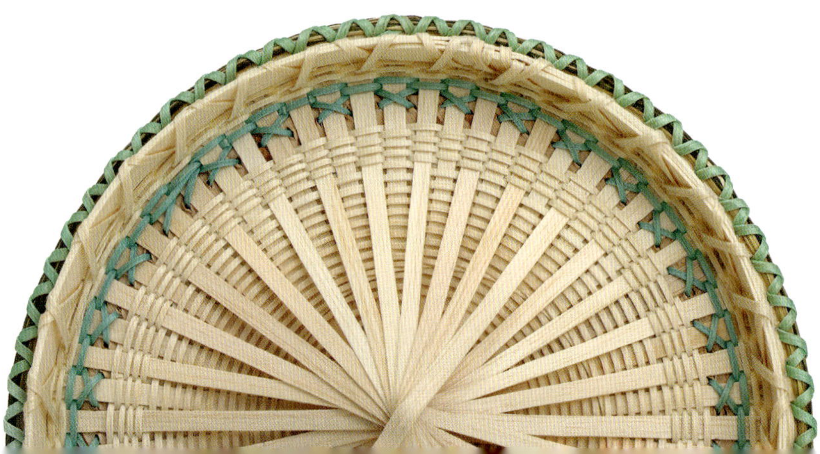

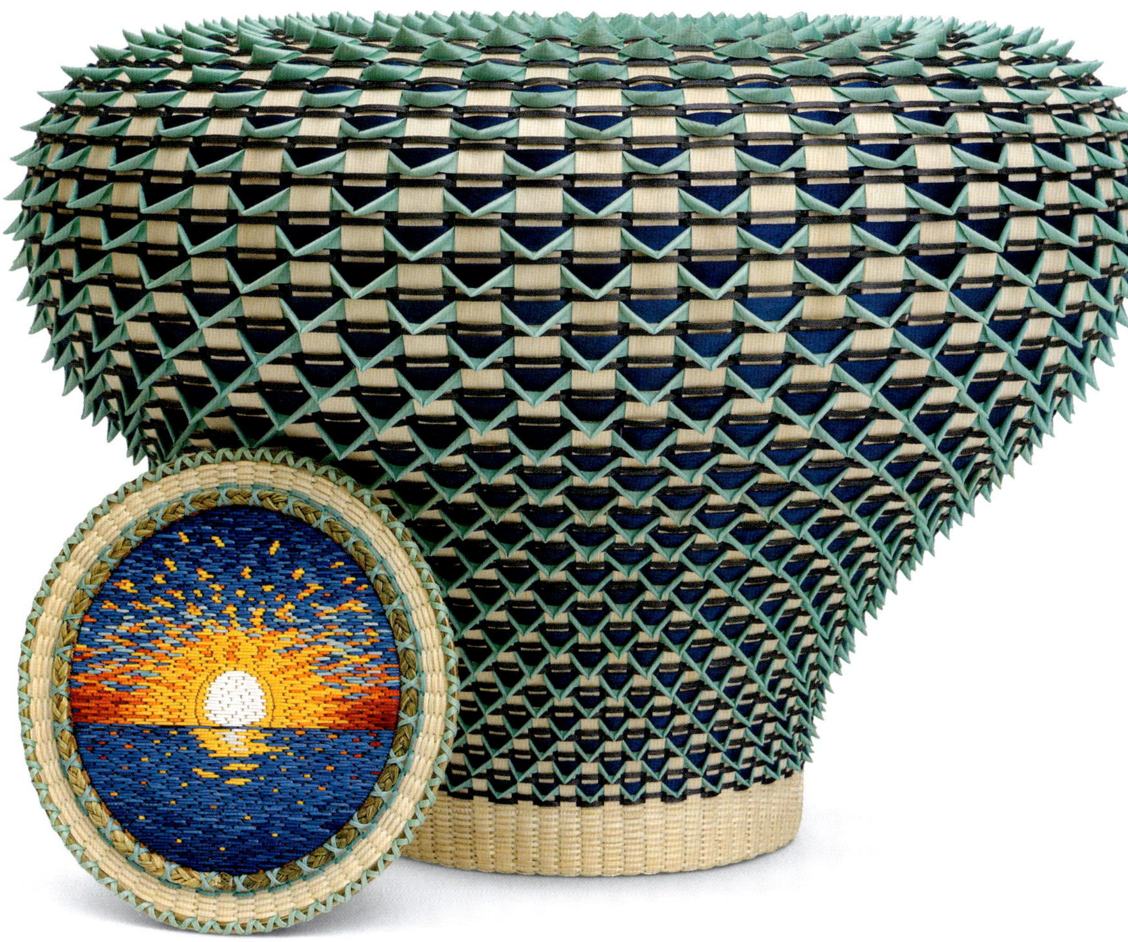

Urchin Baskets

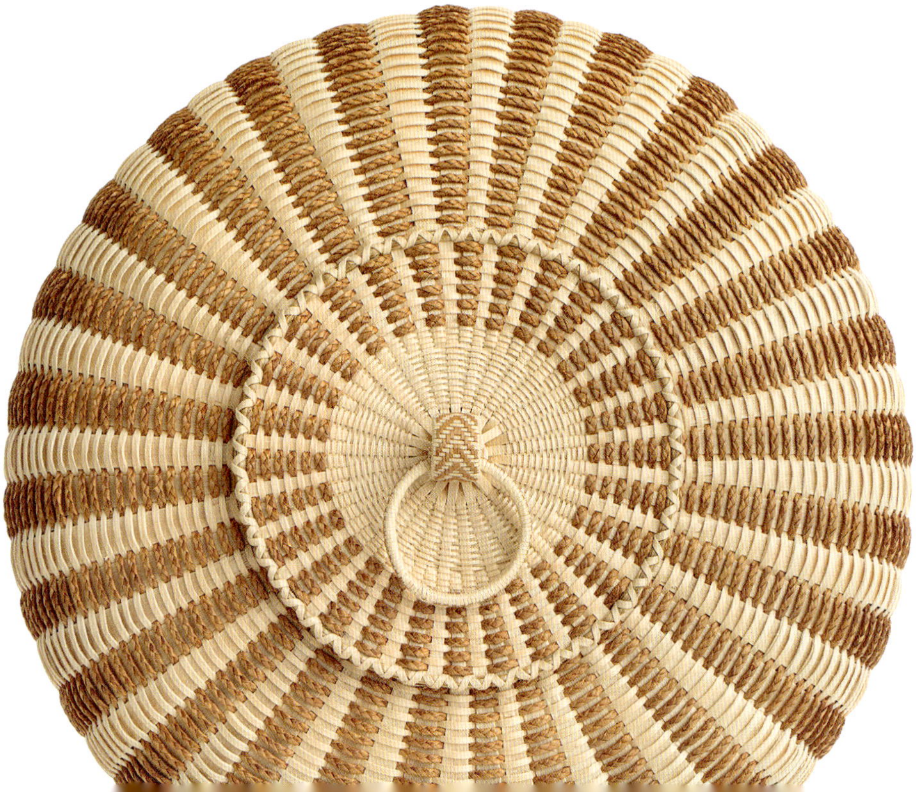

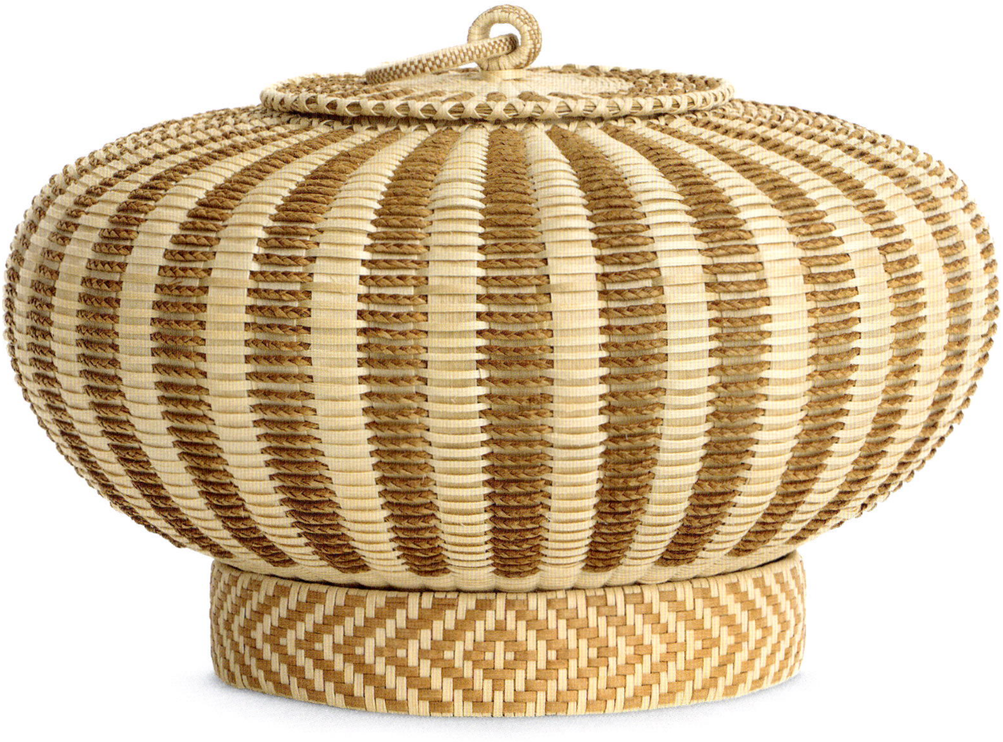

Urchin Basket, 2007

Ash, cedar bark, and sweetgrass
6 × 10½ × 10½ inches
Abbe Museum, Bar Harbor, ME. Museum Purchase,
Diane Kopec Collection Fund, 2007-04-001 A-C

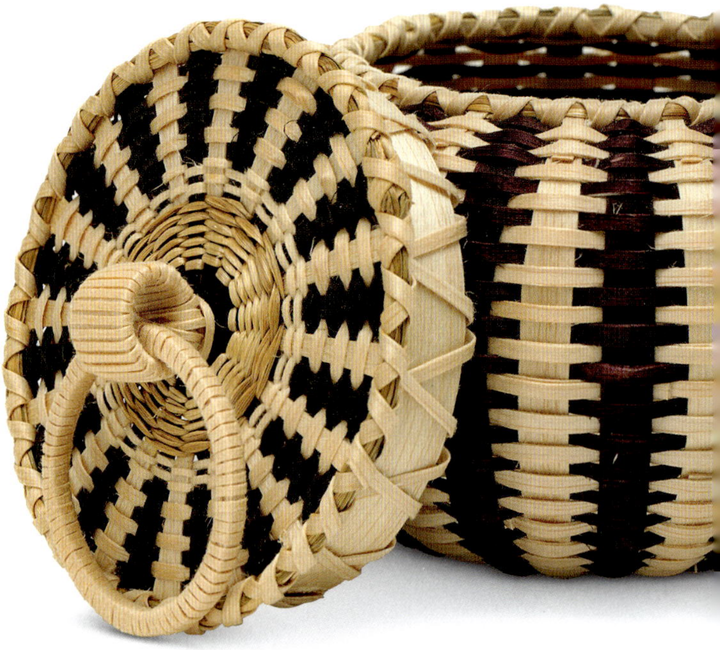

Urchin, 2007

Ash, sweetgrass, and dye
4 × 8 × 8 inches
Hudson Museum, University of Maine, HM8632

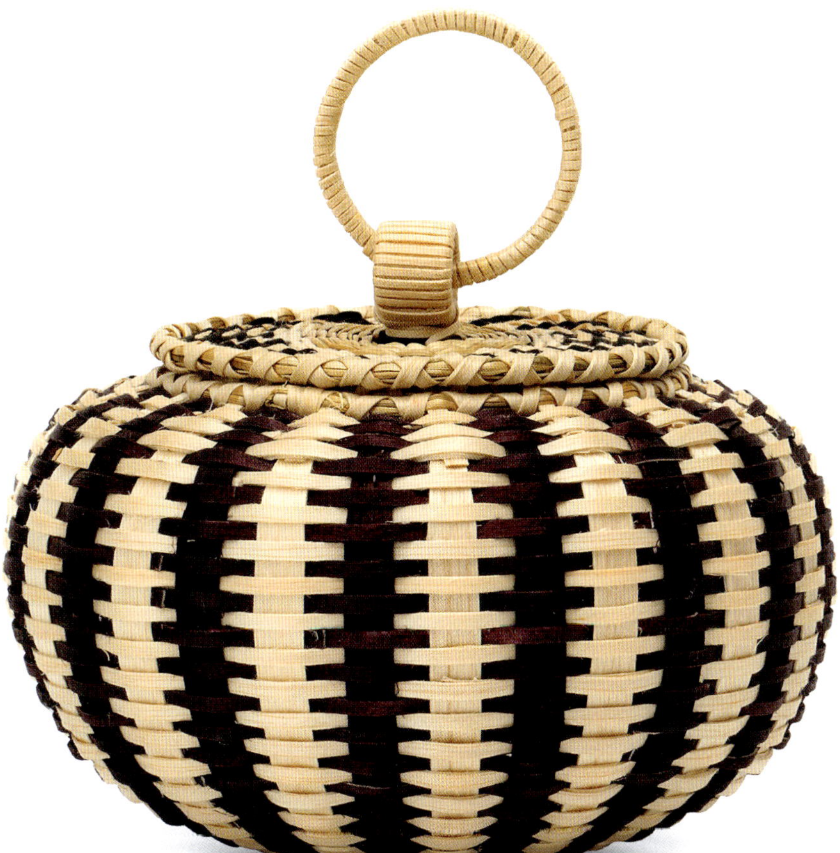

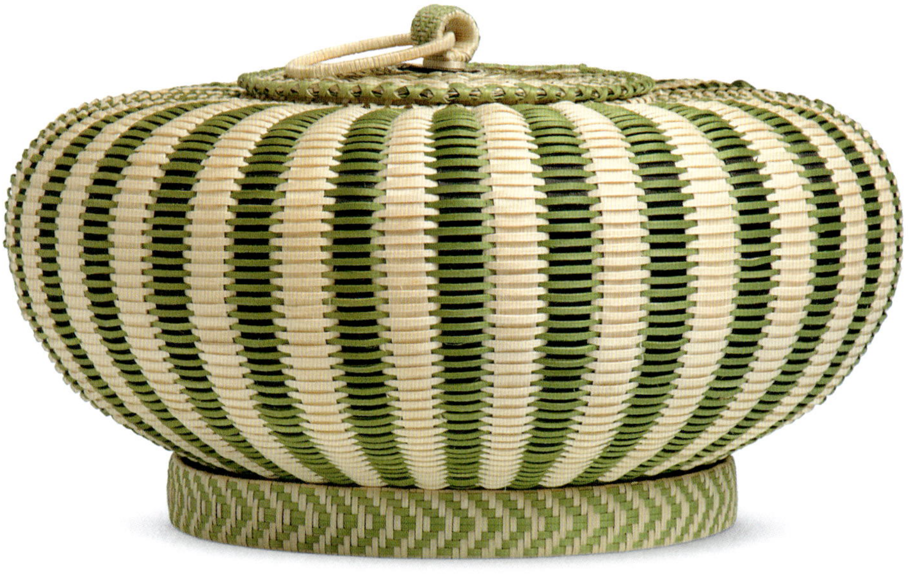

Green Urchin Basket, 2008

Ash, sweetgrass, and dye
$5\frac{7}{8} \times 9\frac{1}{4} \times 9\frac{1}{4}$ inches
Hood Museum of Art, Dartmouth, Hanover, NH: Purchased through the Phyllis and Bertram Geller 1937 Memorial Fund, 2008.51

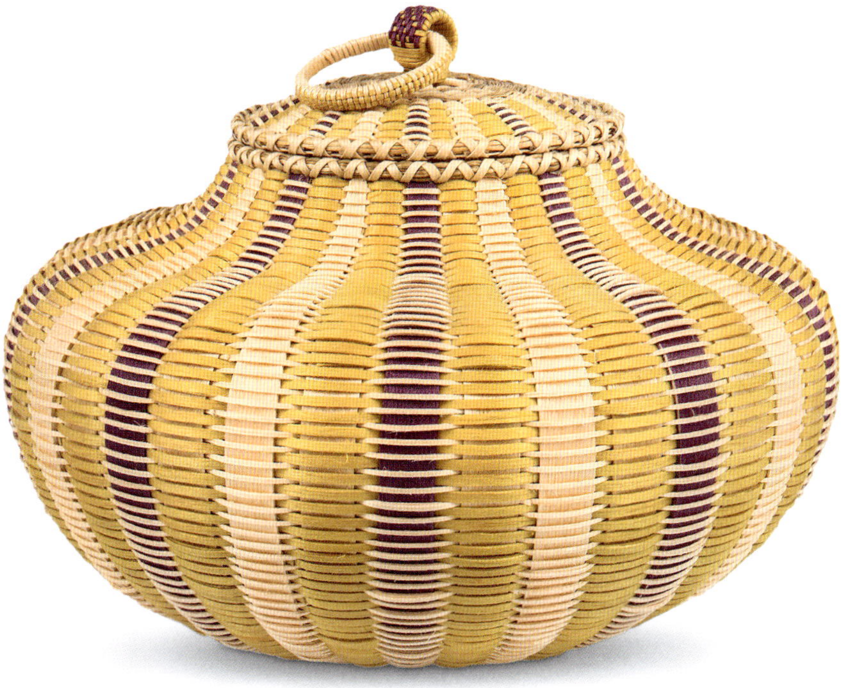

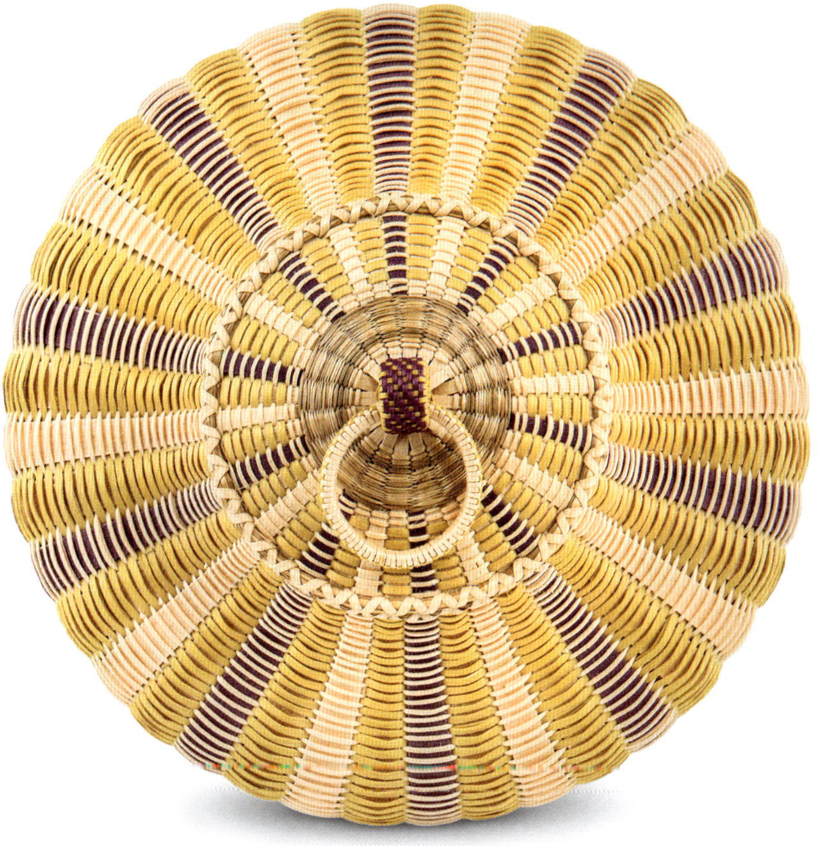

Fluted Neck Urchin, 2009

Ash, sweetgrass, and dye
6 × 9 × 9 inches
Collection of Dr. and Mrs. Ari and Lea Plosker

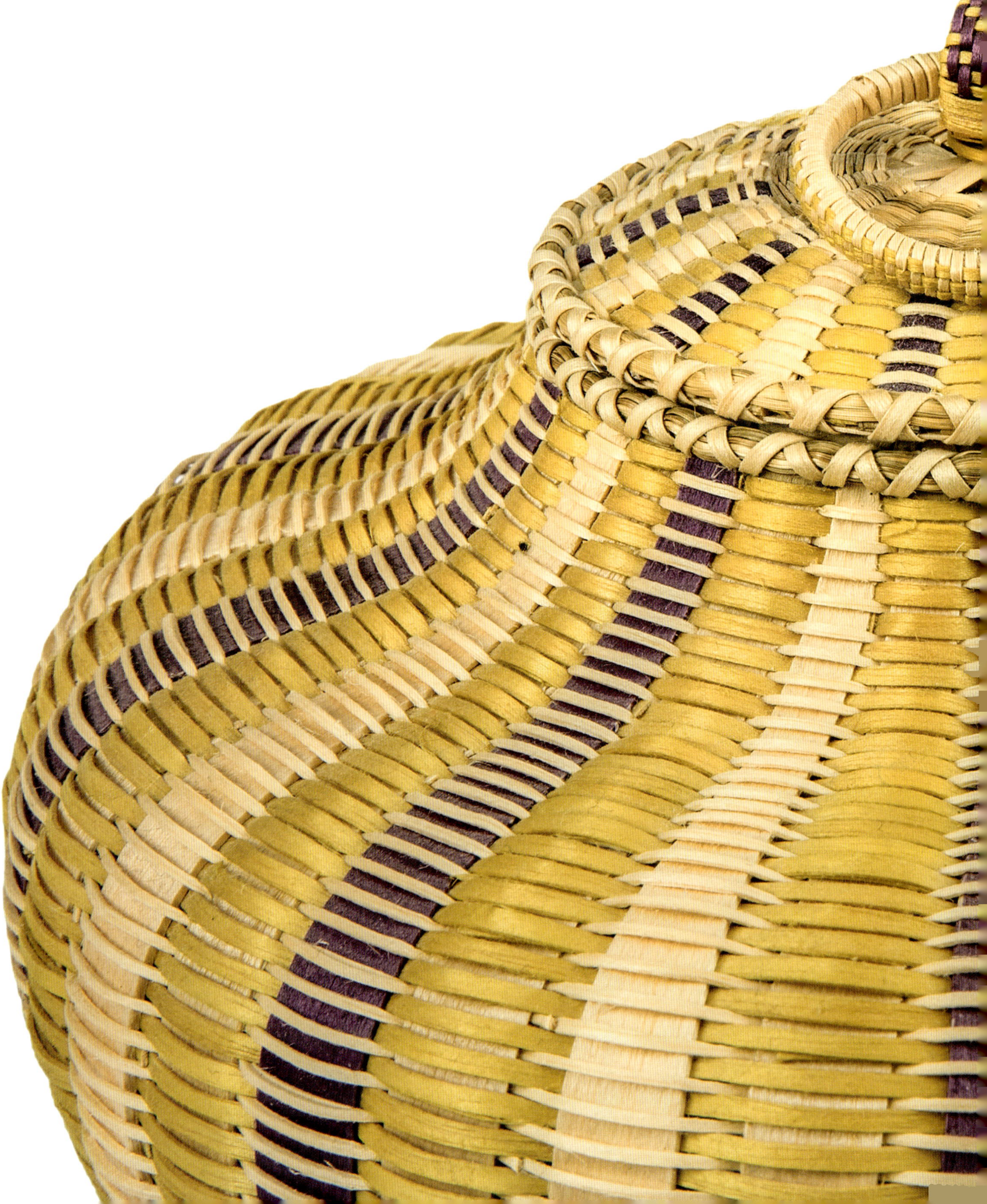

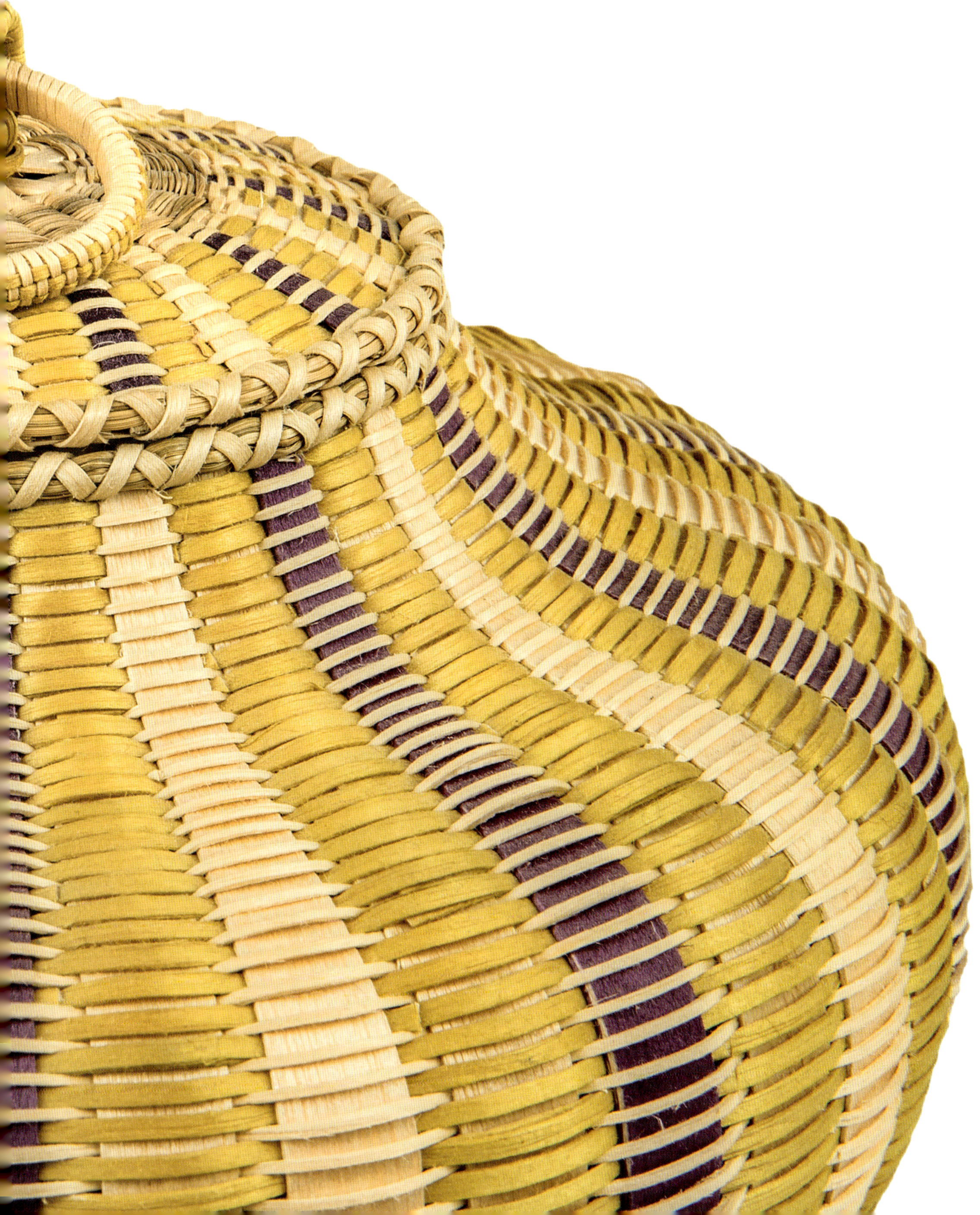

Pointy Urchin, 2011

Ash, sweetgrass, and dye
5½ × 11½ × 11½ inches
Collection of Dr. Marc and Lynn Appelbaum, New Mexico

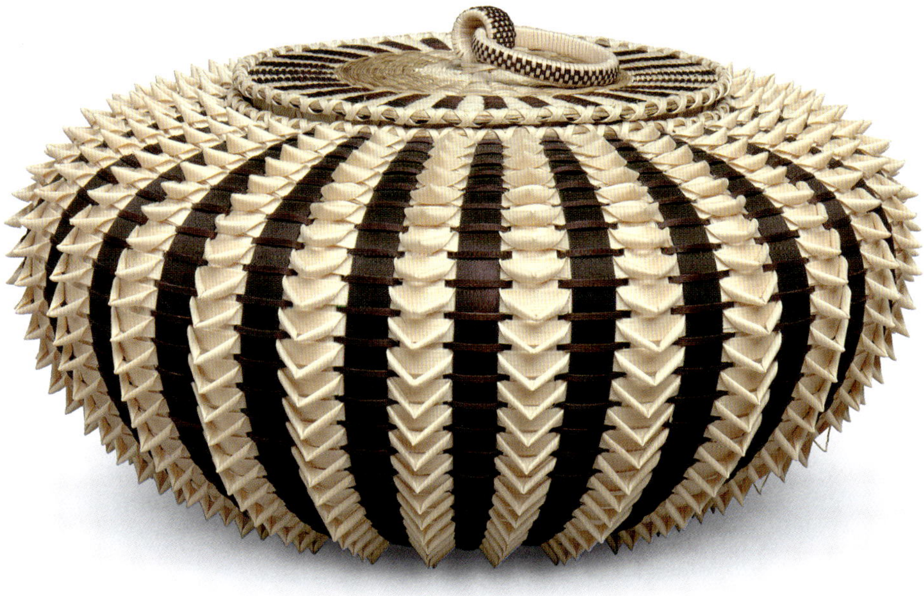

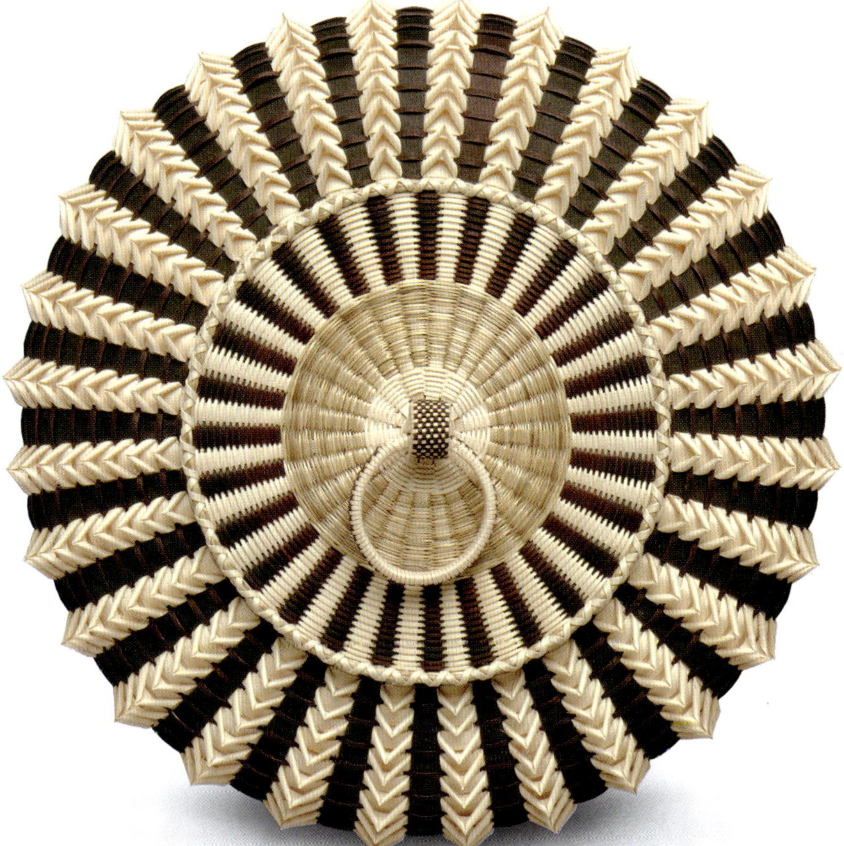

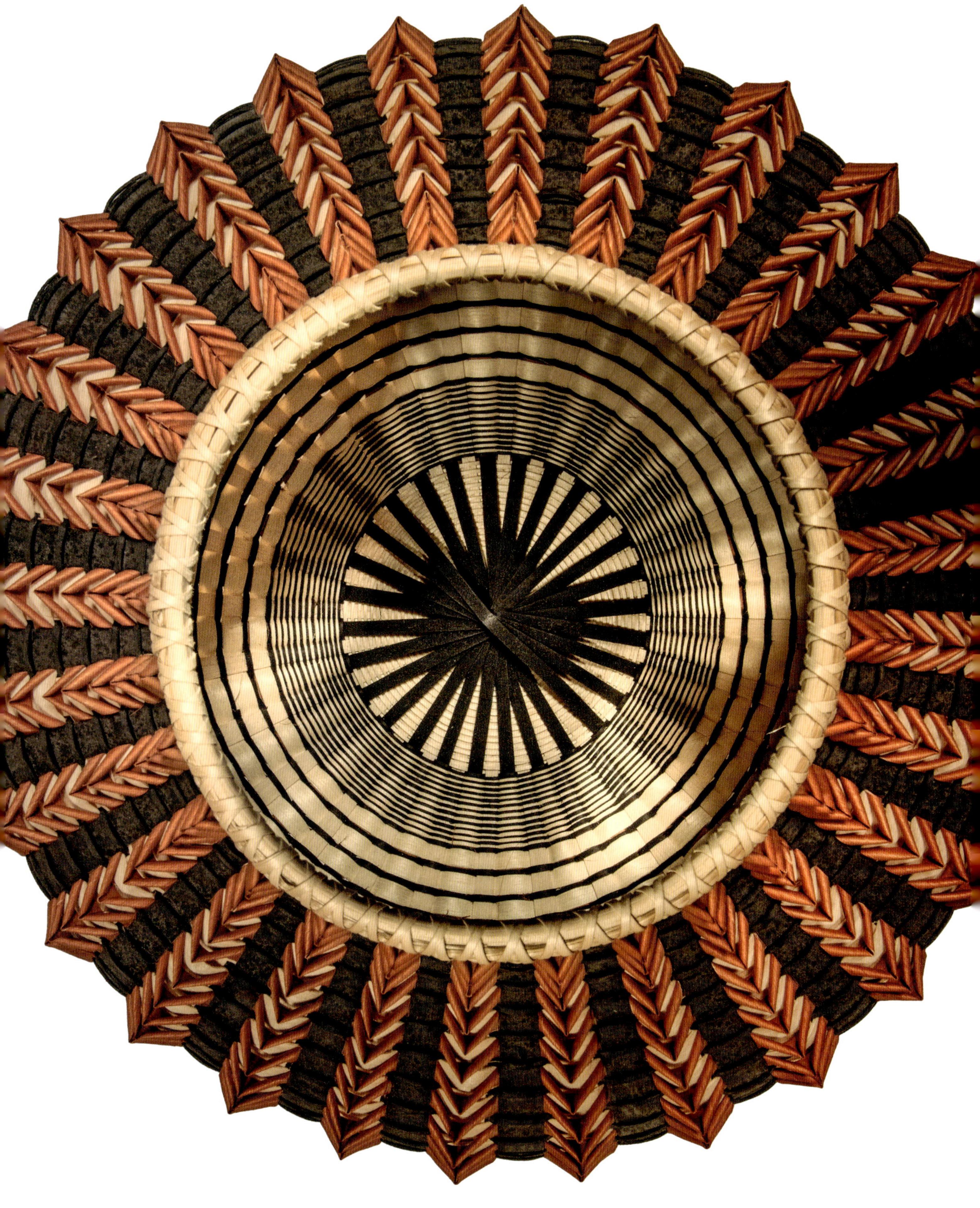

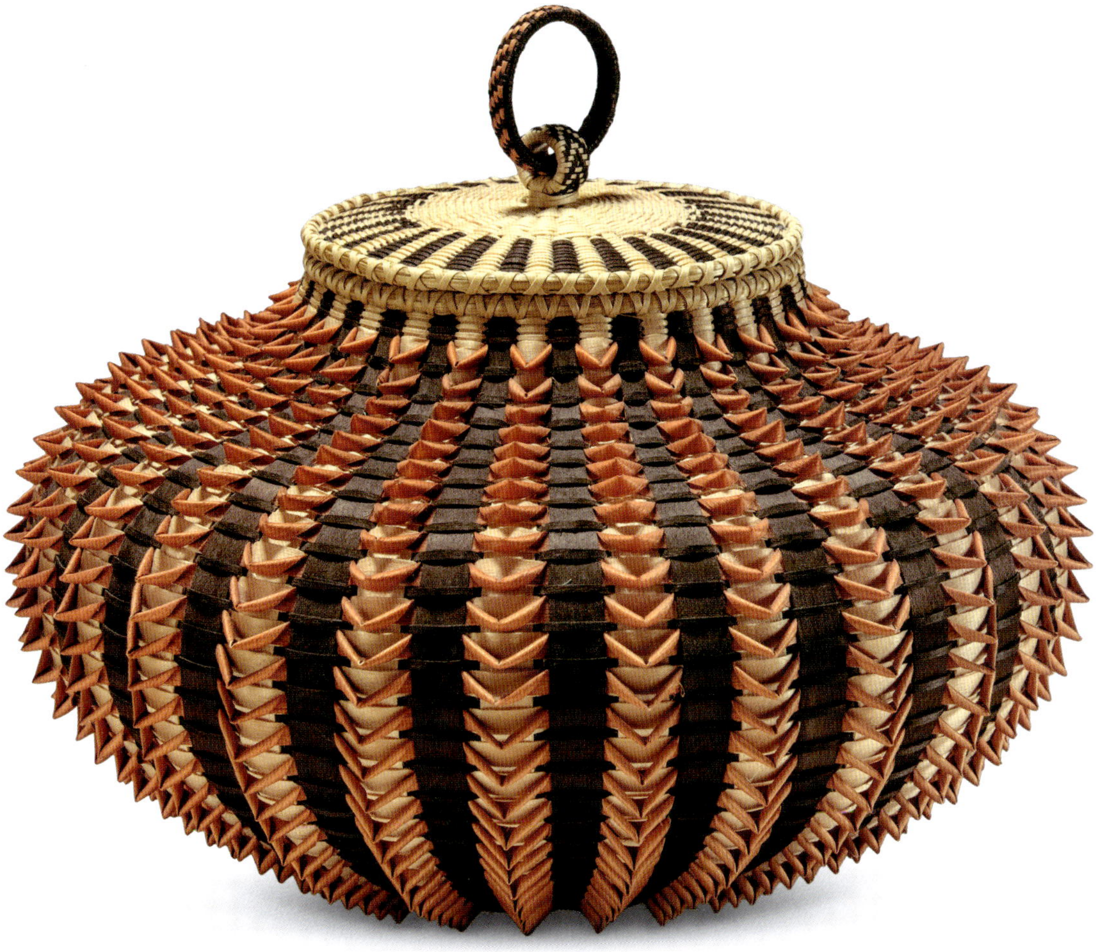

Flute Top Urchin, 2011

Ash, sweetgrass, and dye
7½ × 10½ × 10½ inches
Collection of David and Sue Halpern

102

Urchin, 2011

Ash, sweetgrass, and dye
3¼ × 4 × 4 inches
Collection of Gal Frey

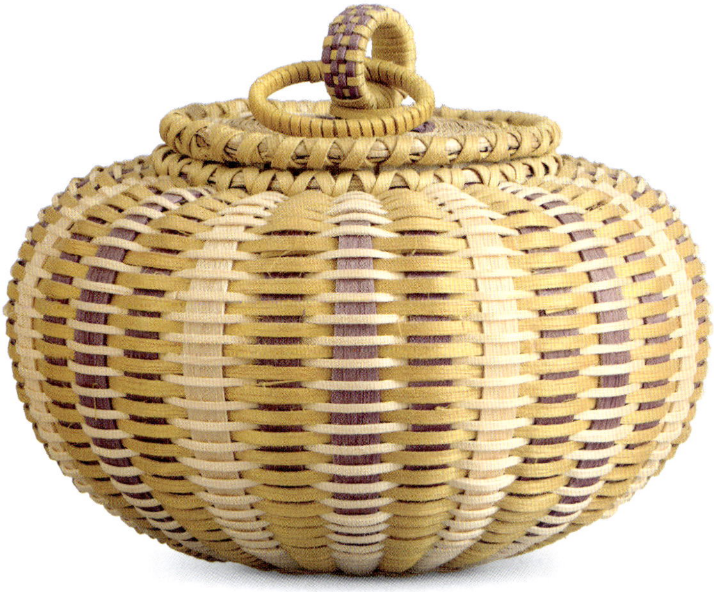

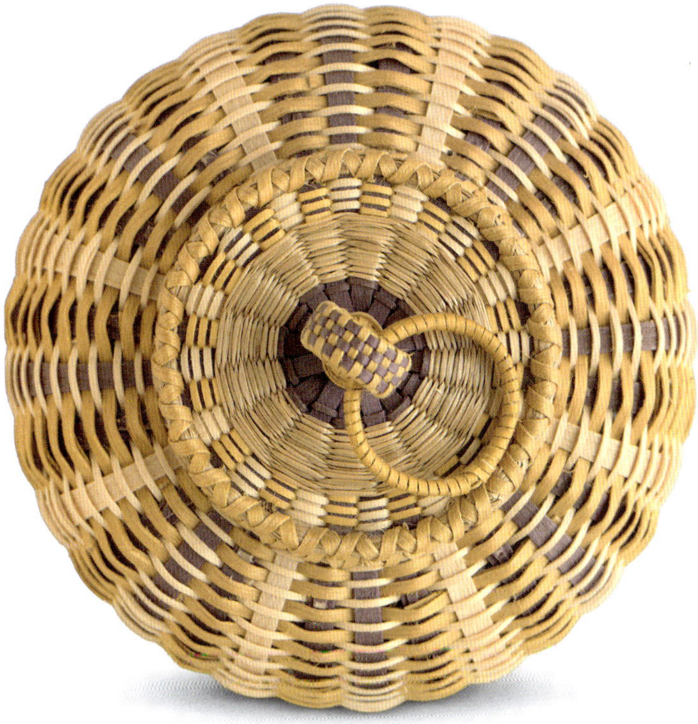

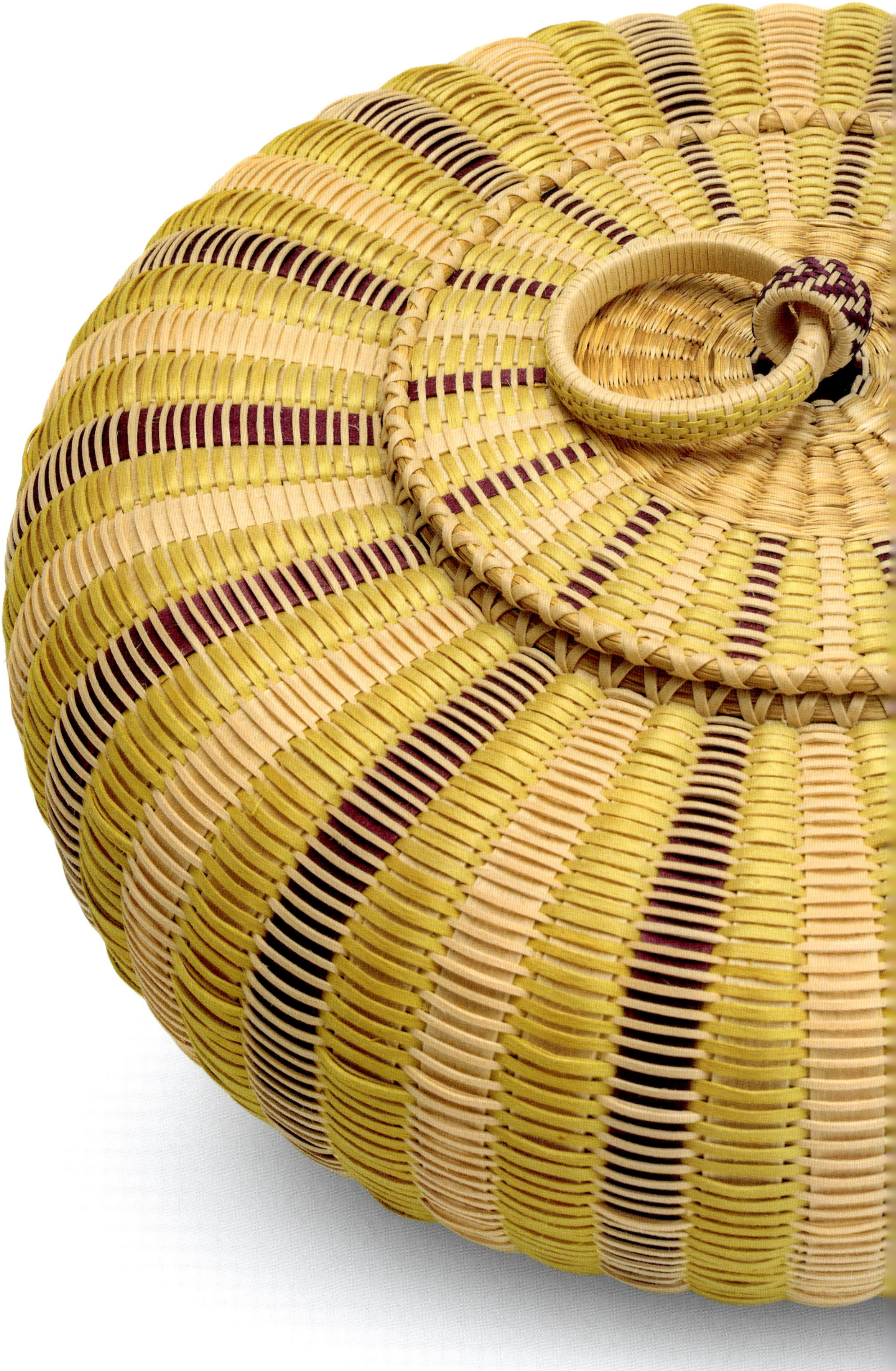

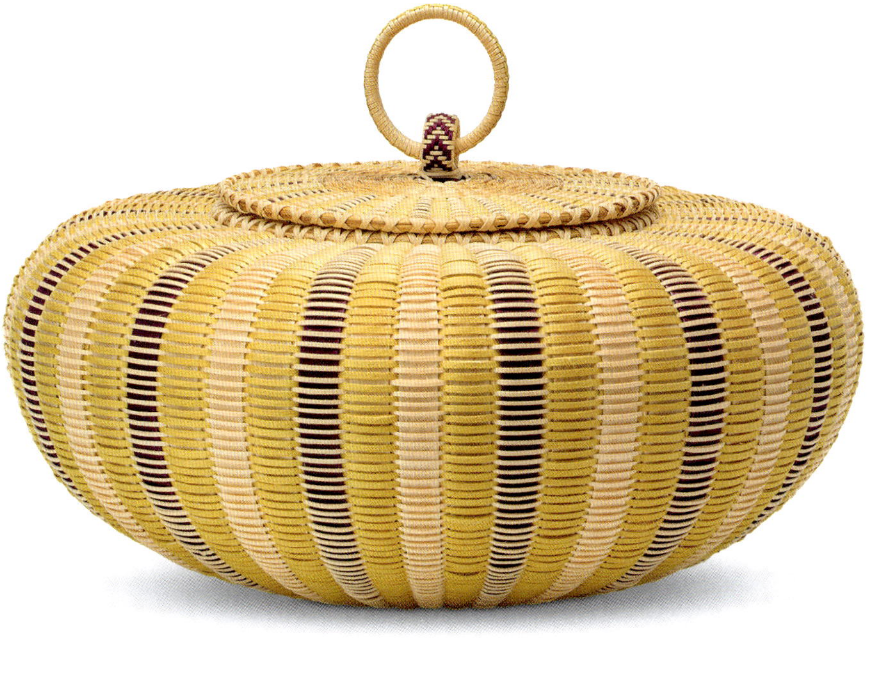

Maine Indian Basketmakers Alliance Commission Basket, 2011

Ash, sweetgrass, and dye
$4\frac{1}{3} \times 11 \times 11$ inches
Maine Indian Basketmakers Alliance

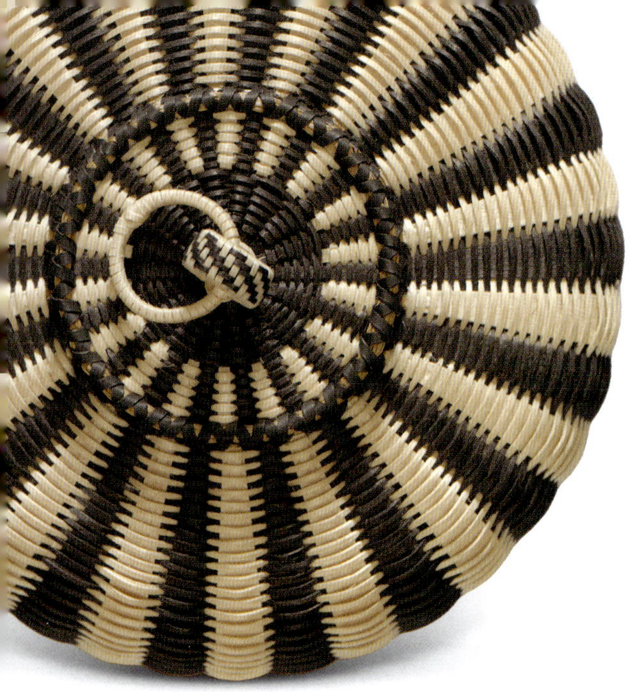

Urchin, 2017-18

Ash, sweetgrass, and dye
$4\frac{1}{2} \times 5\frac{1}{4} \times 5\frac{1}{4}$ inches
Portland Museum of Art, ME .
Gift of Barbara M. Goodbody, 2021.19.7a,b

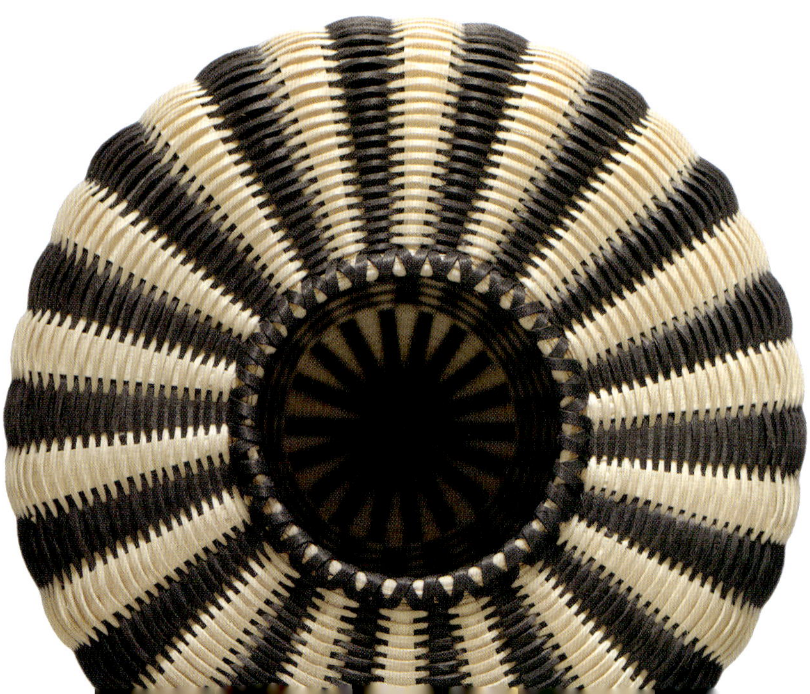

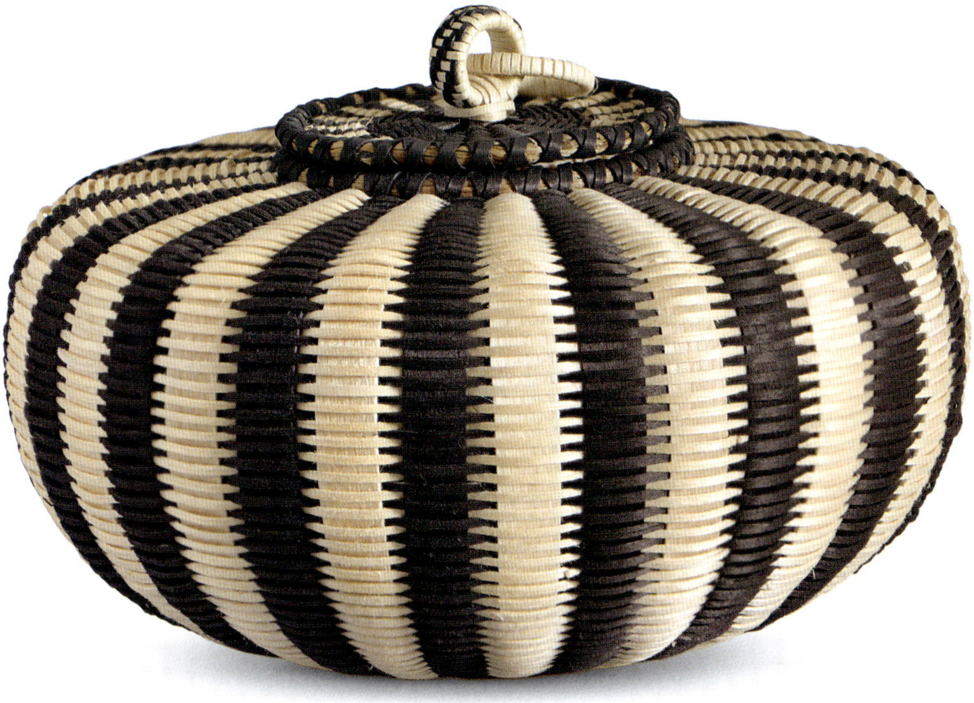

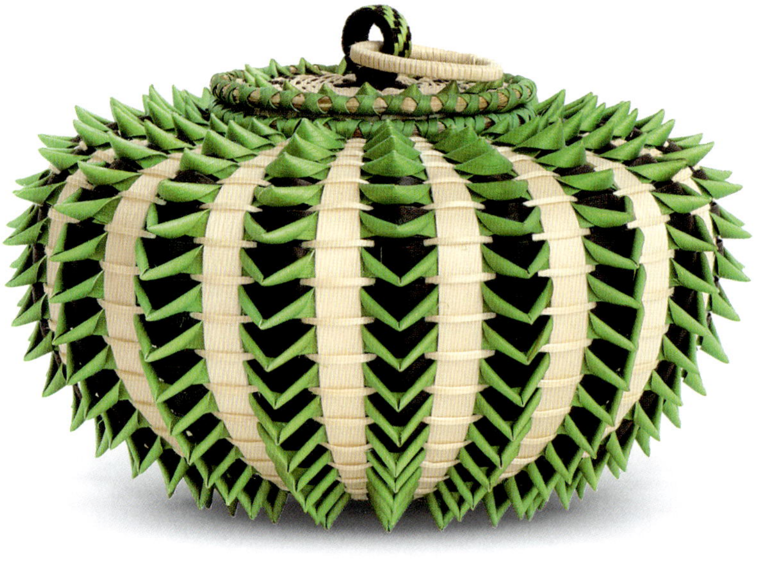

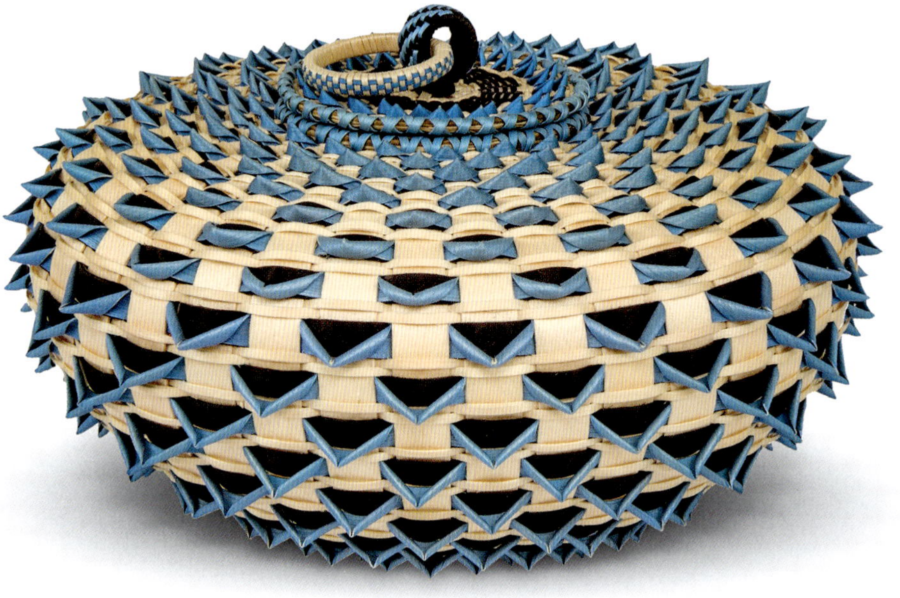

Green Urchin Basket, 2015

Ash, sweetgrass, and dye
4 × 5½ × 5½ inches
Abbe Museum, Bar Harbor, ME. Museum purchase, Native American Festival 2015, 2015-06-004

Blue Point Urchin, 2016

Ash, sweetgrass, and dye
5 × 9 × 9 inches
Collection of Dr. and Mrs. Ari and Lea Plosker

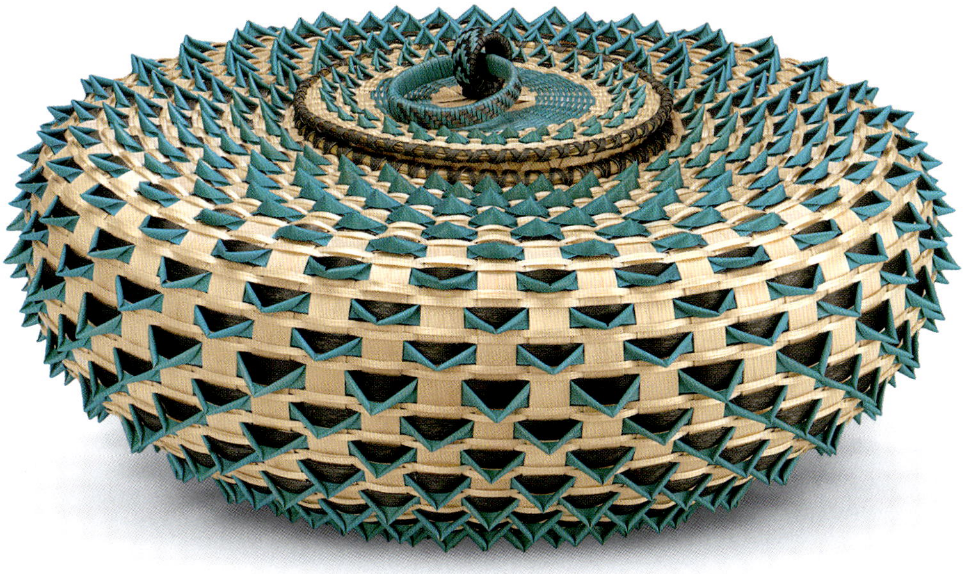

Large Turquoise Urchin Basket, 2019

Ash, sweetgrass, and dye
5¼ × 11½ × 11½ inches
Smithsonian American Art Museum, Washington, D.C., Museum
purchase through the Kenneth R. Trapp Acquisition Fund, 2020.55

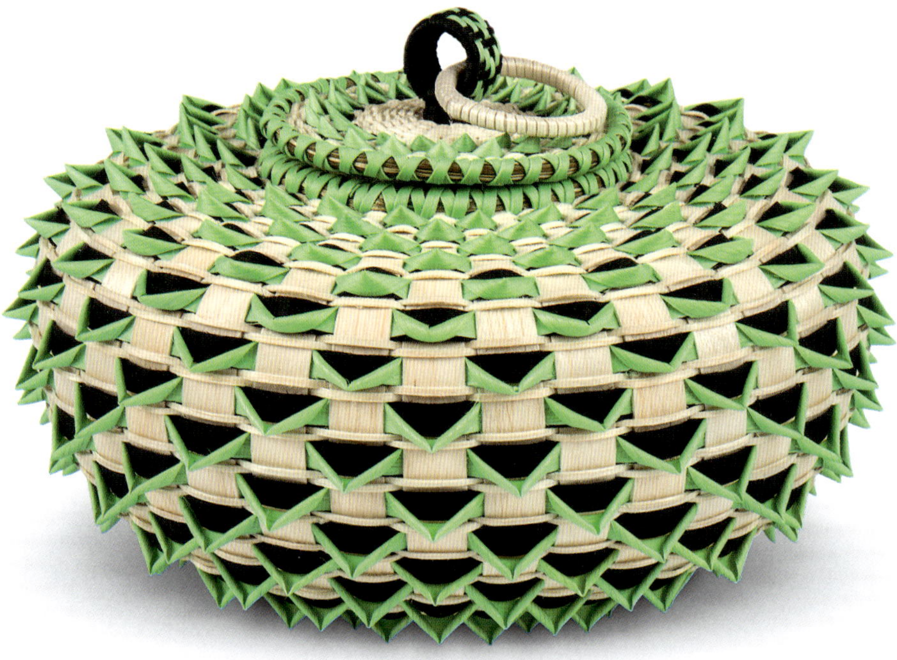

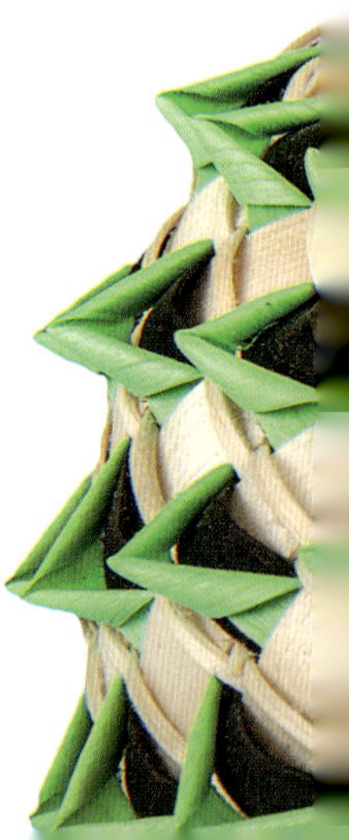

Green Point Urchin, 2022

Ash, sweetgrass, and dye
4 × 6 × 6 inches
Collection of Dr. and Mrs. Ari and Lea Plosker

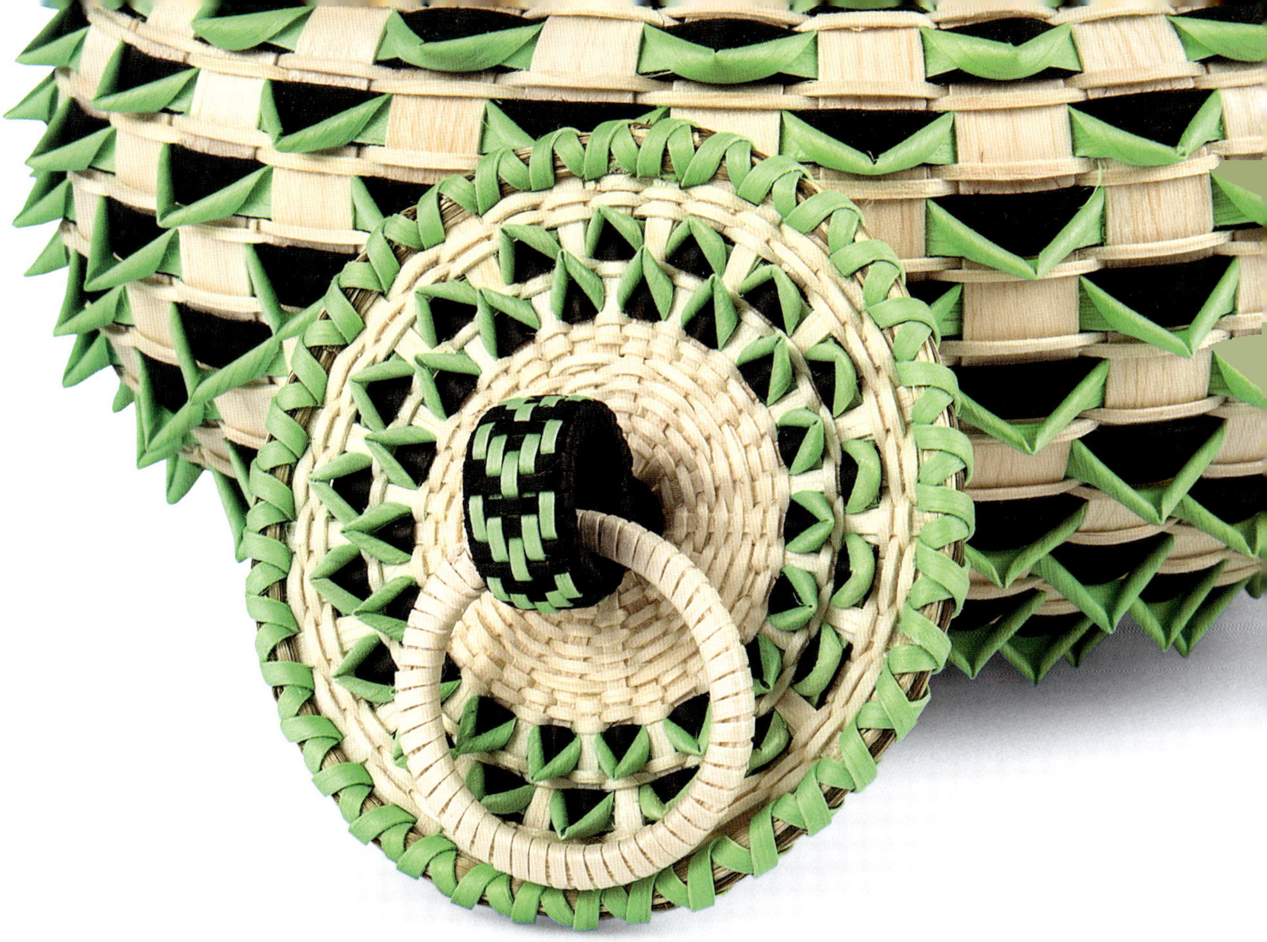

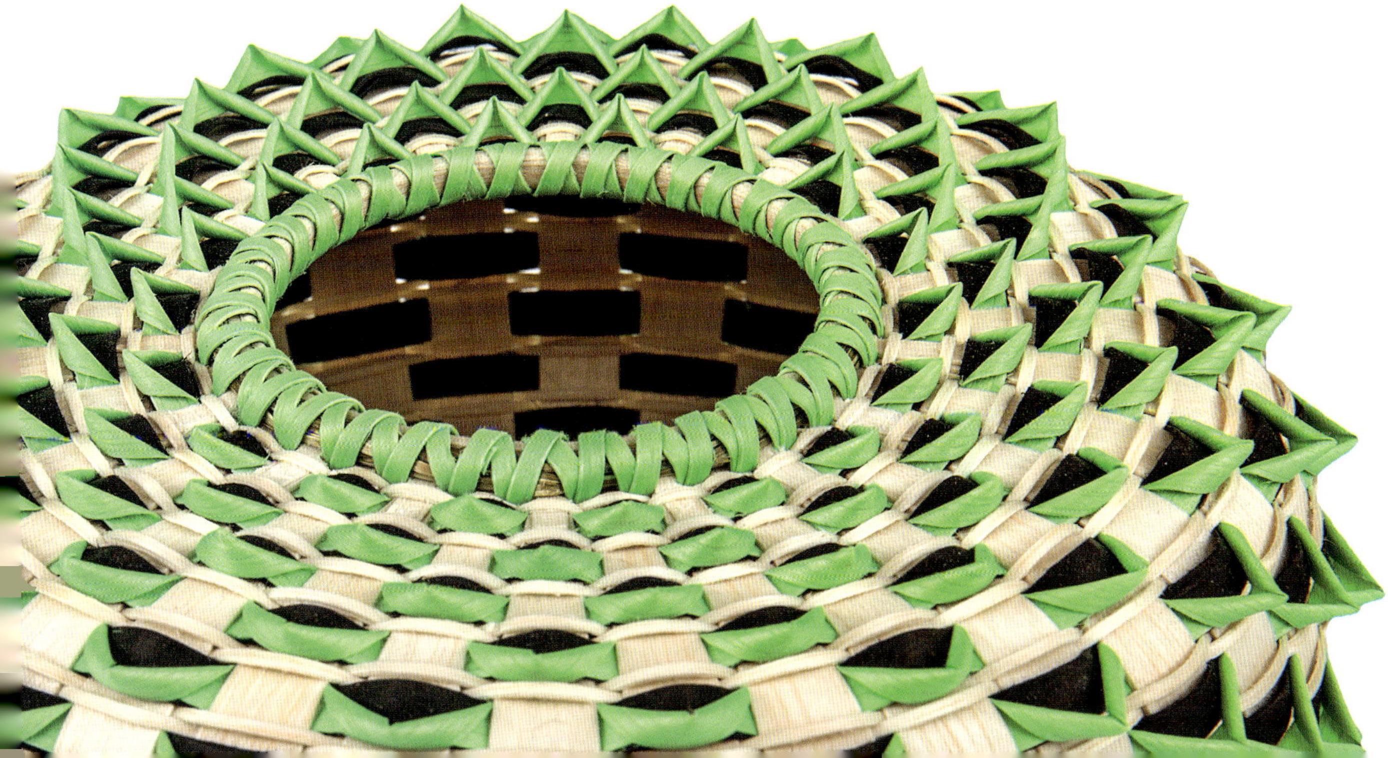

Vase and Double-Walled Baskets

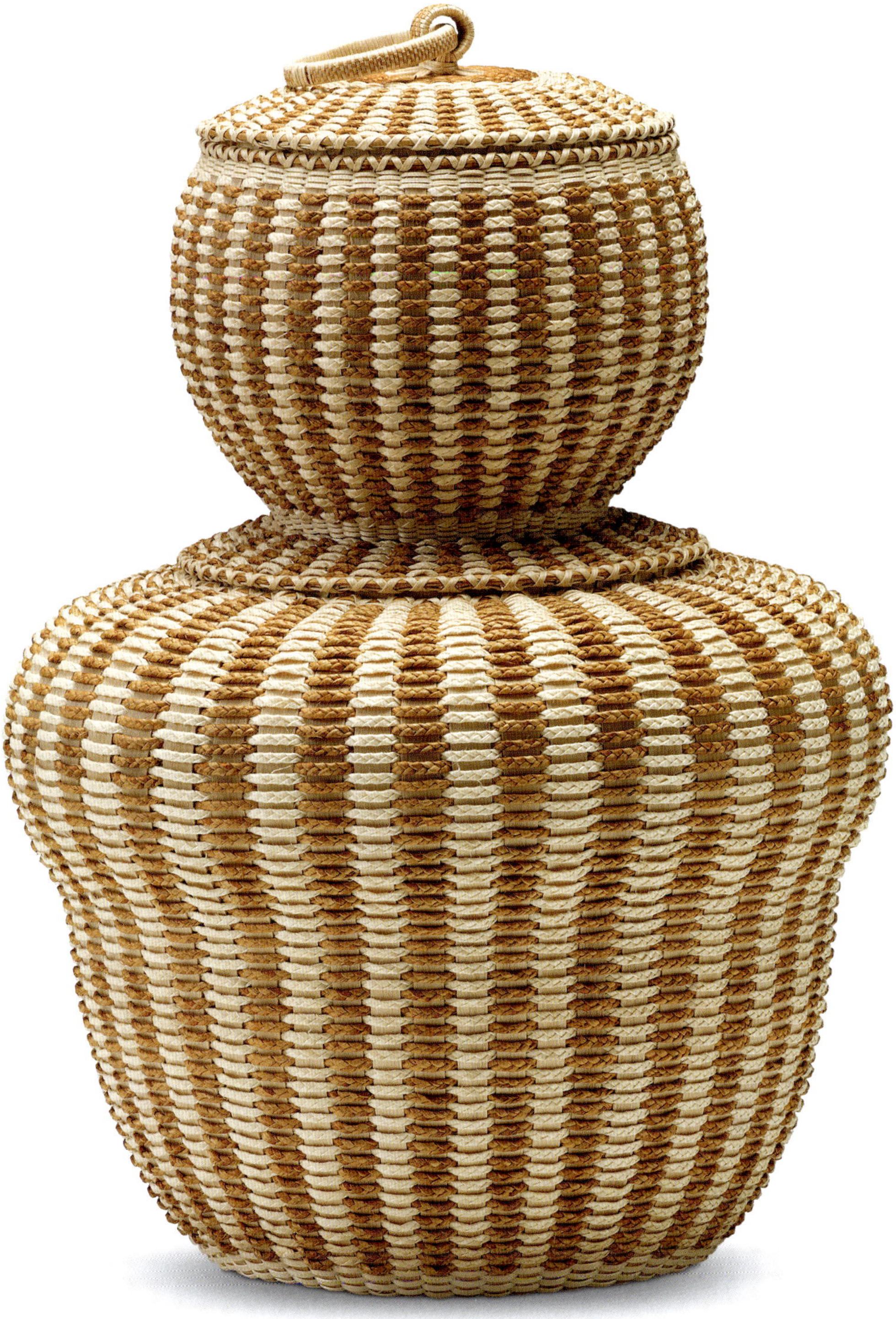

Vase Basket, 2008

Braided ash and braided cedar bark
15 × 10 × 10 inches
Hood Museum of Art, Dartmouth, Hanover, NH: Purchased through
the Phyllis and Bertram Geller 1937 Memorial Fund, 2008.88

114

Point Basket, 2011

Ash, sweetgrass, and dye
16 × 12 × 12 inches
Collection of Dr. and Mrs. Ari and Lea Plosker

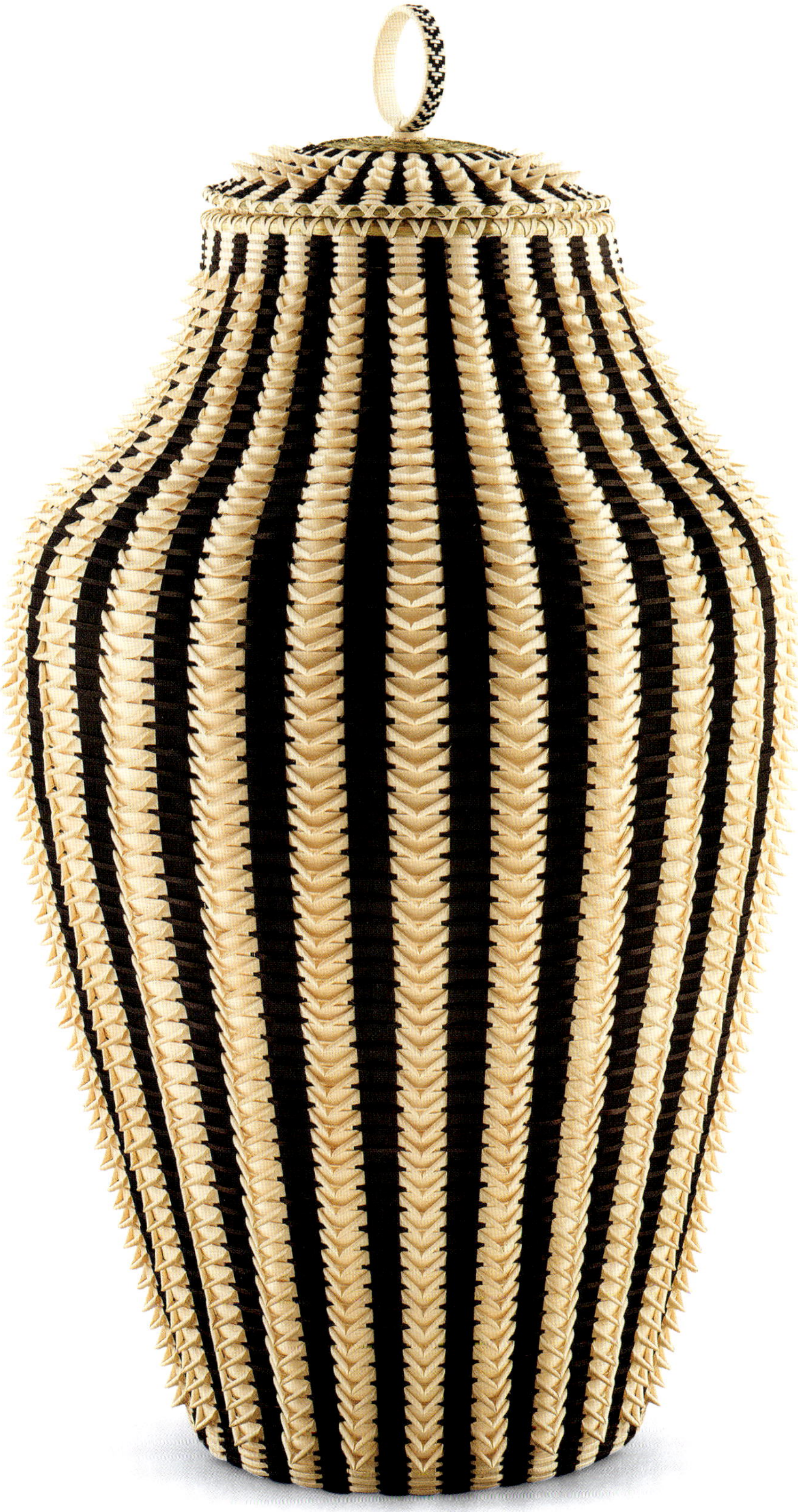

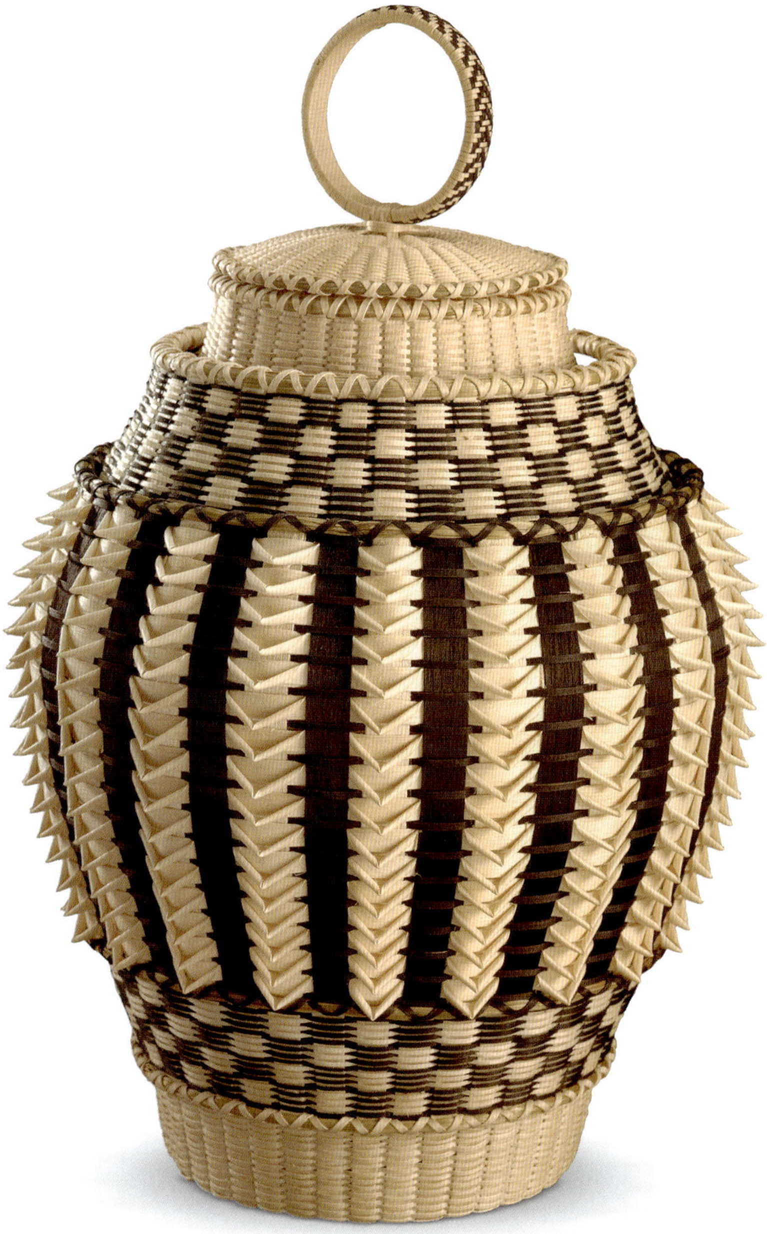

Basket with Cover, 2012

Ash, sweetgrass, and dye
12⅛ × 8⅜ × 8⅜ inches
National Museum of the American Indian, Smithsonian Institution, Washington, D.C., 269237.000

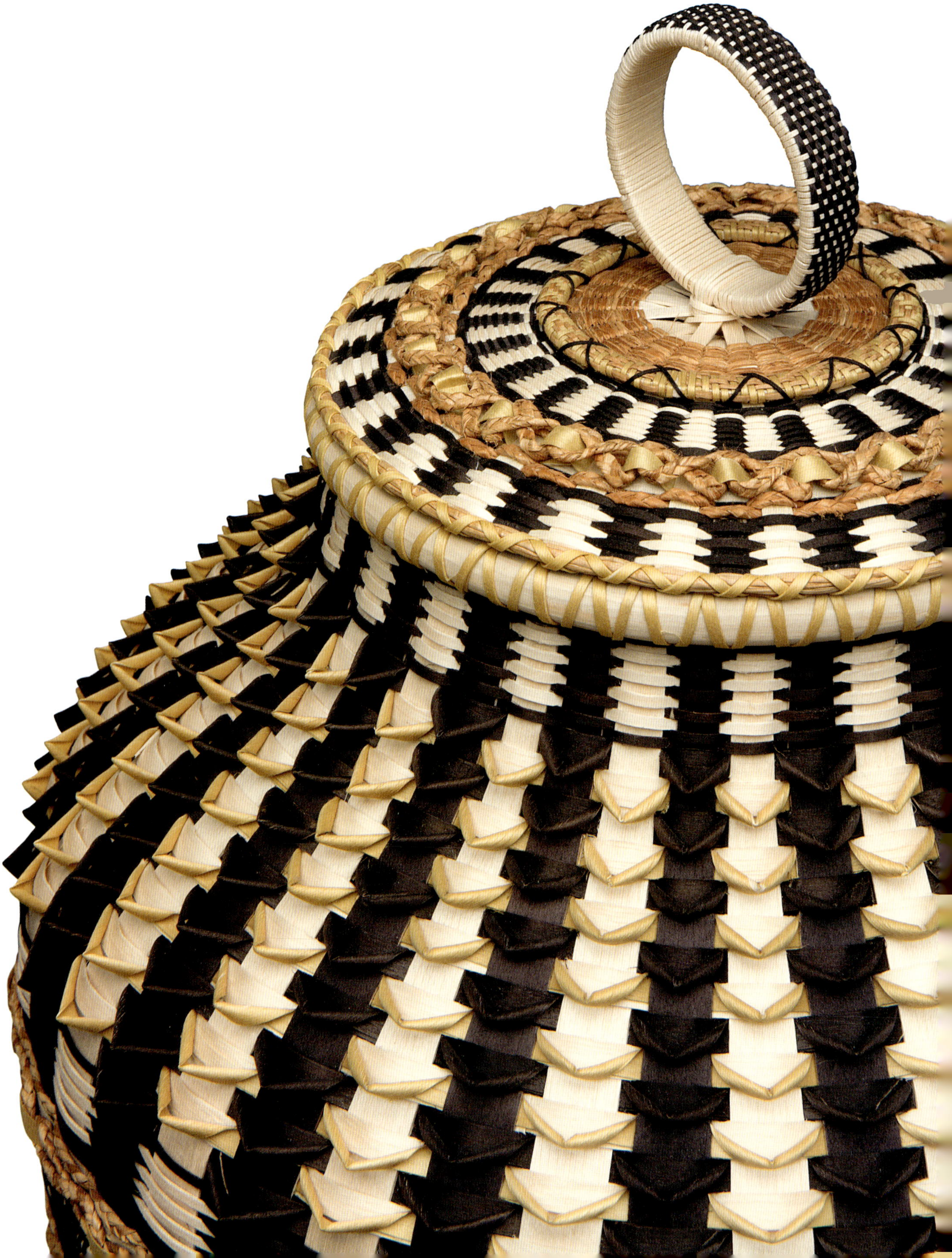

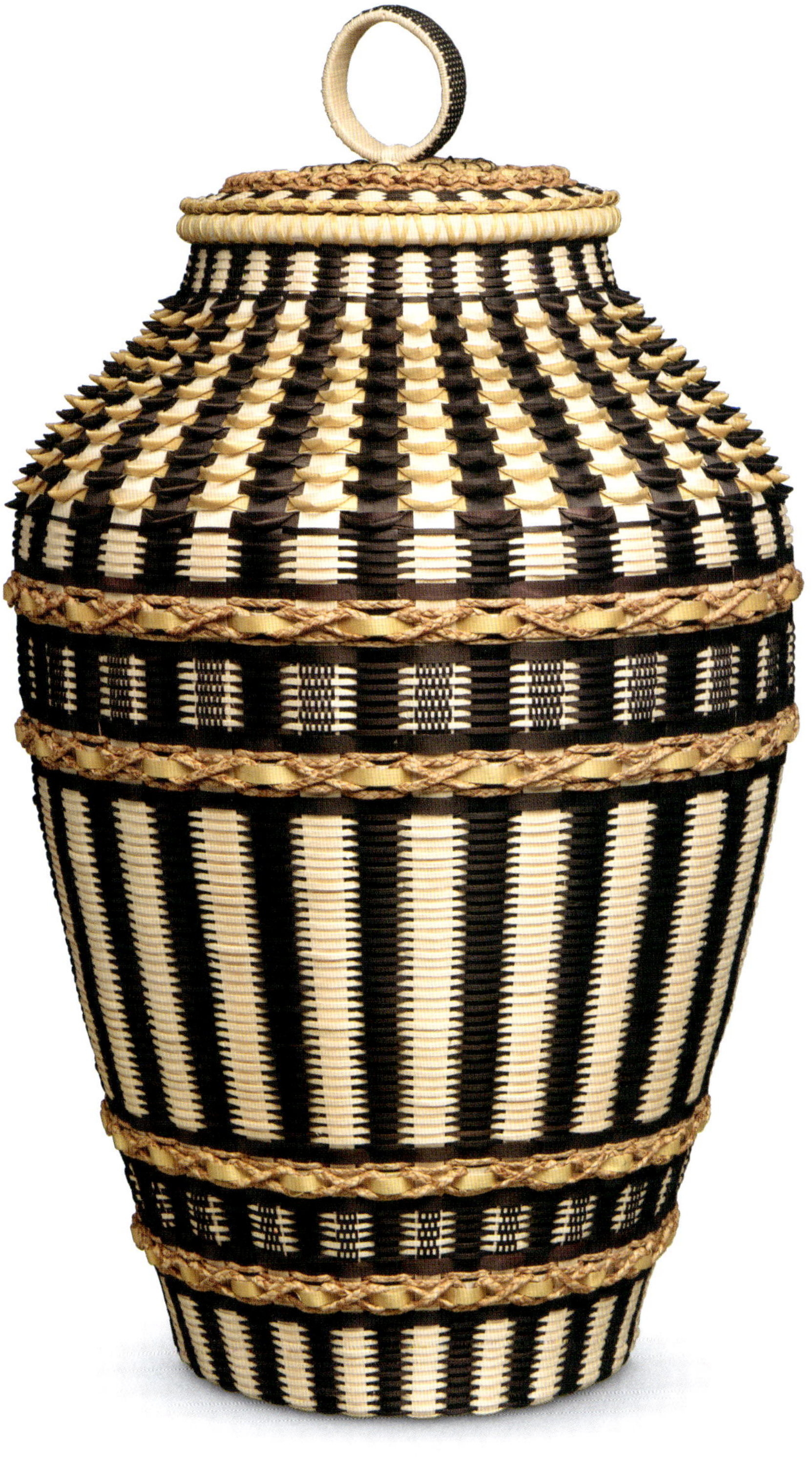

Covered Vase, 2012

Ash, cedar bark, sweetgrass, and dye
18½ × 12 × 12 inches

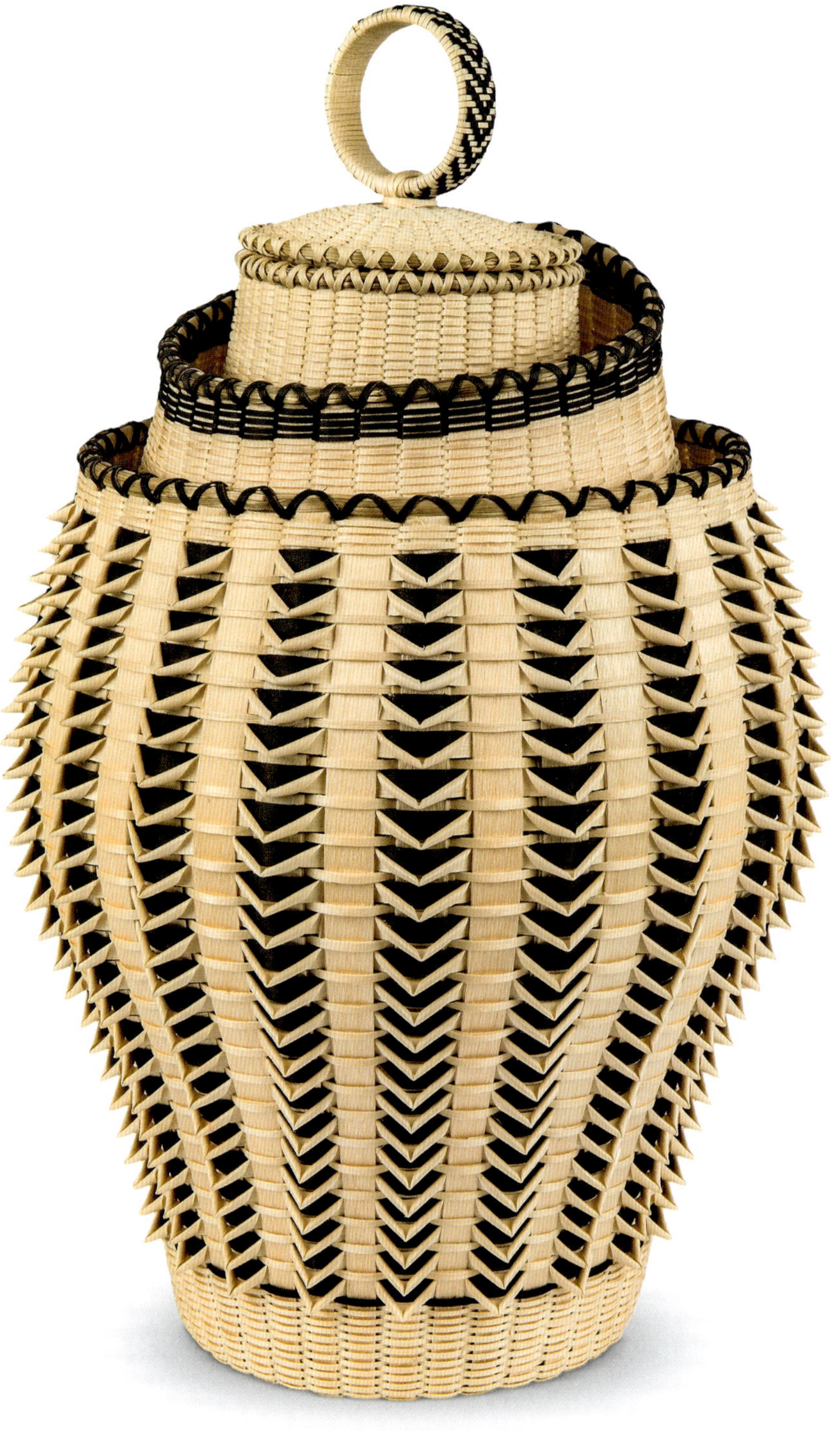

Biased Top Basket, 2013

Ash, sweetgrass, and dye
13 × 9 × 9 inches
Collection of Dr. and Mrs. Ari and Lea Plosker

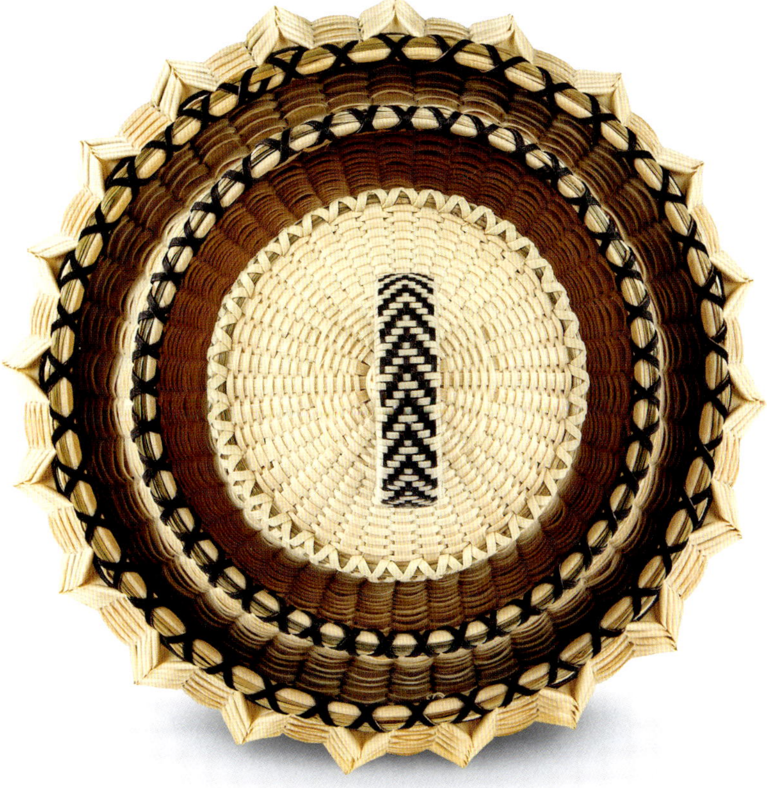

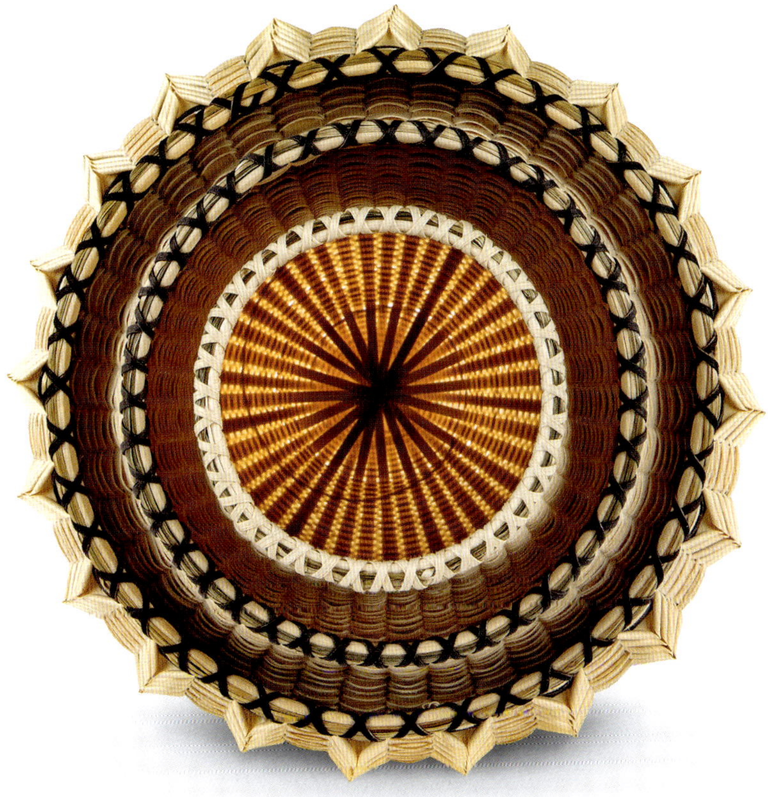

122

Emergence, 2013

Ash, sweetgrass, and dye
23 × 13 × 13 inches
Southwest Museum of the American Indian Collection, Autry Museum of the American West. Donated by W. Richard West, Jr. and Mary Beth West in honor of the Autry staff, 2013.33.1

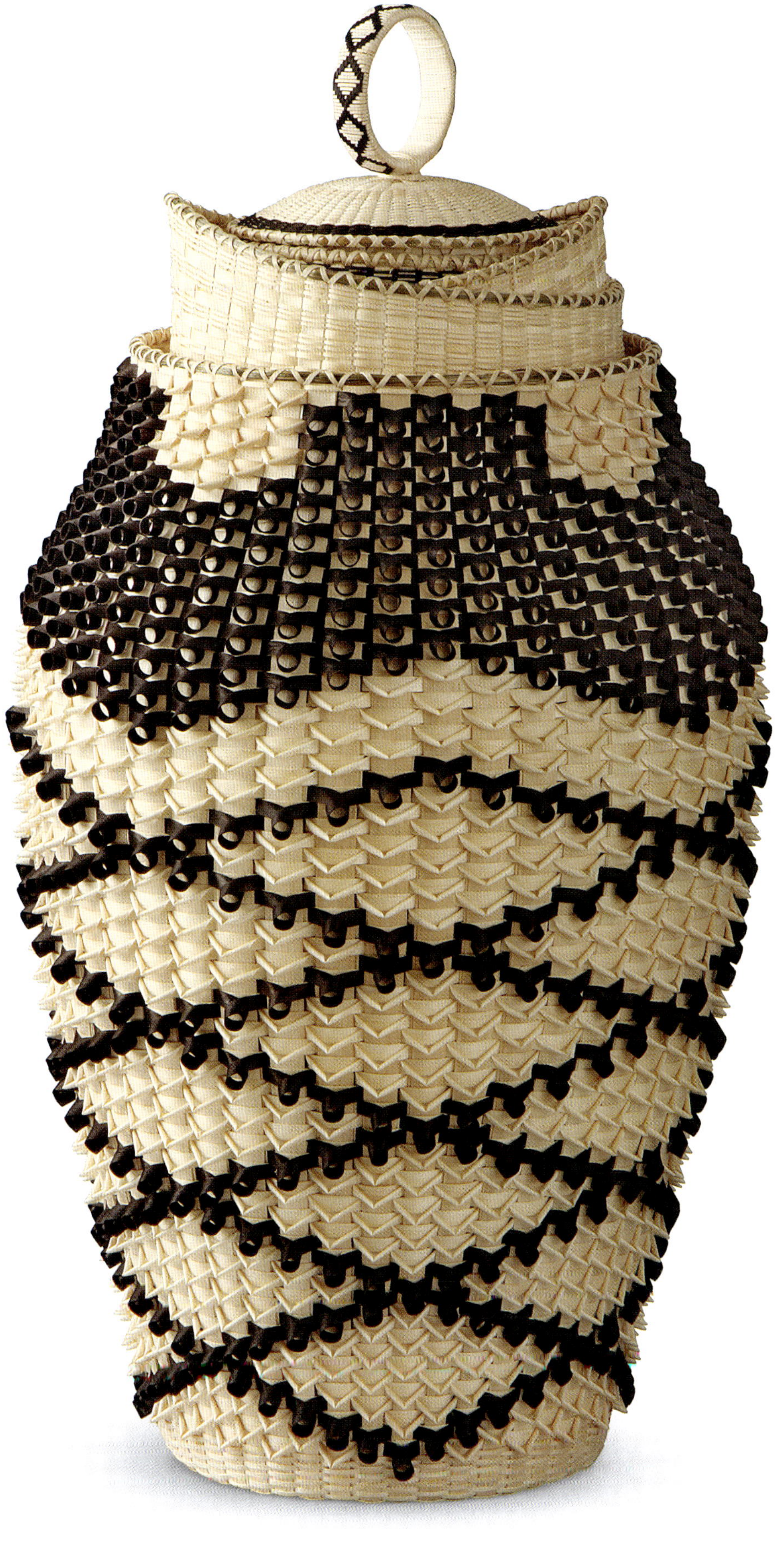

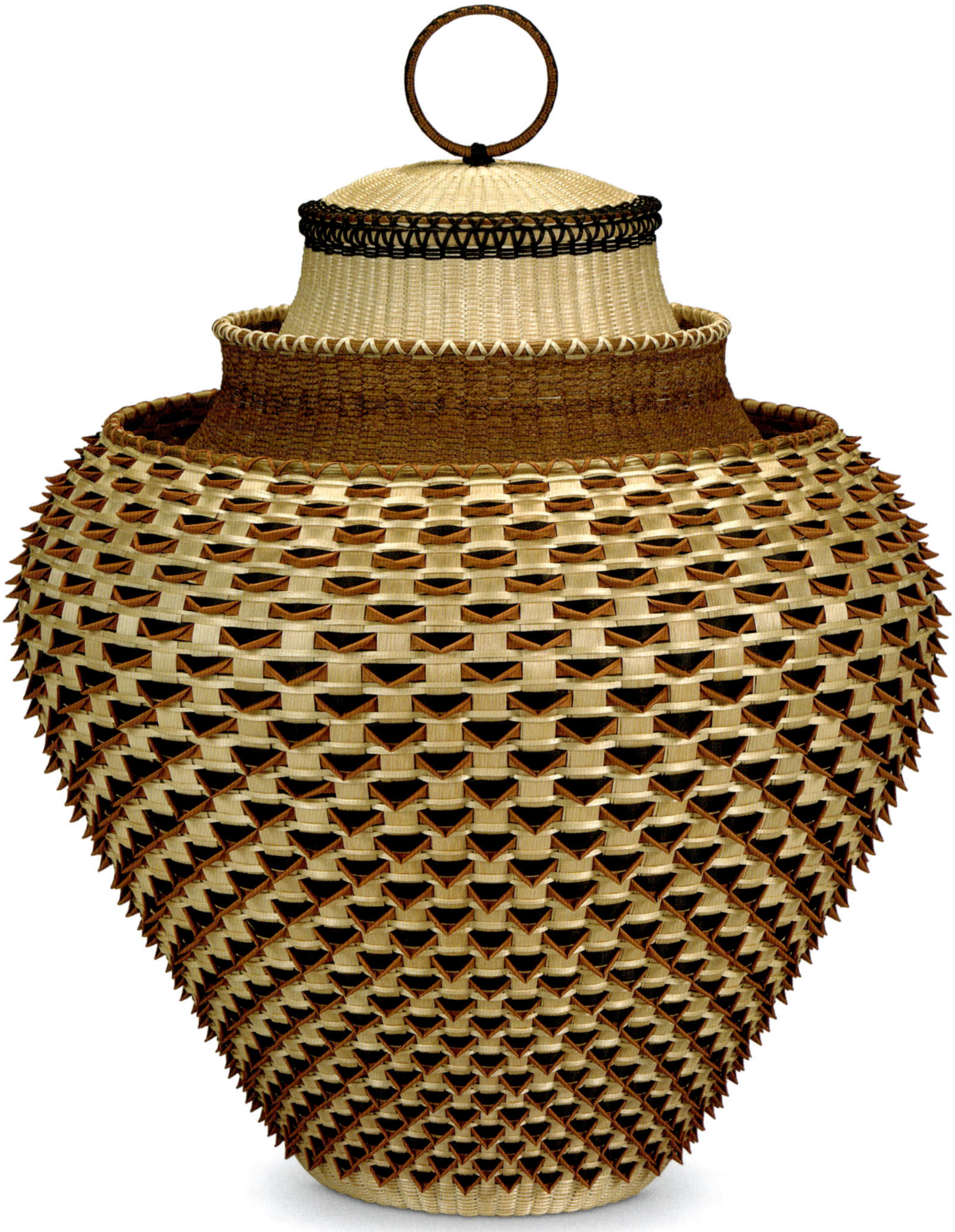

Deception, 2014

Ash, braided cedar bark, spruce root, and dye
17⅛ × 16 × 16 inches
Virginia Museum of Fine Arts, Richmond, 2016.11a-b

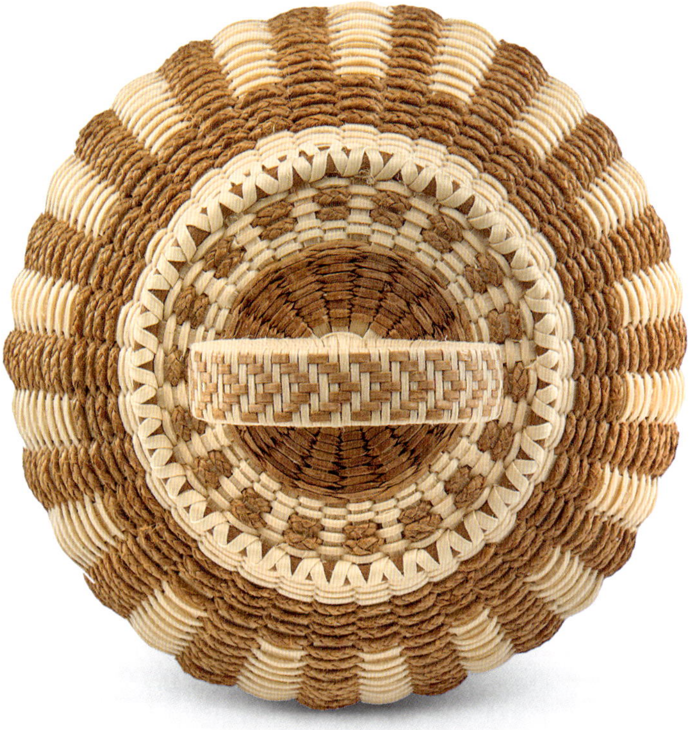

126

Fine Weave Vase, 2015

Ash and braided cedar bark
9 × 4½ × 4½ inches
Collection of Dr. and Mrs. Ari and Lea Plosker

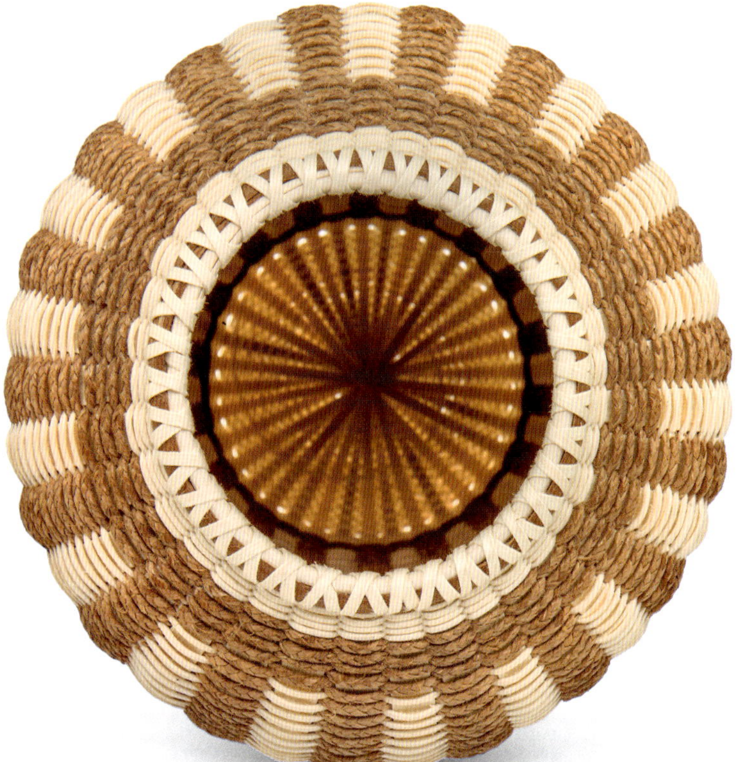

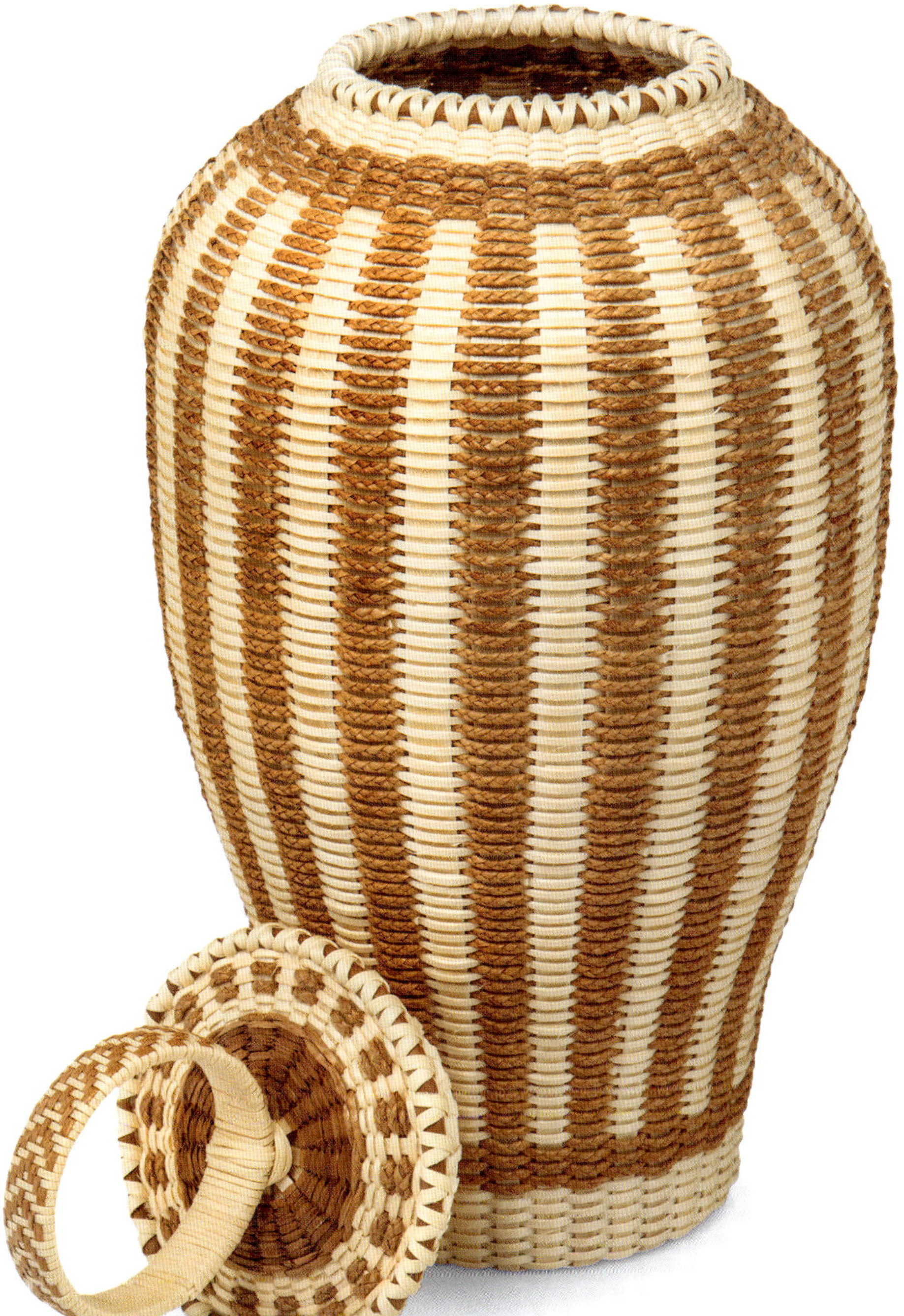

128

Covered Vase, 2016

Ash, cedar bark, cherrywood, sweetgrass, and spruce root
14¾ × 7 × 7 inches
Portland Museum of Art, ME.
Gift of Barbara M. Goodbody, 2021.19.6a,b

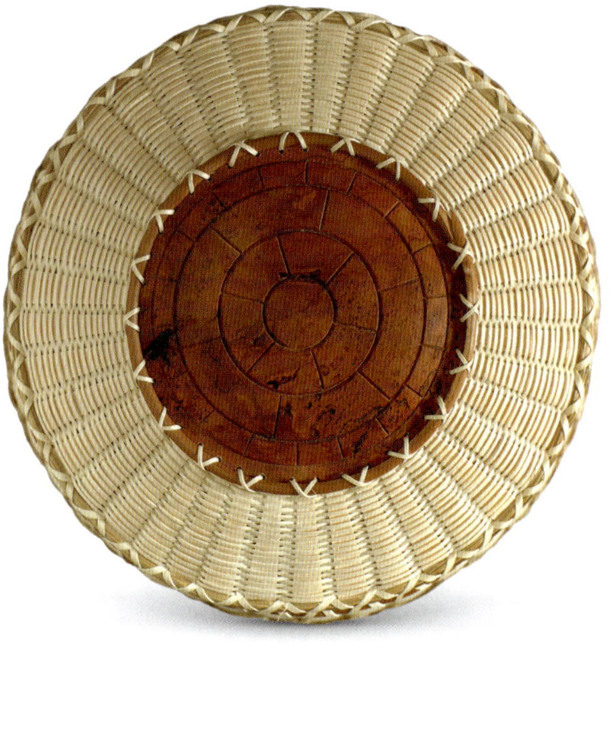

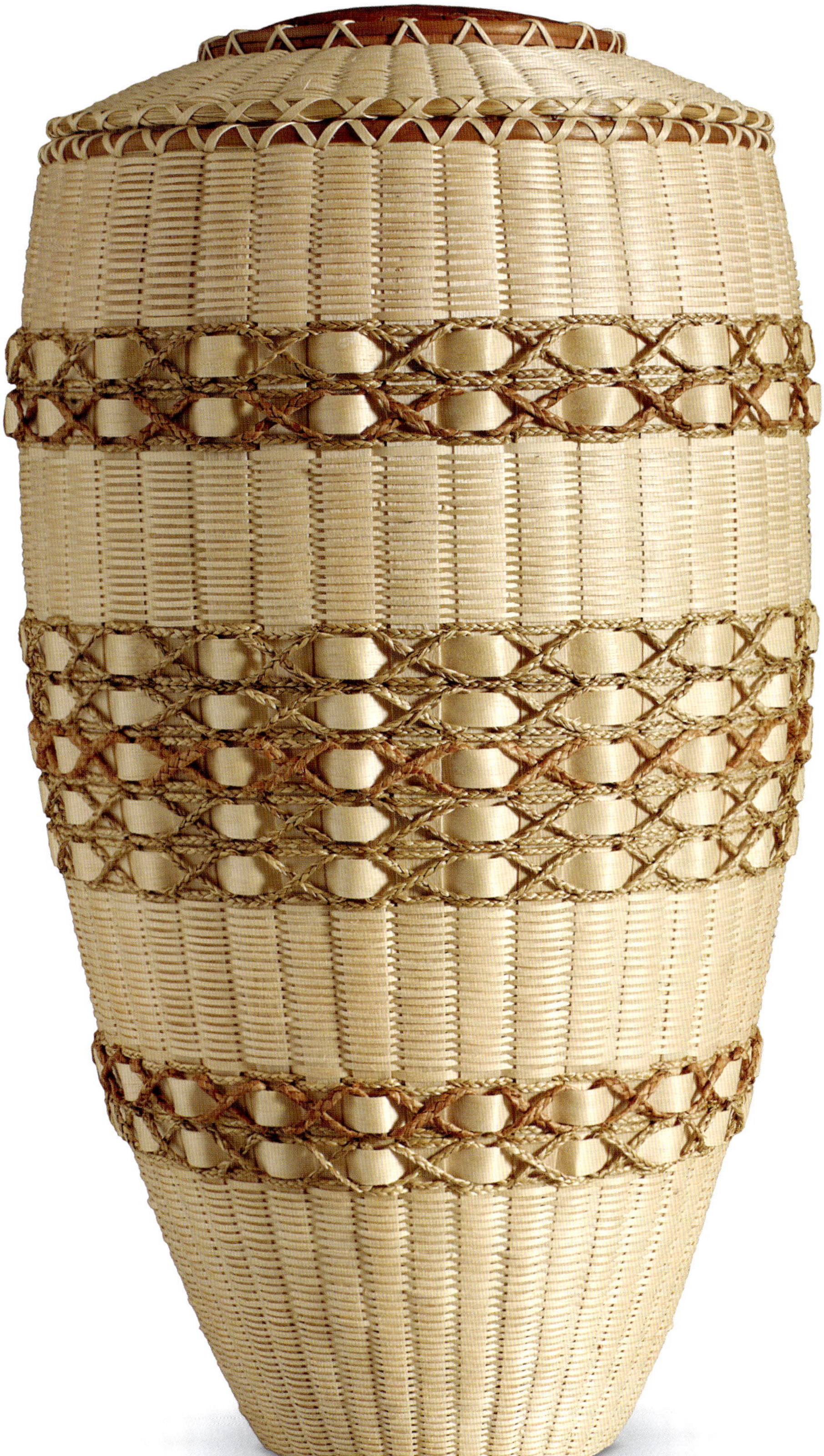

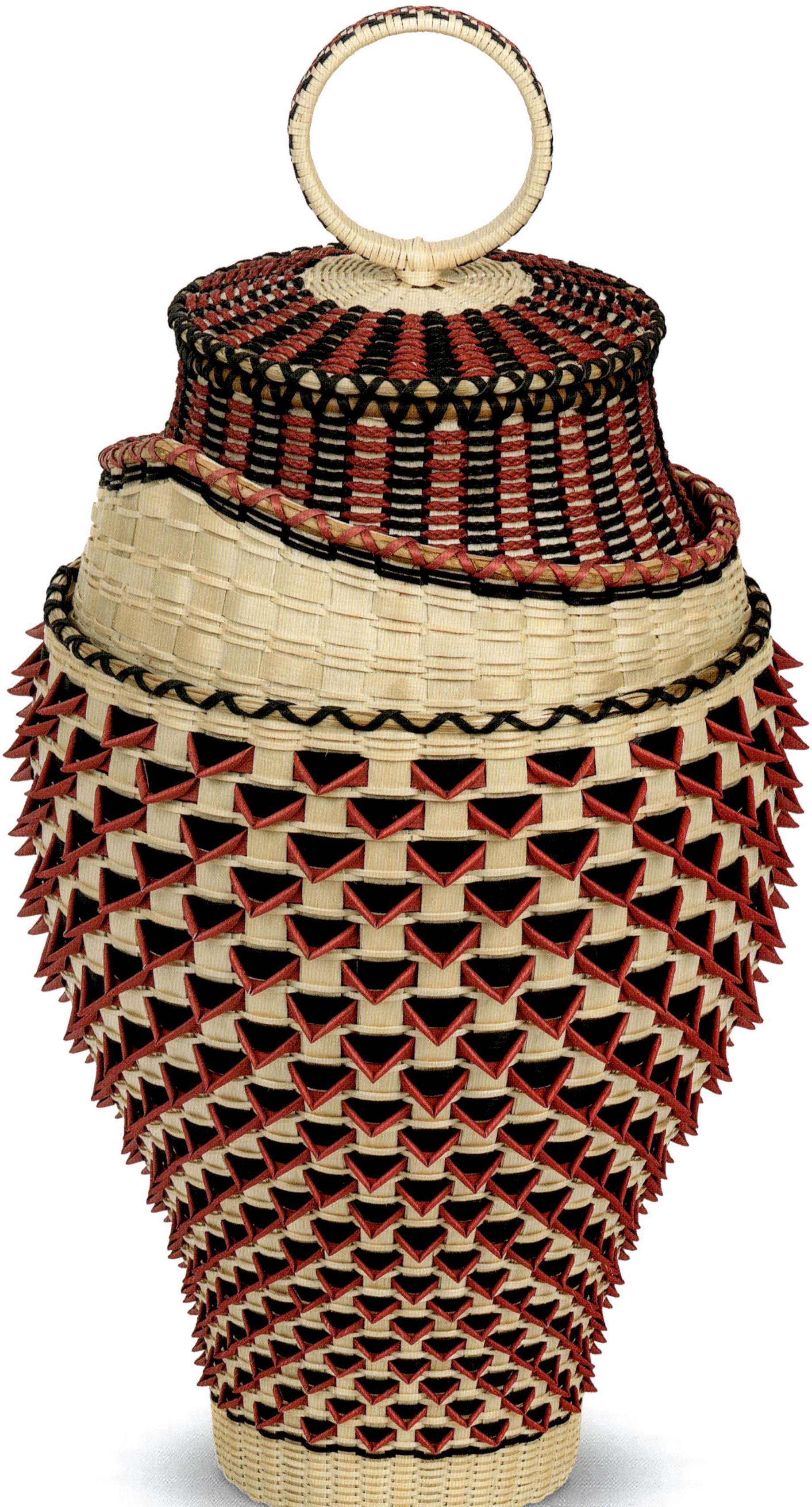

Phoenix, 2017

Ash, cedar, sweetgrass, spruce root, and dye
8 × 6 × 6 inches
The Buker Collections

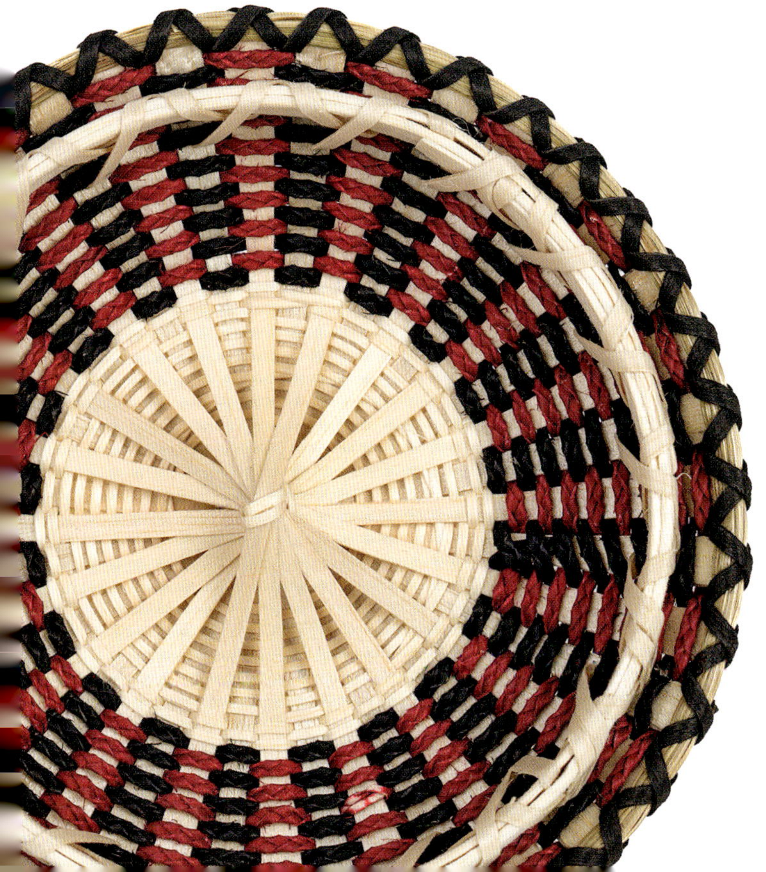

Untitled, 2017

Ash and braided cedar bark
16¾ × 9½ × 9½ inches
Collection of David and Sue Halpern

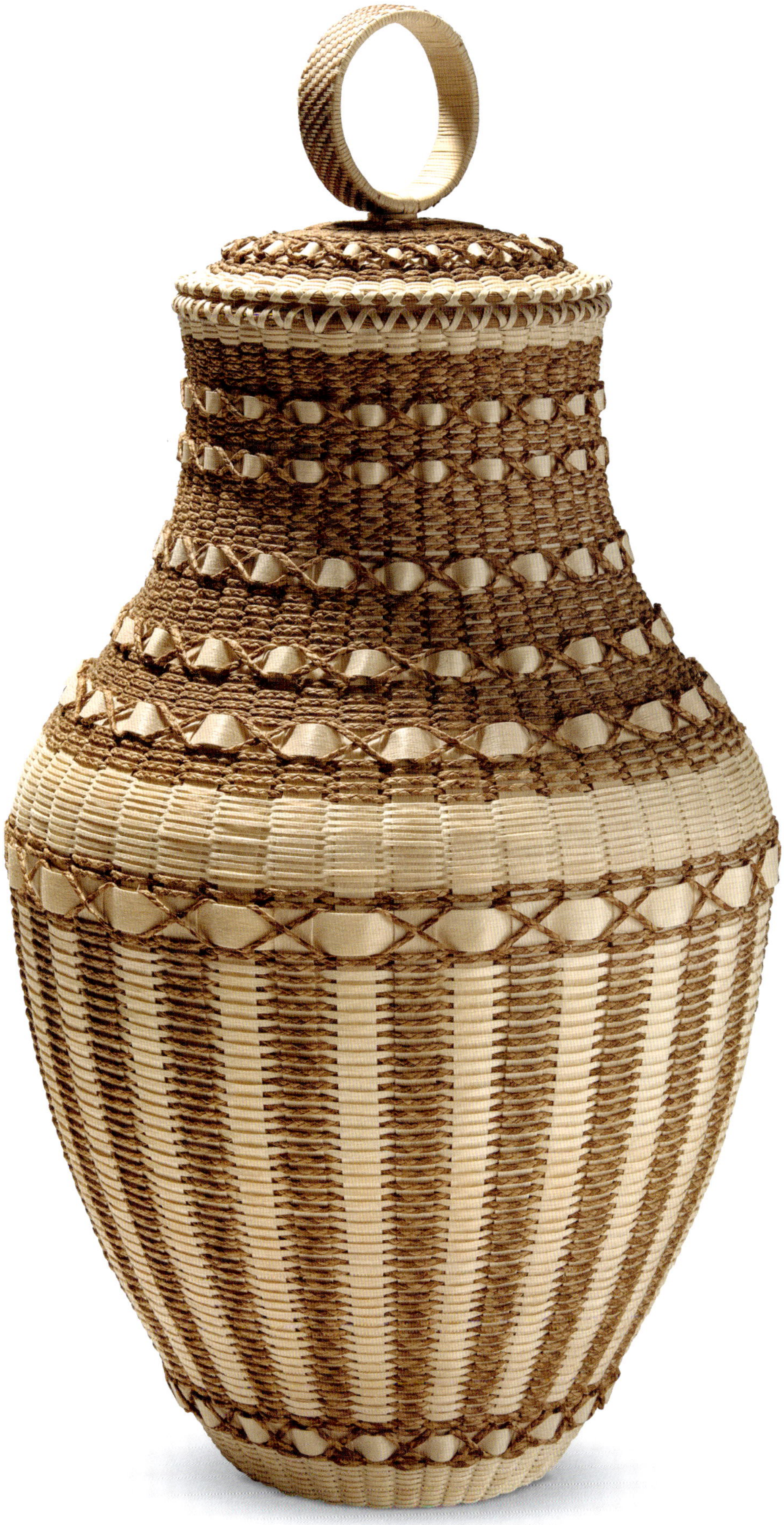

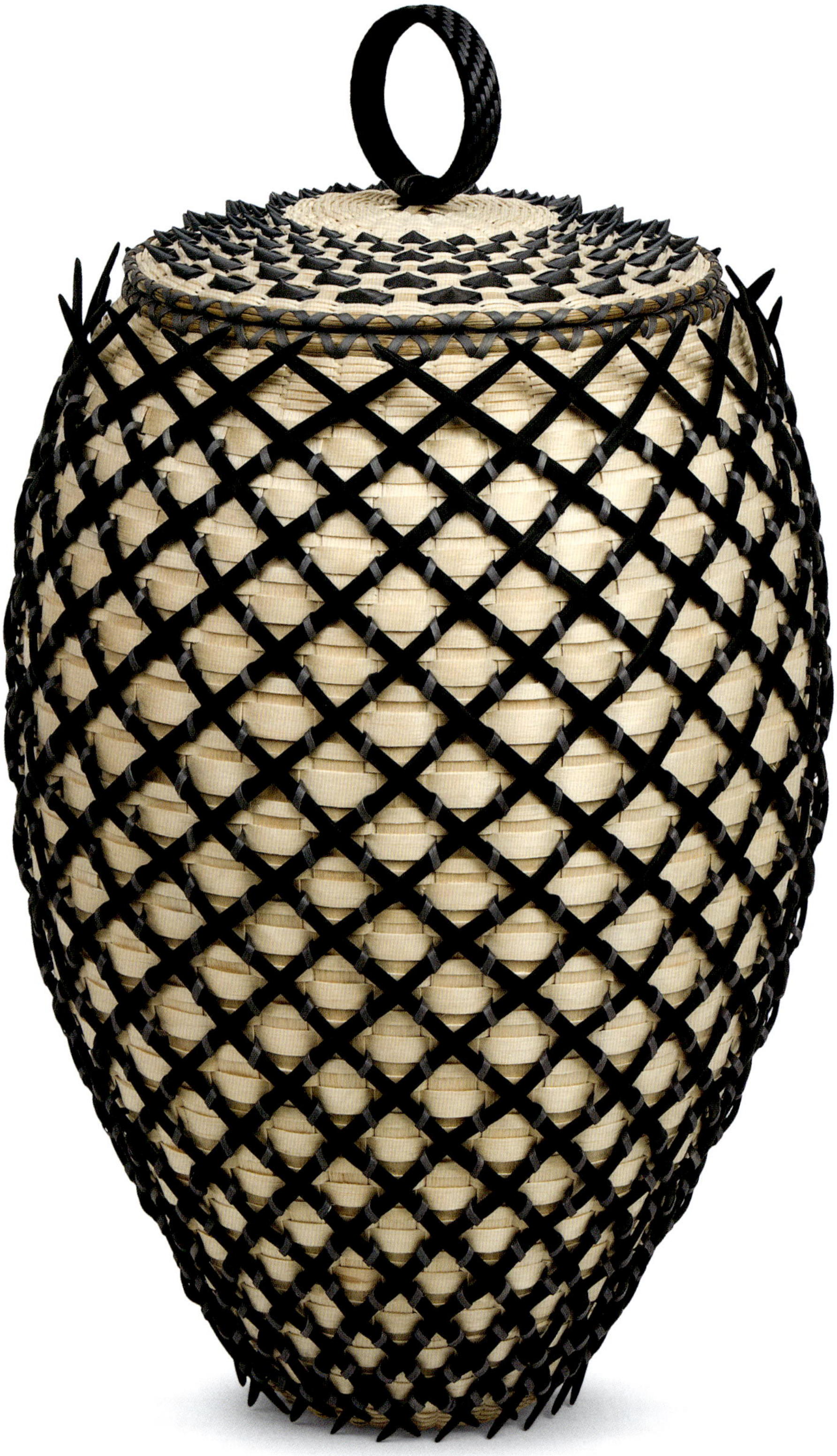

Caged, 2018

Ash, sweetgrass, and dye
13 × 7 × 7 inches
The Buker Collections

Cathedral, 2018

Ash, sweetgrass, and dye
21¼ × 10 × 10 inches
Portland Museum of Art, ME. Museum purchase with support from the Peggy and Harold Osher Acquisitions Fund, Bernstein Acquisition Fund, and Barbara Goodbody, 2018.15a,b

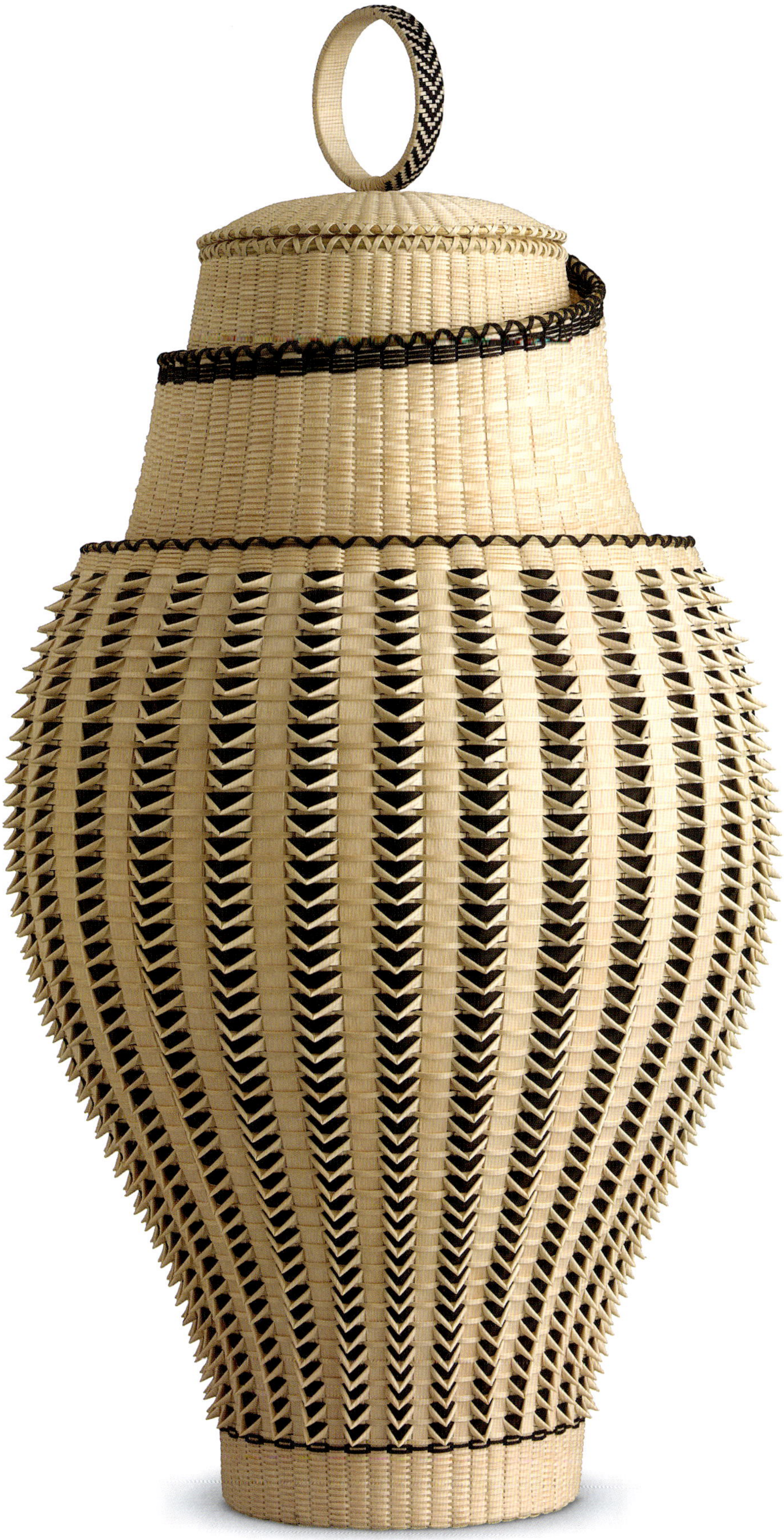

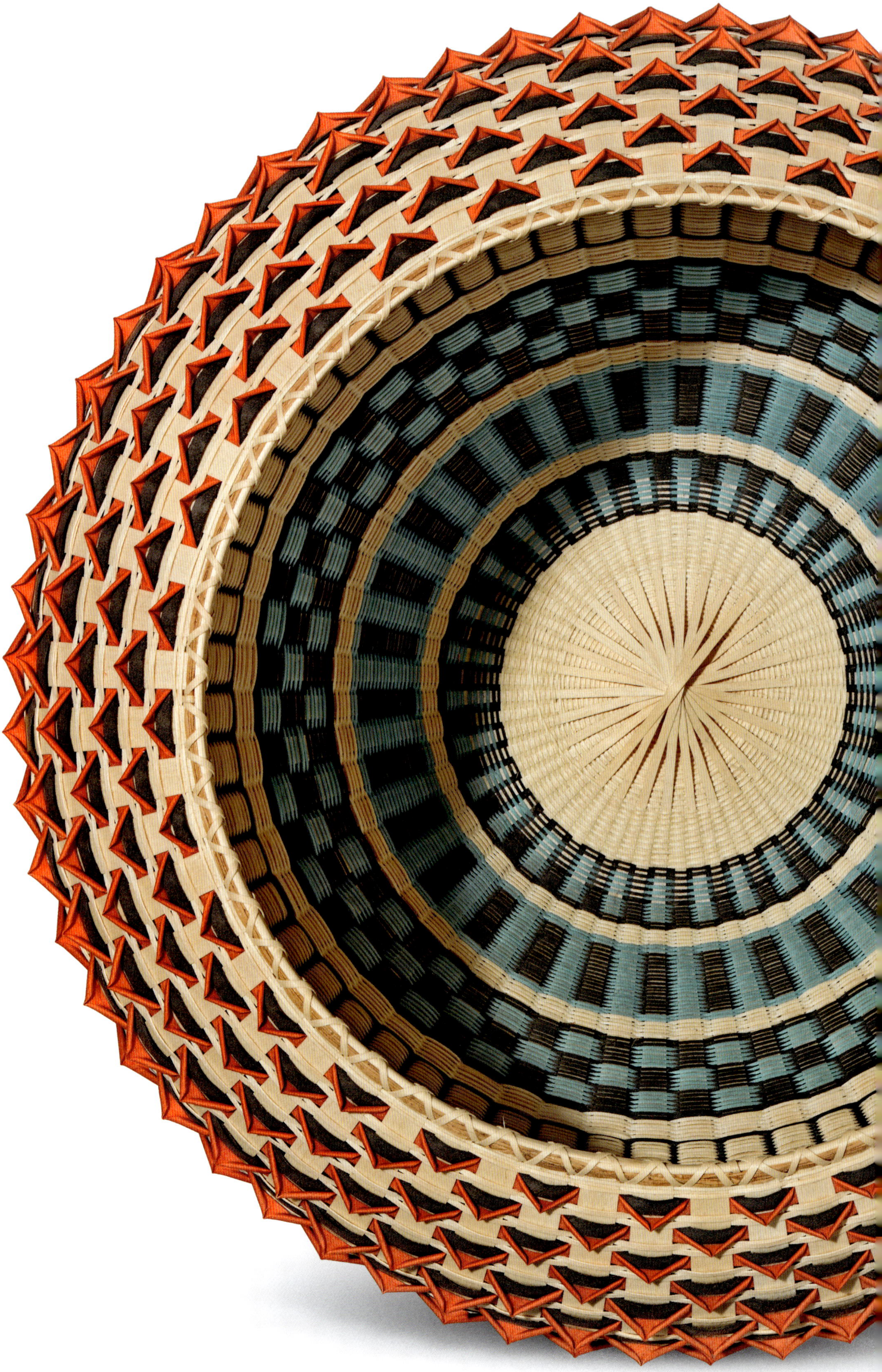

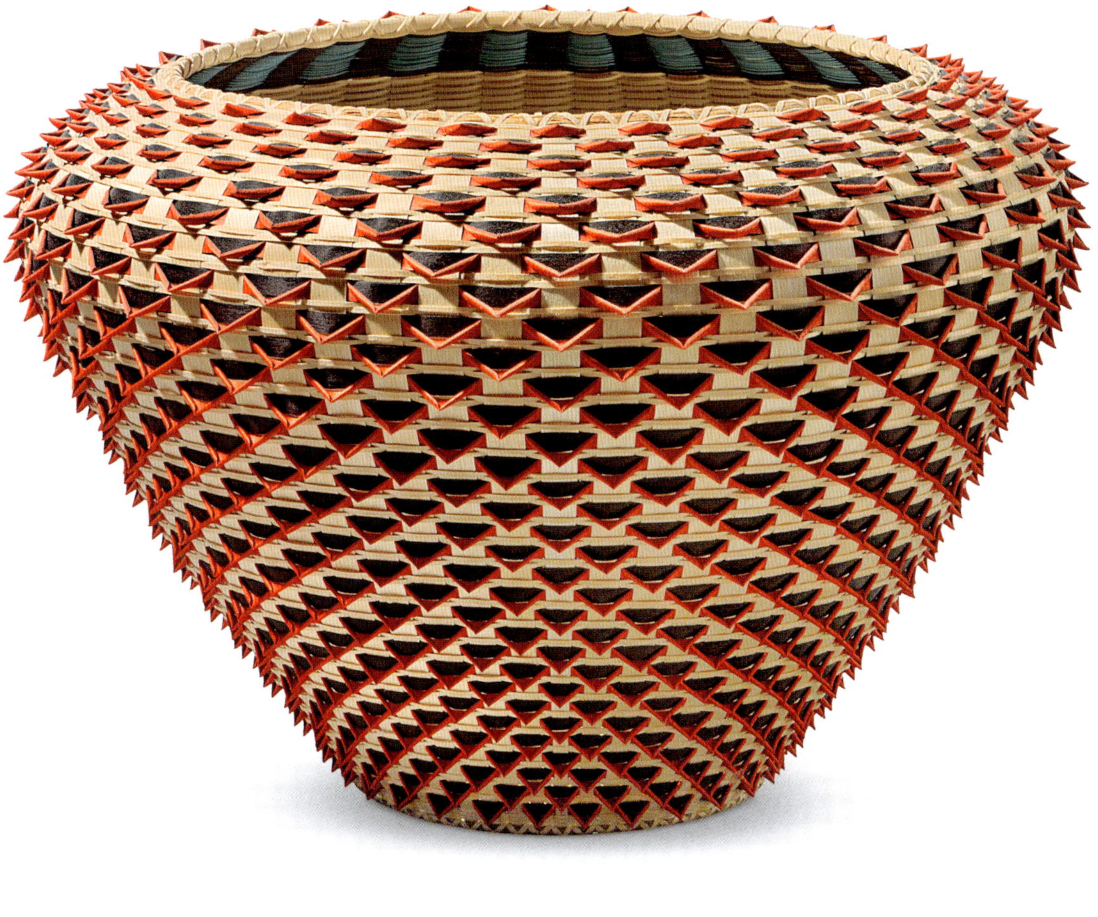

Double-Walled Point Basket, 2018

Ash, cedar bark, and dye
12 × 18 × 18 inches
Private collection

Ghost Bear, 2018

Ash, sweetgrass, moose antler, and dye
21 × 10 × 10 inches
The Buker Collections

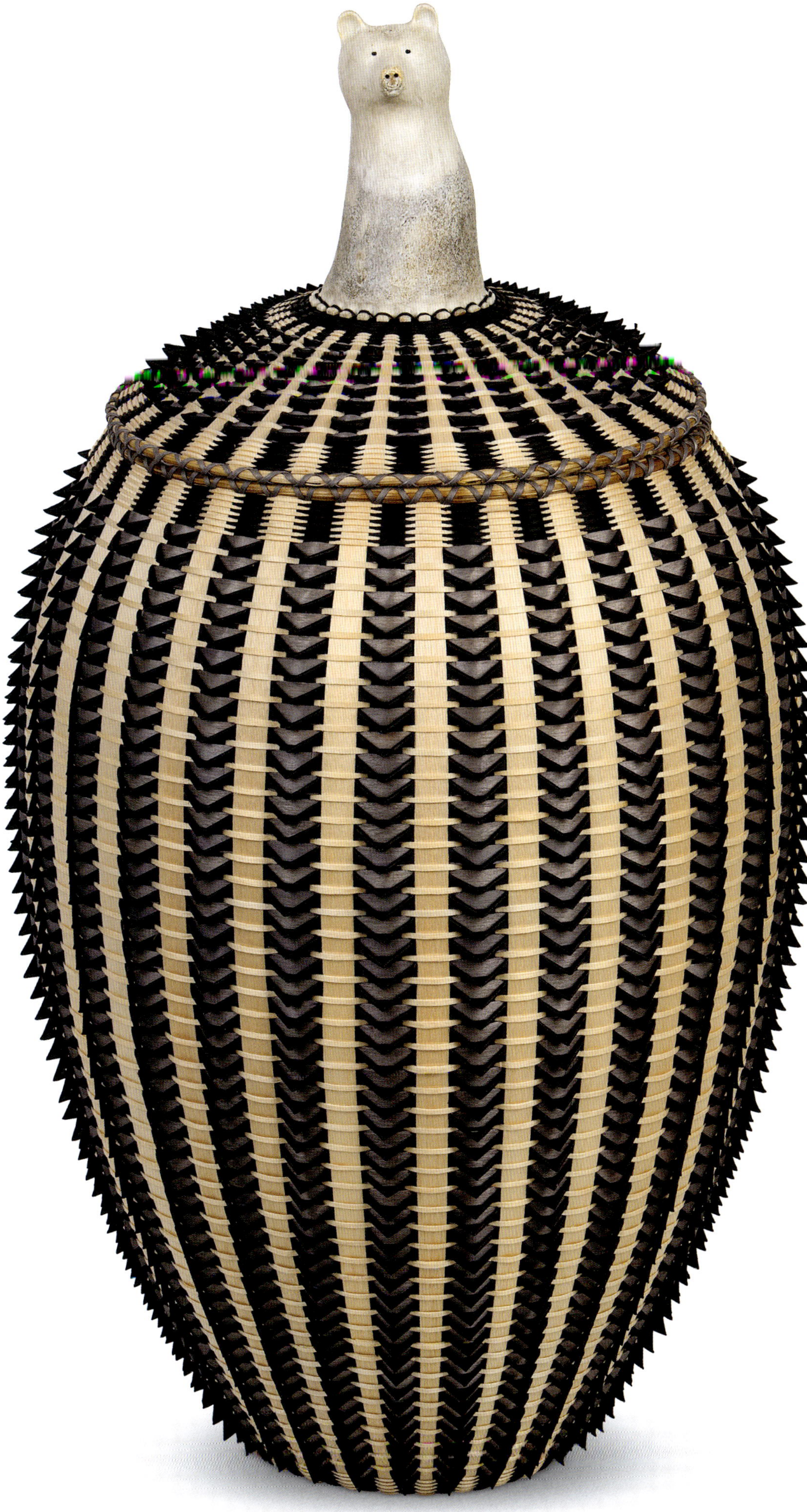

142

Quilted Cedar Bark Multi-Top, 2020

Ash, braided cedar bark, sweetgrass, and dye
18 × 9 × 9 inches
The Buker Collections

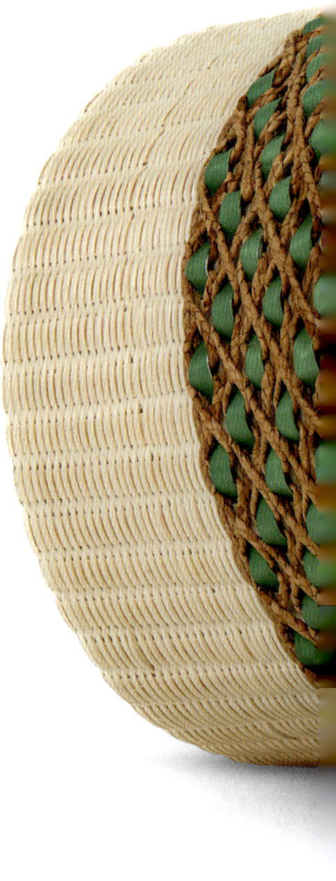

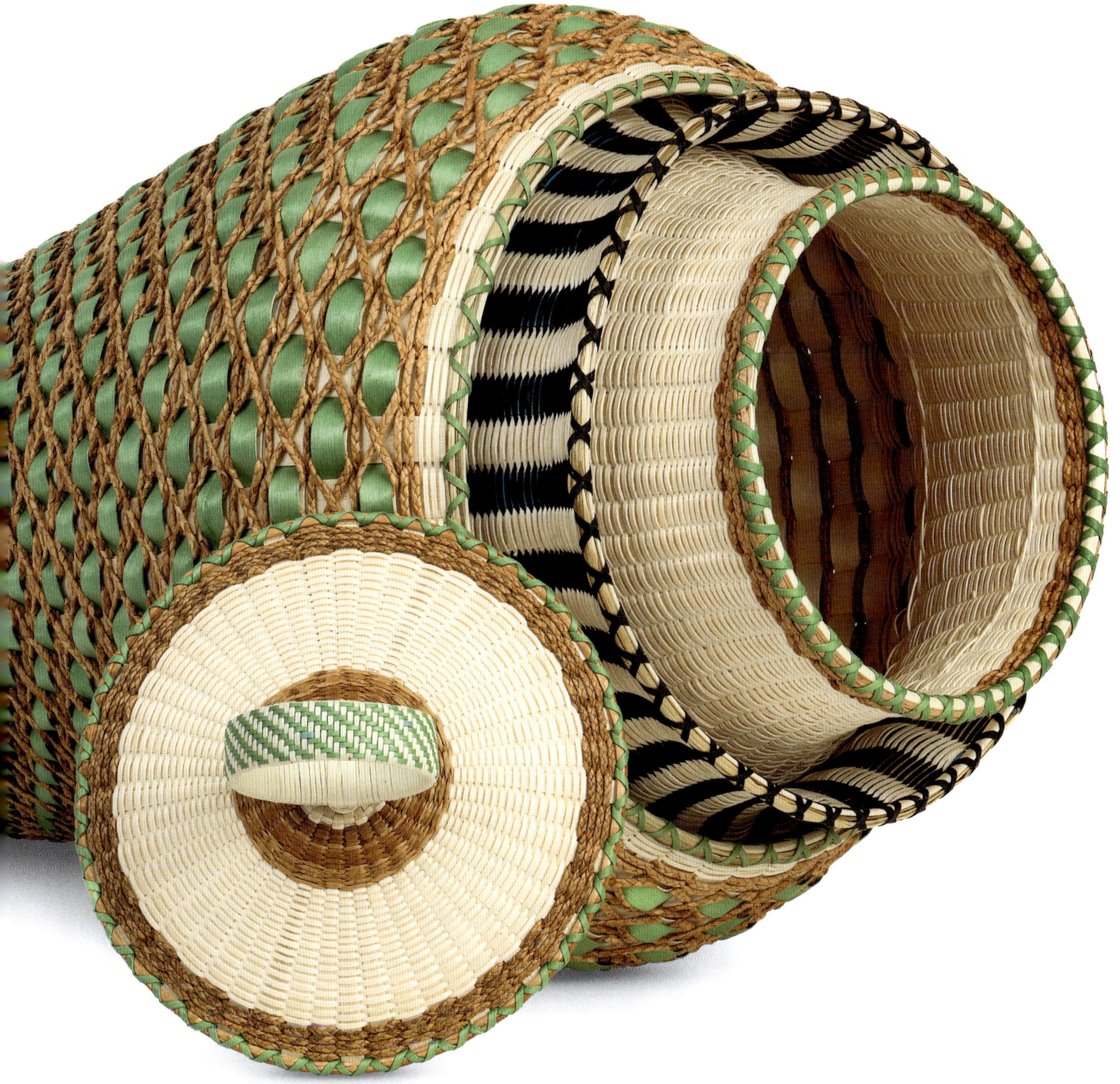

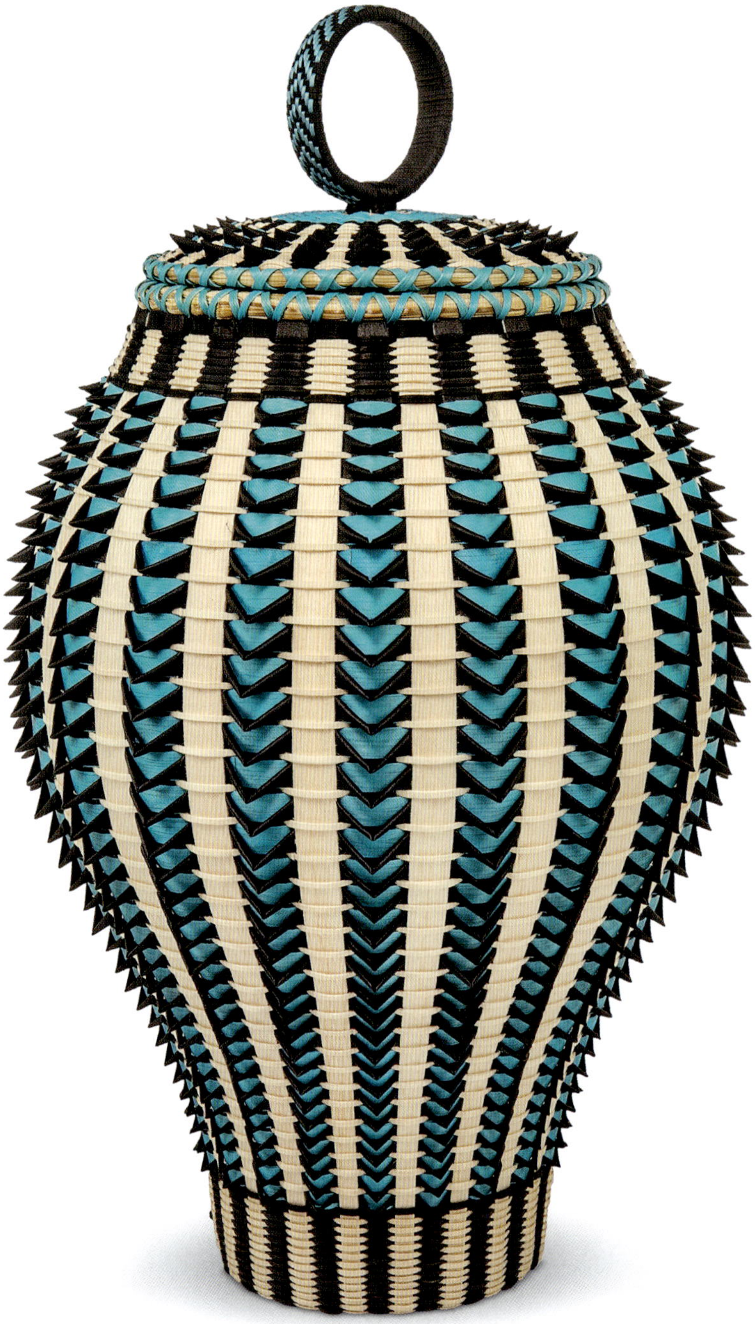

Blue Point Vase, 2021

Ash, sweetgrass, and dye
11½ × 8 × 8 inches
Collection of Dr. and Mrs. Ari and Lea Plosker

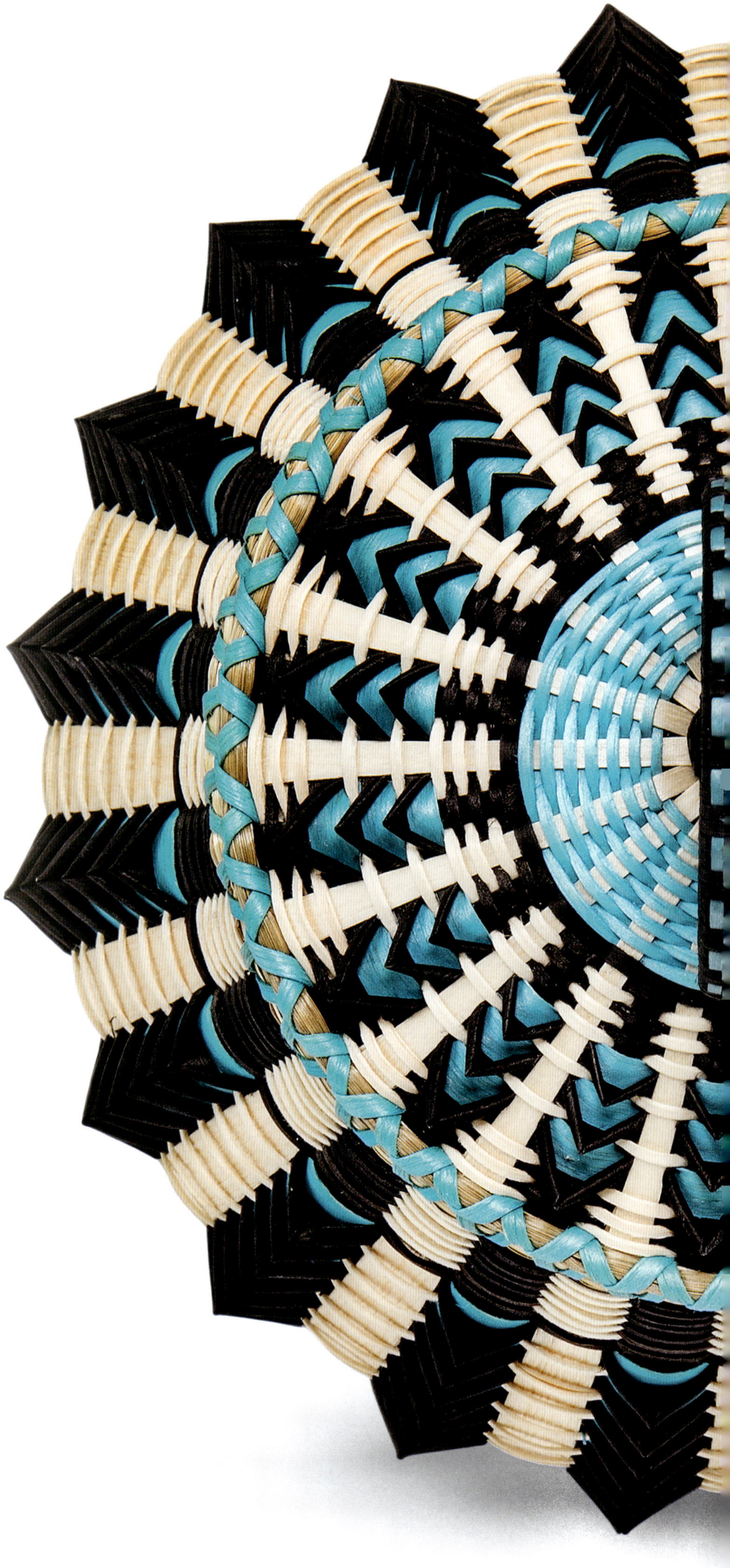

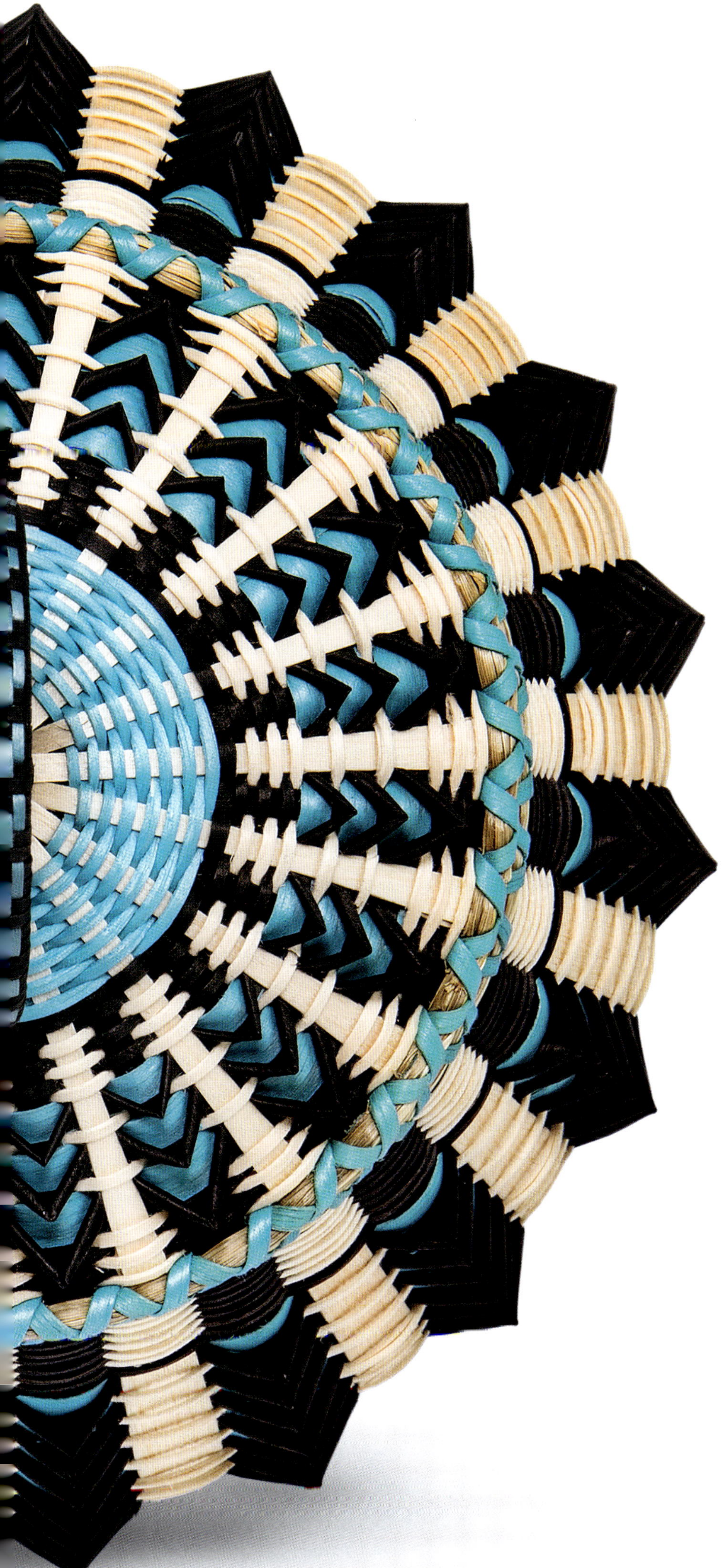

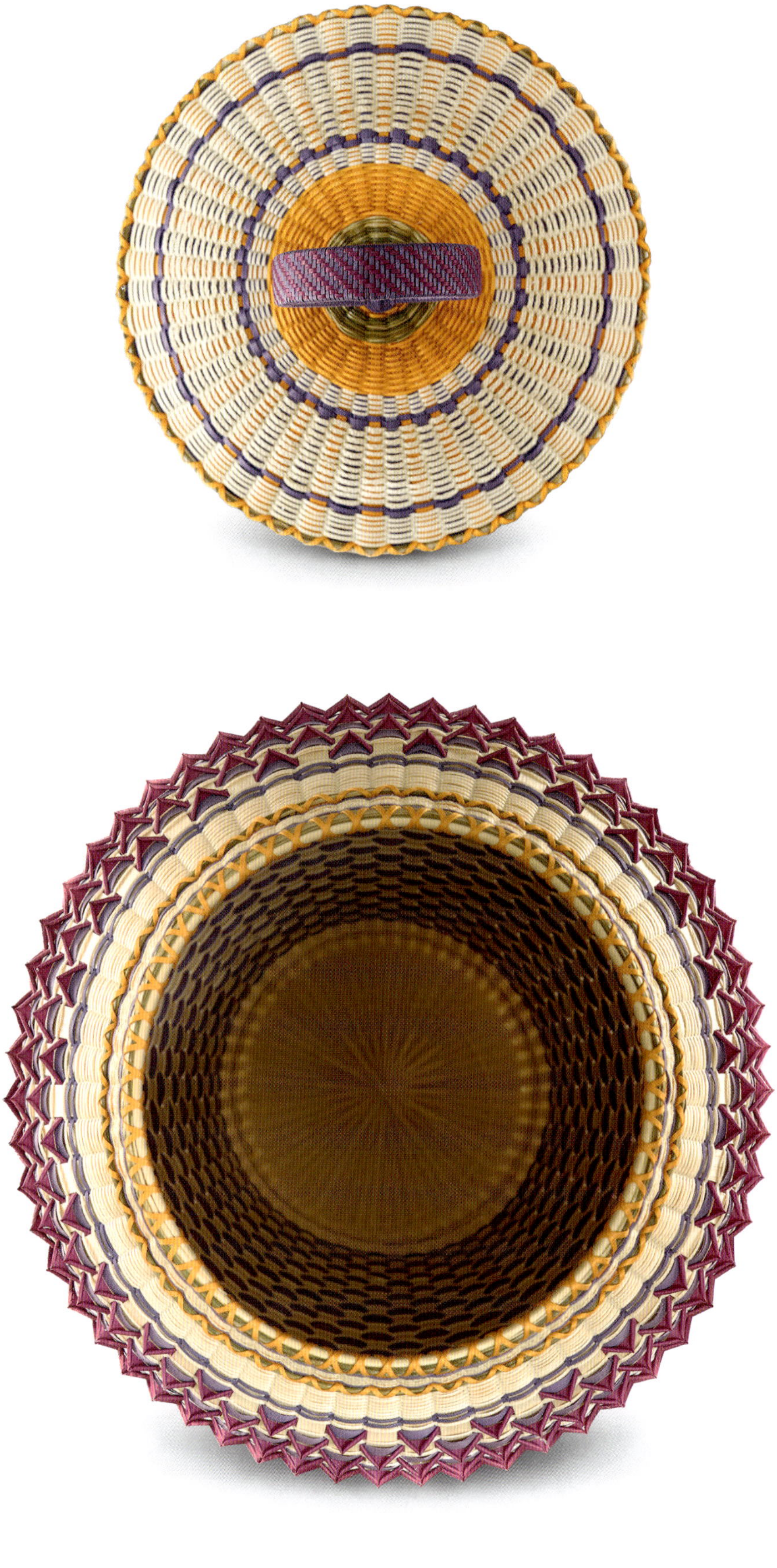

Dawnland, 2022

Ash, sweetgrass, and dye
17½ × 11½ × 11½ inches
Collection of Jim and Sara TenBroek

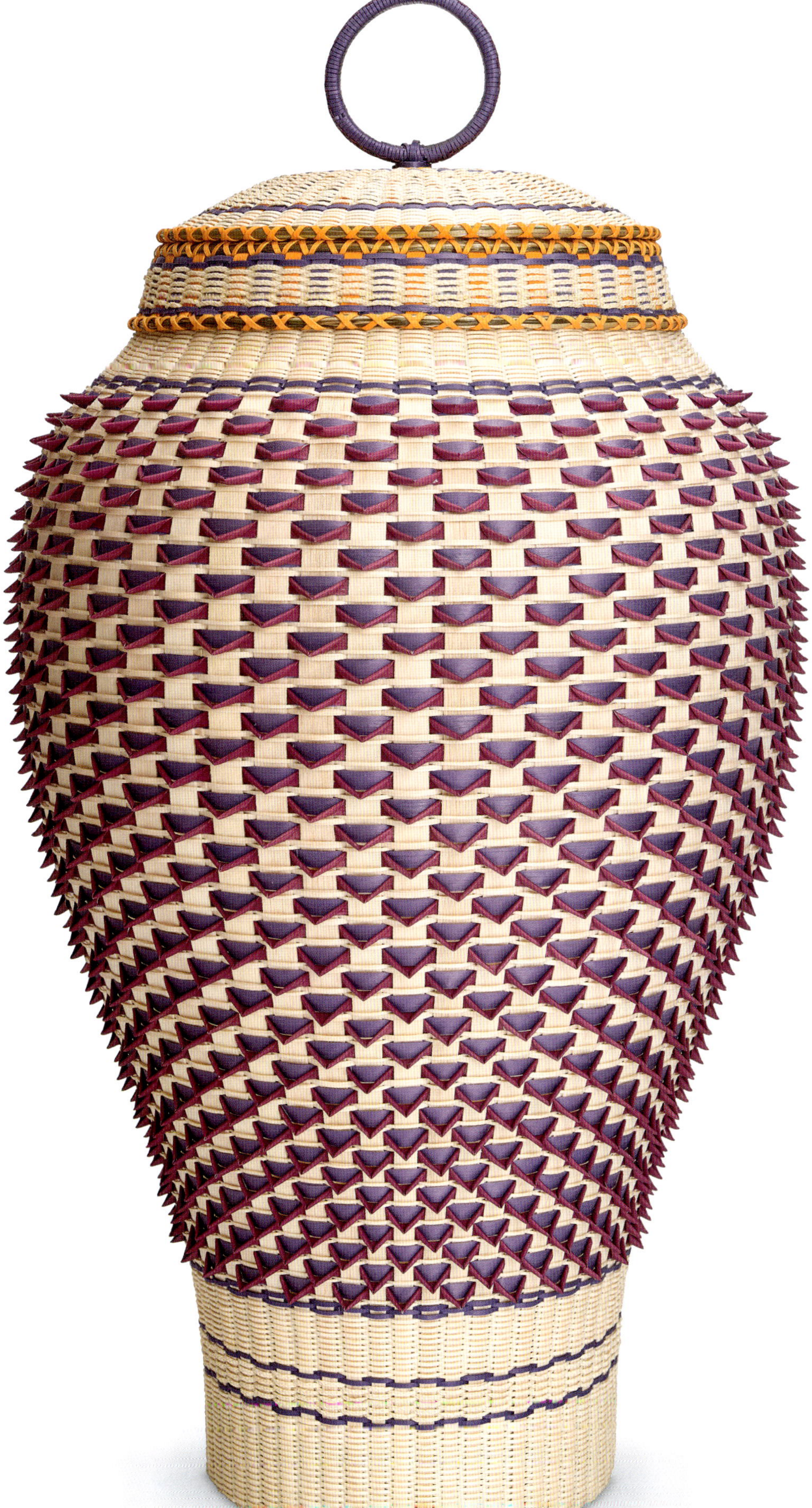

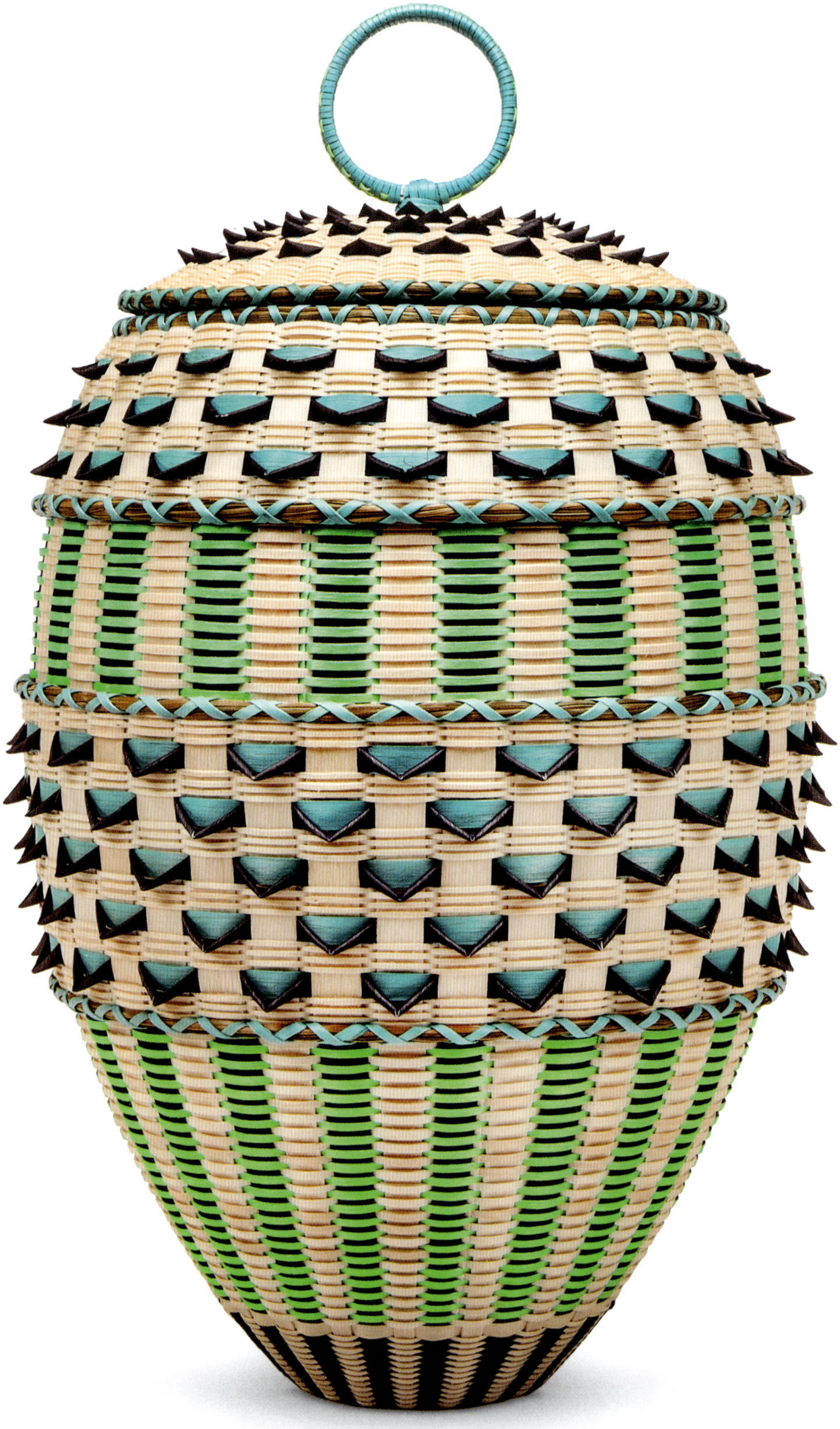

Defensive, 2022

Ash, sweetgrass, and dye
12½ × 7½ × 7½ inches
Collection of Carole Katz

Nearly Monochrome, 2022

Ash, braided ash, cedar bark, and dye
31½ × 16$\frac{5}{16}$ × 16$\frac{5}{16}$ inches
Art Institute of Chicago. Mrs. Leonard S. Florsheim Jr. Fund; purchased with funds provided by the bequest of Fred E. Spreitzer. 2022.1824a-b

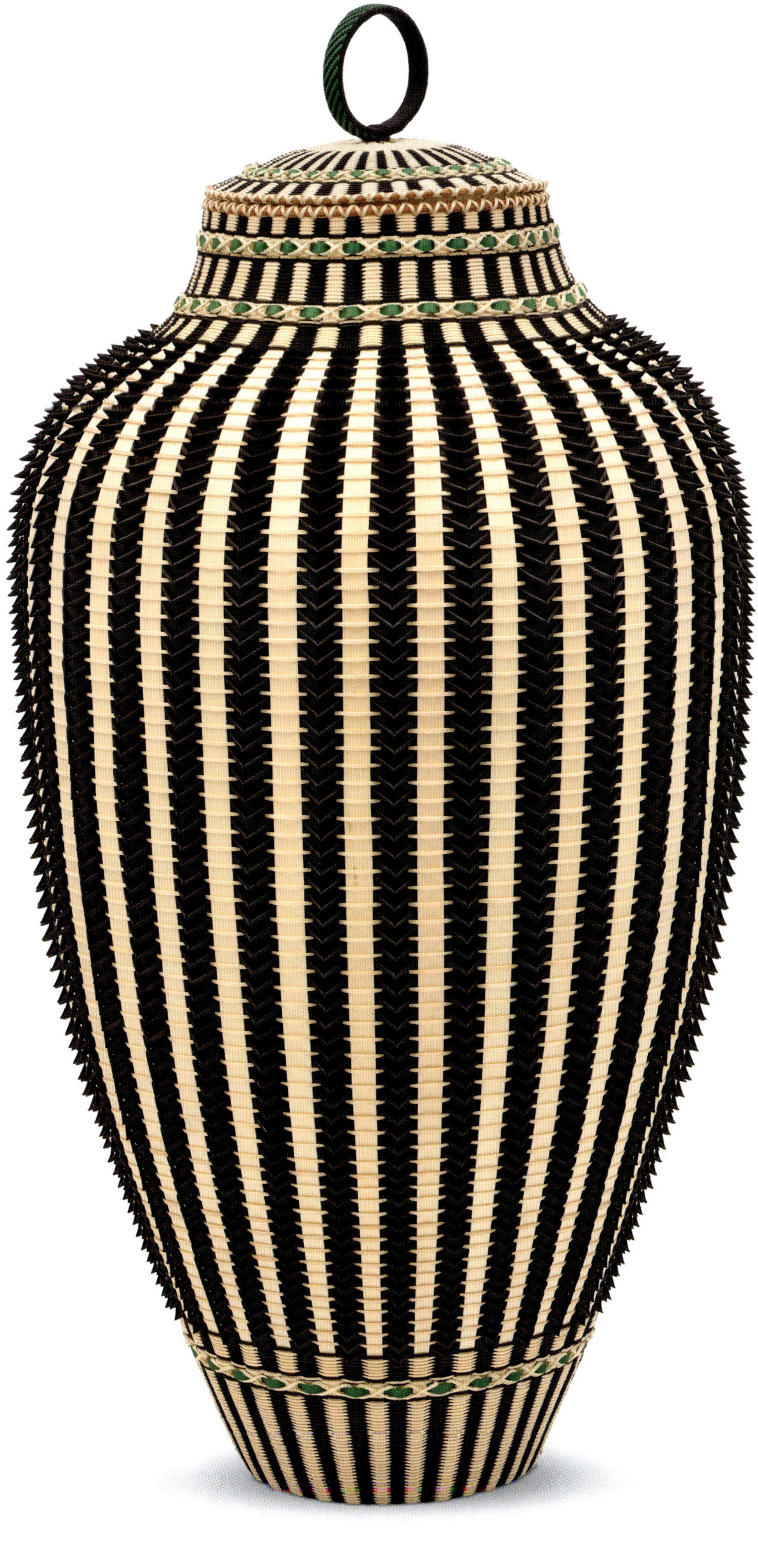

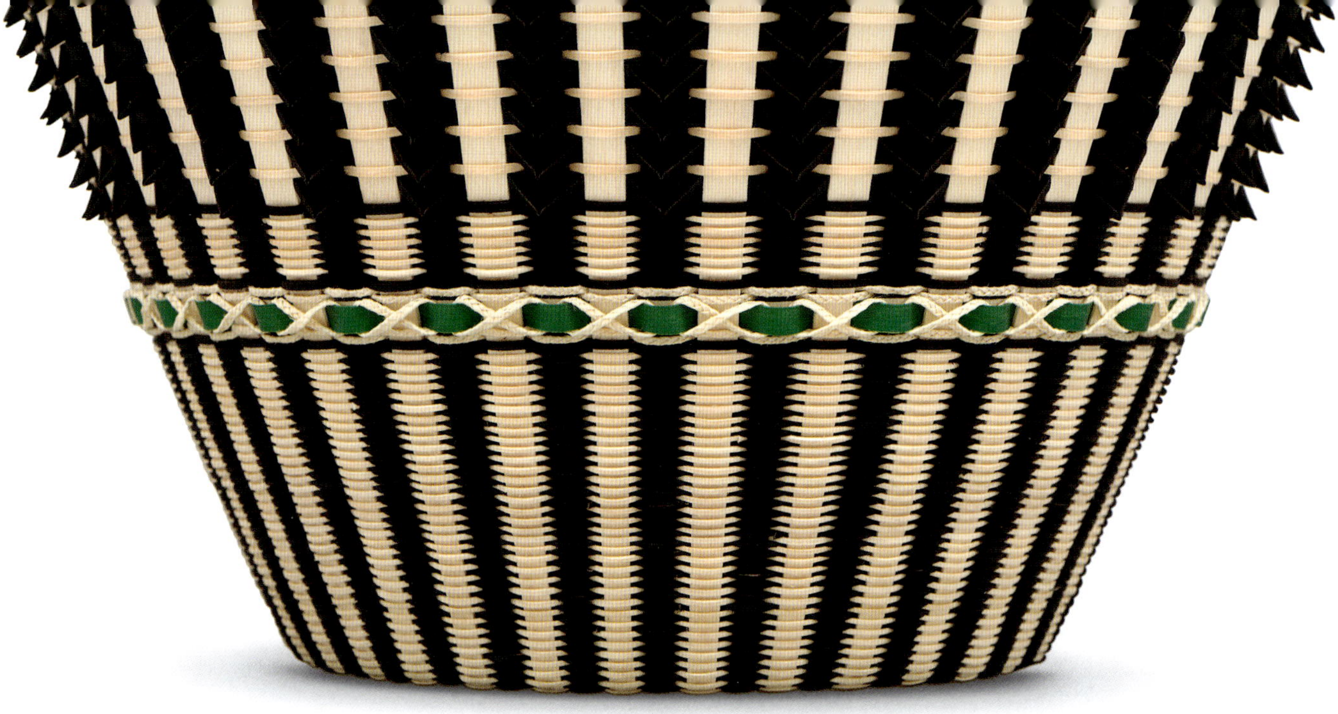

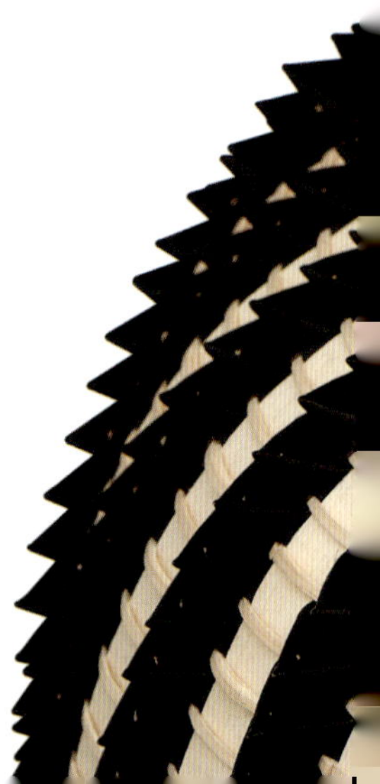

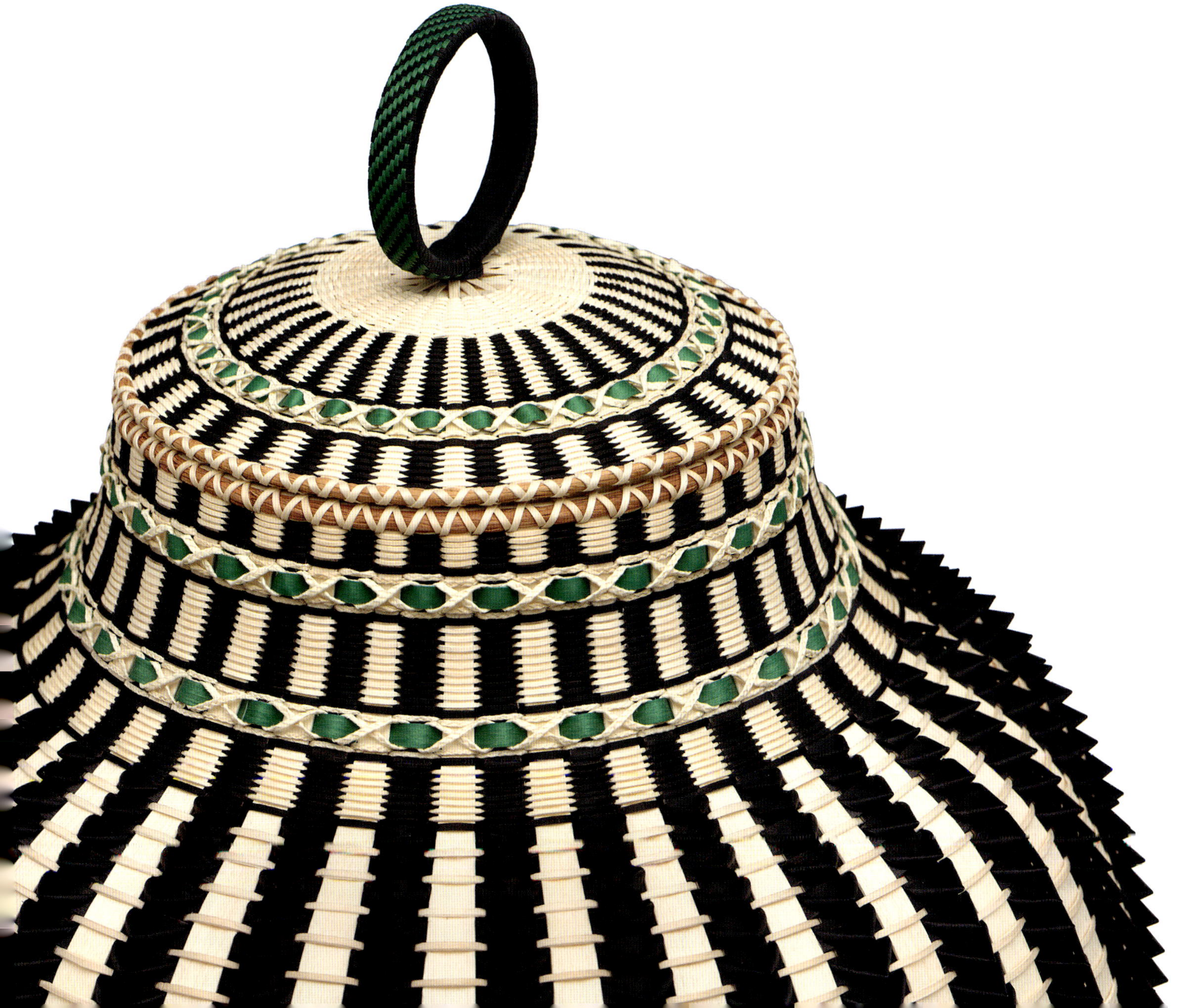

156

Symphony in Wood, 2022

Ash, sweetgrass, and dye
18½ × 11½ × 11½ inches
Collection of Dr. Marc and Lynn Appelbaum, New Mexico

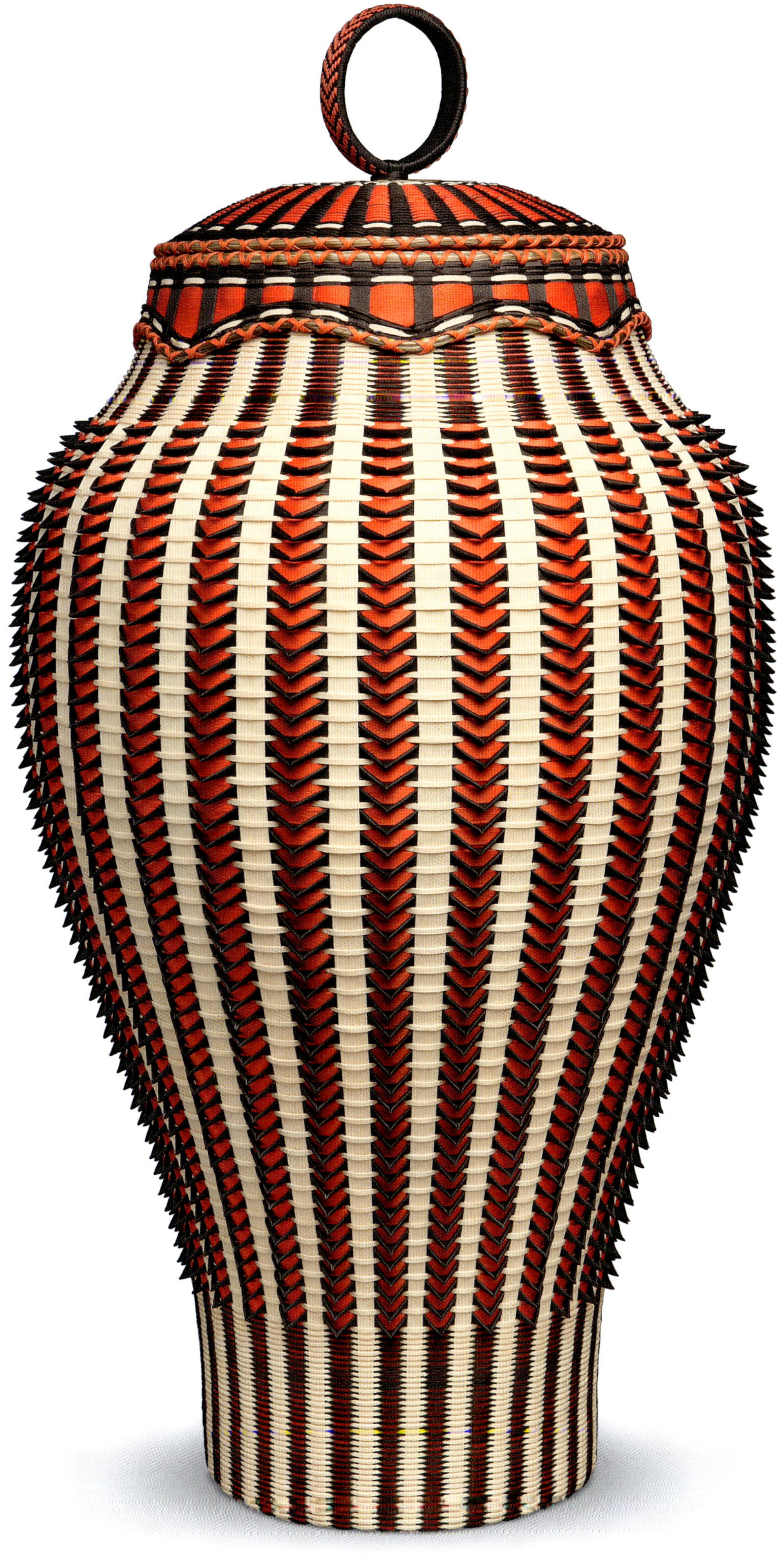

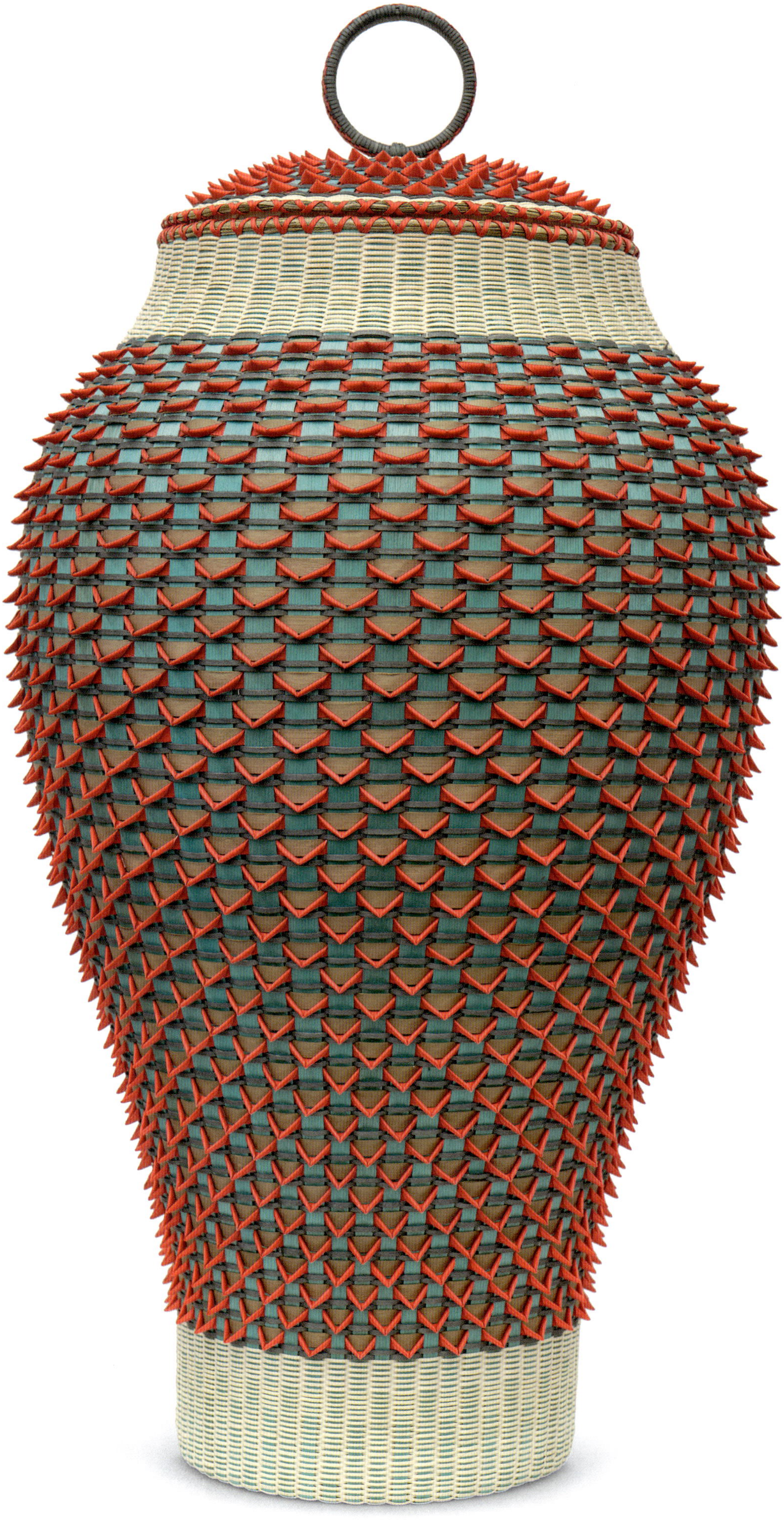

Aura, 2023

Ash, sweetgrass, and dye
21 × 12 × 12 inches

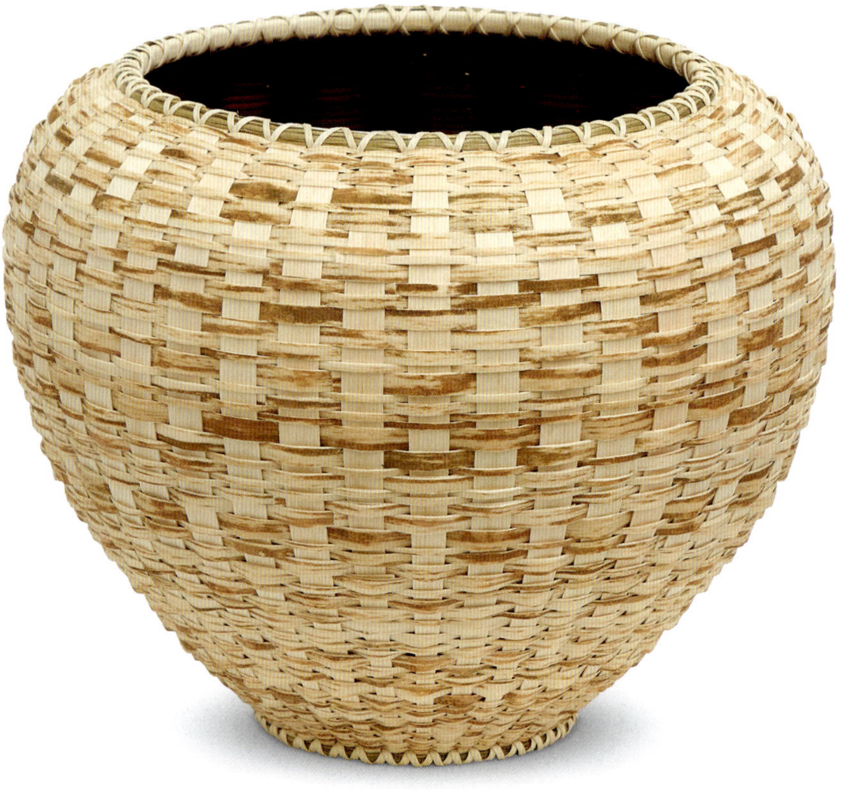

Navigating Tradition, 2023

Ash, sweetgrass, and dye
6¾ × 9½ × 9½ inches
Portland Museum of Art, ME. Museum purchase with exchange funds
from the gift of Joseph and Ruth Sataloff, 2023.35

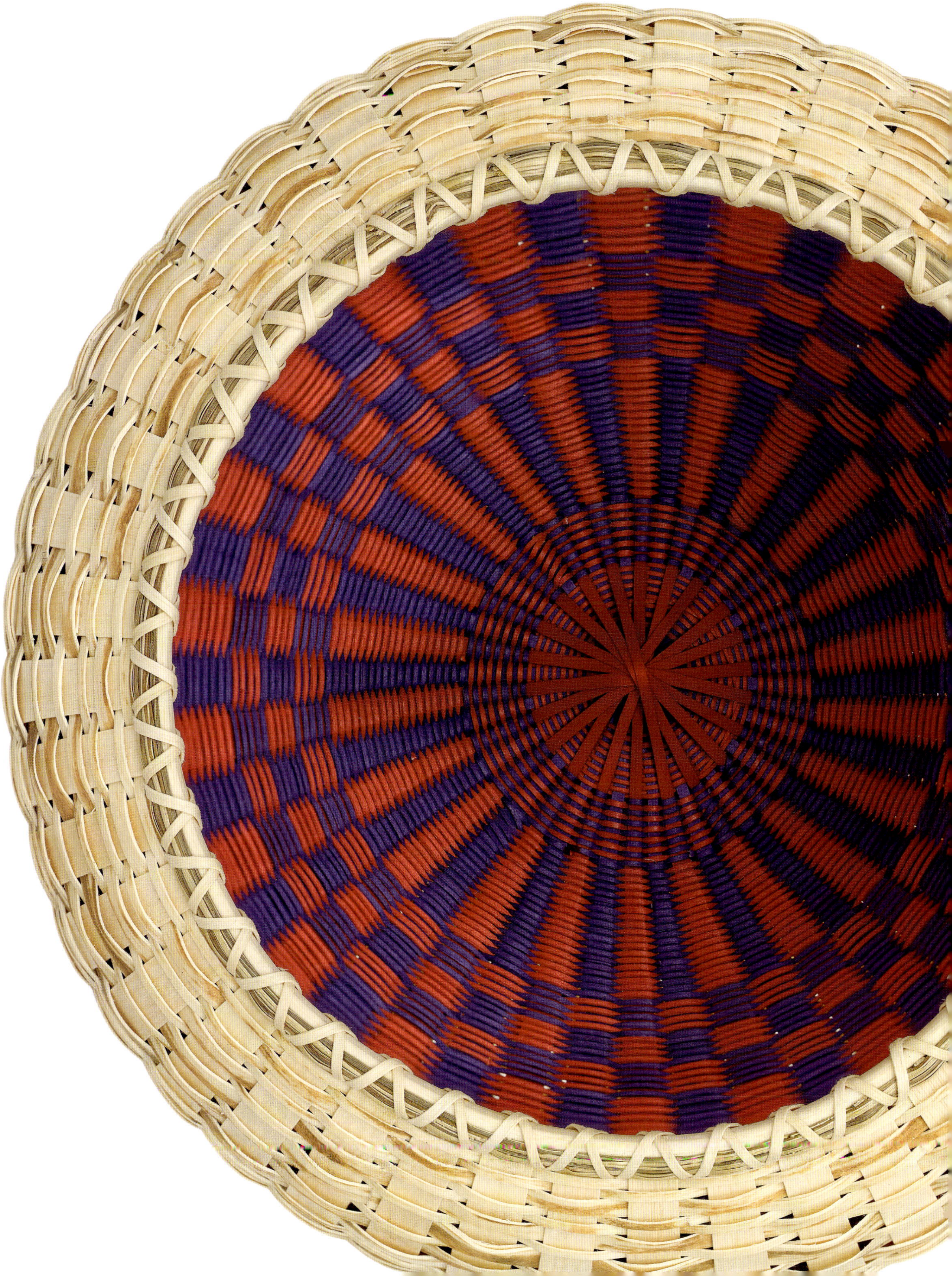

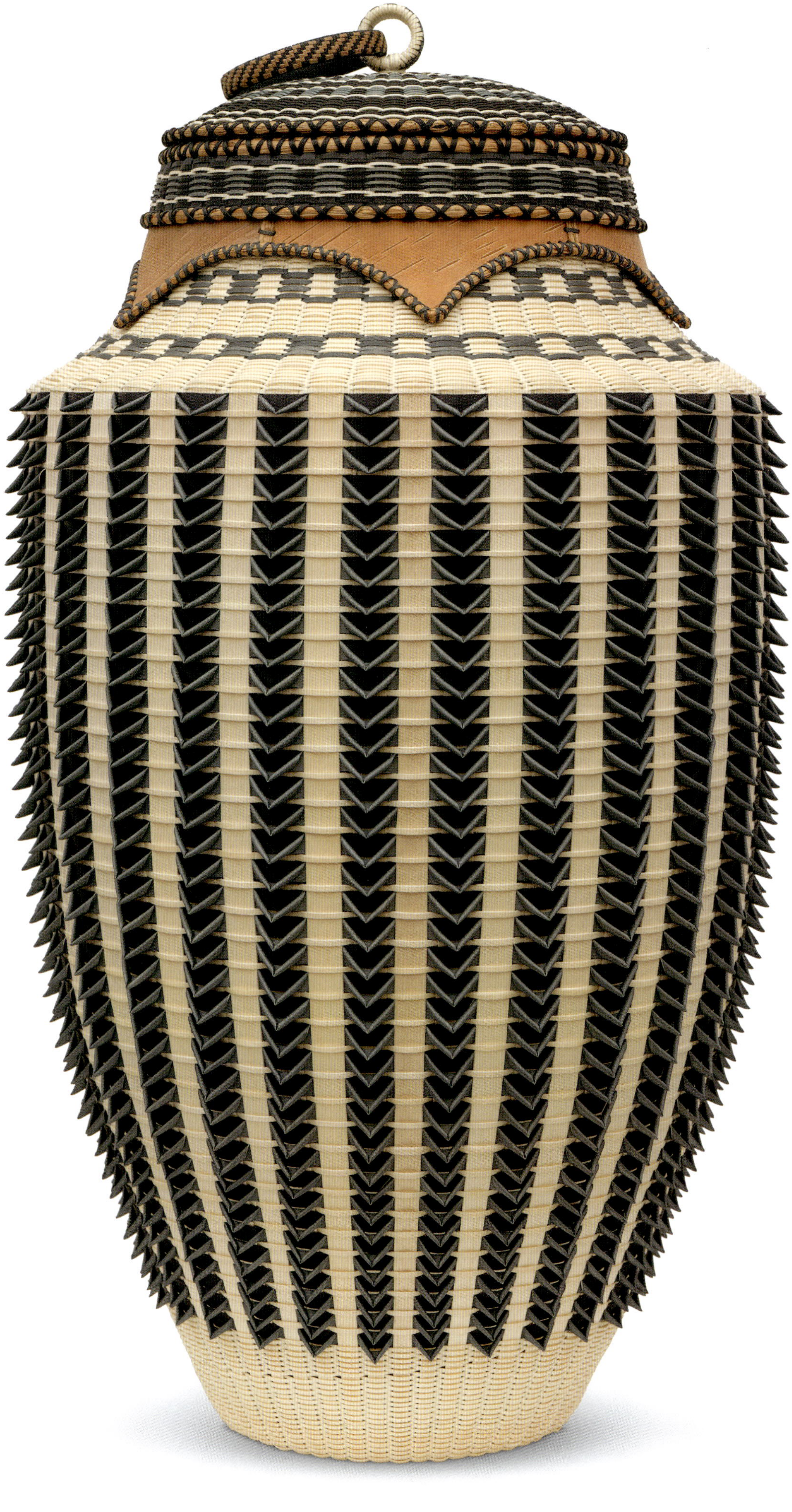

Permanence, 2023

Ash, cedar bark, birch bark, sweetgrass, and dye
19½ × 11¼ × 11¼ inches
Bowdoin College Museum of Art, Brunswick, Maine, Museum Purchase,
Jane H. and Charles E. Parker, Jr. Art Acquisition Fund

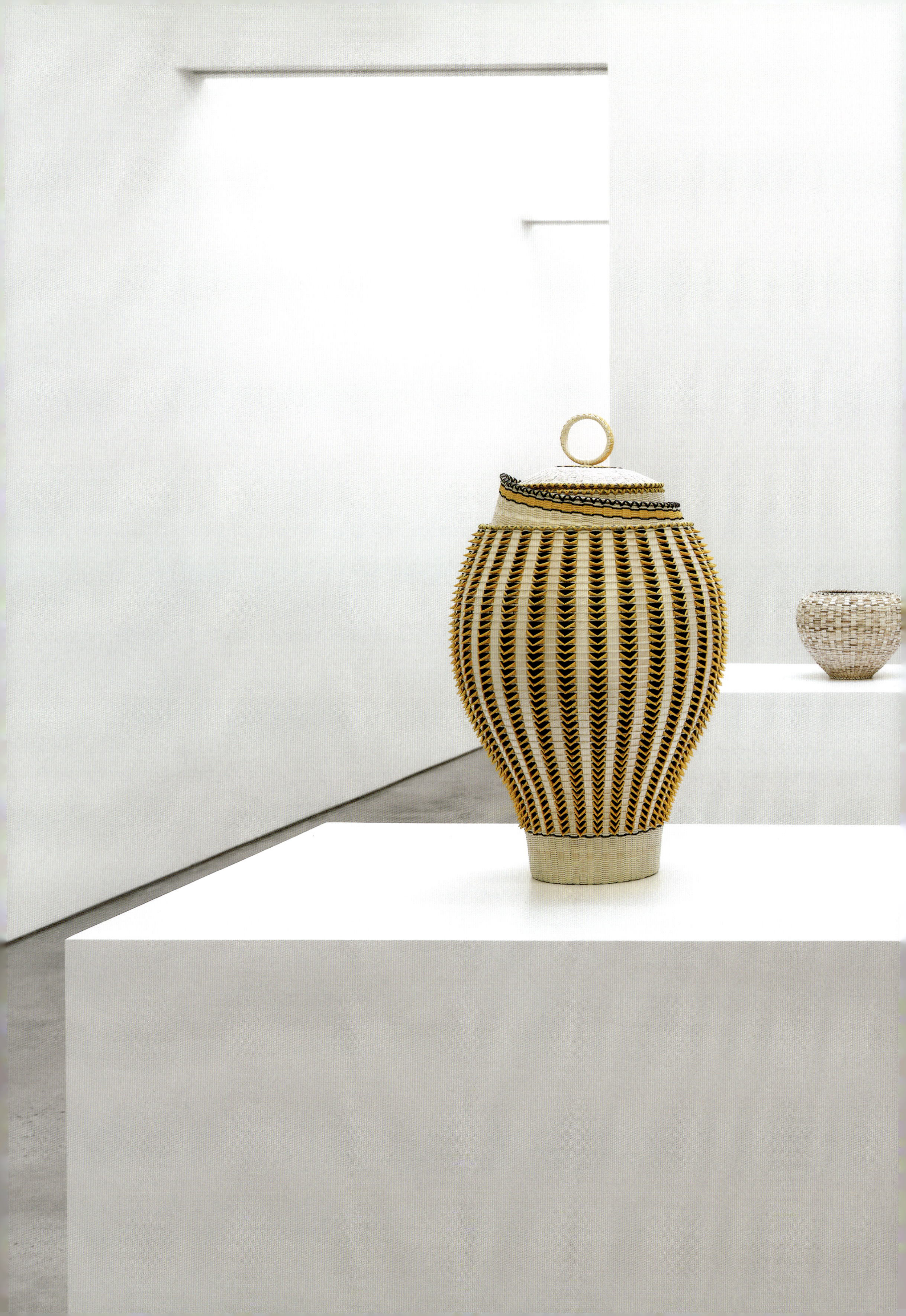

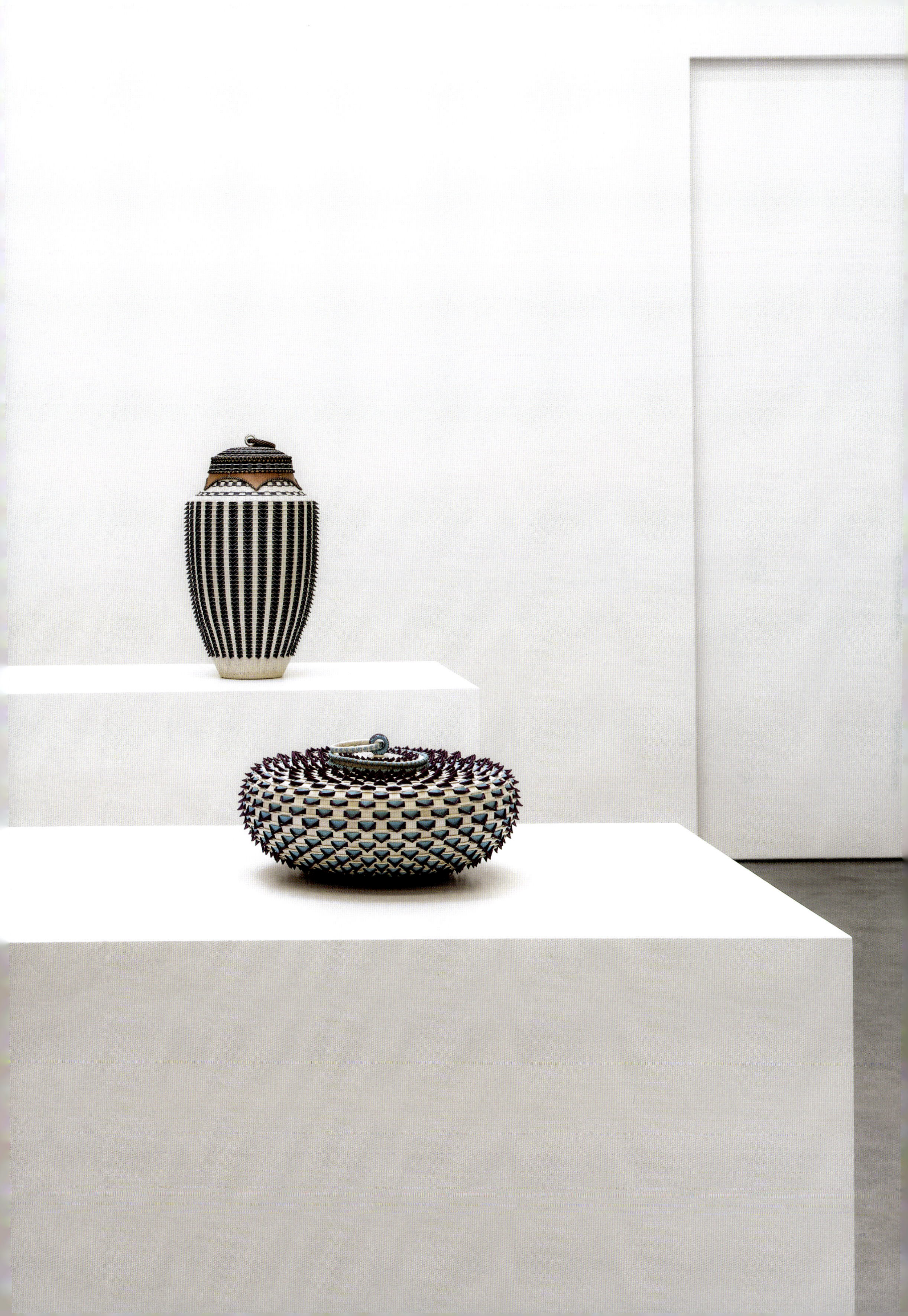

Director's Afterword

Jeremy Frey: Woven commemorates the extraordinary artistic achievements of one of the most celebrated basket makers in the country. Over the past two decades, Frey has emerged as a leading knowledge keeper of Passamaquoddy basketry and has made unprecedented innovations within and beyond his medium—from early point baskets and urchin forms to more recent monumental multicolored vases with meticulous porcupine quillwork, as well as new work in video, prints, and large-scale woven sculpture—all while remaining grounded in tradition and community. Basketry represents a core mode of cultural expression for Passamaquoddy people, whose tribal nation is one of five known collectively as the Wabanaki, "People of the Dawnland," along with the Penobscot, Mi'kmaq, Maliseet/Wolastoqiyik, and Abenaki. Their ancestral territory encompasses parts of present-day Canada and northern New England, including the land on which the PMA sits.

This publication and exhibition are a tribute to Frey's many accomplishments in a powerful and culturally significant art form. In 2010, Frey was selected as a USA Fellow by the United States Artists, a prestigious award which recognizes the most compelling artists working and living in the United States, in all disciplines, at every stage of their careers. A year later, in 2011, he was awarded "Best of Show" at both the Heard Museum Guild Indian Fair and Market and the Santa Fe Indian Market. Frey repeated the Best of Show award at the Heard again in 2015—an astonishing achievement. Since that time, he has won numerous awards for "Best of Basketry" at numerous art markets. Such national recognition, as well as his prodigious technical expertise and artistic ingenuity, positions Frey as one of the foremost basket makers of his generation.

While it is common for museum directors to contribute the foreword, it felt appropriate in this case to locate these comments at the end of the catalogue. This sequence is due to the historic nature of the project and the long-overdue recognition of Wabanaki artists by art museums. *Jeremy Frey: Woven* marks a momentous occasion: it is the first solo exhibition of a Wabanaki artist in an art museum in the United States. As Theresa Secord reminds us in her essay in this volume, Wabanaki art was only recently considered for acquisition by these types of institutions. For our part, Wabanaki basketry entered the Portland Museum of Art's collection in 2016, when we purchased Secord's own *Barrel Basket* on the occasion of the 2015 Biennial. This Biennial, titled *you can't get there from here*, was guest curated by Alison Ferris and marked one of the earliest exhibitions to feature Wabanaki baskets in an art museum in Maine. Four years later, the landmark installation *Wíwənikan . . . the beauty we carry*, organized by Jennifer Sapiel Neptune (Penobscot) and Kathleen Mundell for the Colby College Museum of Art, represented the first major group exhibition to exclusively feature contemporary Wabanaki art in an art museum. These projects joined longer-term commitments to Wabanaki art and culture stewarded by other institutions and organizations in our region, including the Abbe Museum in Bar Harbor, the Hudson Museum in Orono, and tribal museums such as Penobscot Nation Museum, the Sipayik Museum and the Passamaquoddy Cultural Heritage Museum. All these efforts, of course, are indebted to the vital advocacy of Wabanaki leaders, artists, and culture bearers—including the notable Maine Indian Basketmakers Alliance—who have worked tirelessly to preserve and share their cultural traditions.

The wooden mold that Secord used to weave *Barrel Basket* was made by none other than Frey, which he based on an earlier precedent possessed by Secord's great-grandmother, Philomene Saulis Nelson (Wolastoquey/Penobscot, 1886–1977). Frey produced this essential tool for Secord in exchange for her guidance throughout his creative and professional development. This beautiful symmetry bespeaks the patterns of relationship and reciprocity that have always supported Wabanaki basketry, which is rooted in intergenerational exchange that ensures the extension of the art form for future generations. We are honored to have Secord's guidance not only as a member of the PMA's Board of Trustees, but also as the coeditor of this volume. Secord's role as a longtime mentor to Frey makes her participation in this project even more meaningful and, indeed, essential.

Frey's 2018 *Cathedral* basket (retitled as of 2023) represents another first for our institution: the inaugural commission of a work of art by a Wabanaki artist (p.136). At that time, Frey collaborated with the then Curator of American Art Diana Greenwold to develop a concept for the piece. Together, they determined that the commission would honor and emulate the *Biased Top Basket* (2013), one of the artist's signature vase baskets that also appeared in the PMA's 2015 Biennial (pp. 120-21). *Cathedral* is an exceptionally striking example of Frey's inventive approach to weaving: instead of a single rim, the artist has layered multiple rims in this piece, including one that wends gracefully around the basket's neck. We are grateful to the Peggy and Harold Osher Acquisitions Fund, the Bernstein Acquisition Fund, and Barbara Goodbody for helping to make this commission possible. Since then, the PMA has been fortunate to welcome four additional works by the artist to the collection—two gifts from Barbara Goodbody, *Urchin* and *Covered Vase*, and two purchases, *Shooting Star* and *Navigating Tradition* (pp. 106-7, 128-29, 58-59, 160-61). Most recently, the PMA commissioned Frey's first video, *Ash* (pp. 38-43), a thought-provoking journey about Passamaquoddy history, people, art, and loss. Filmed by Joshua Reiman, *Ash* was born out of conversations between Frey and then Robert and Elizabeth Nanovic Curator of Contemporary Art Jaime DeSimone. Together, these works establish the PMA as one of the largest public repositories of Frey's work, and we are proud to be able to showcase such a wide range of his practice in both this exhibition and the years to come.

The prospect of a mid-career exhibition (and the artist's first solo show) for Frey was first explored by DeSimone, who is now the Chief Curator at the Farnsworth Art Museum in Rockland. DeSimone and the artist worked together on the PMA's exhibition *Untitled, 2020: Art from Maine in a ____ Time*, for which Frey served as a juror; they had met the previous year during a basketry demonstration Frey performed at the museum as a program for the exhibition *Open Ended: New Acquisitions at the Portland Museum of Art*. Frey's interest in extending his work into contemporary art contexts sparked these preliminary conversations at the artist's booth in the SWAIA Santa Fe Indian Market in August 2021. We thank DeSimone for championing this project in its early stages and remaining on as cocurator following her move to the Farnsworth in 2022.

The PMA team went above and beyond to realize this watershed exhibition for our institution. Ramey Mize, Assistant Curator of American Art, stepped in as cocurator alongside DeSimone and coeditor of the present publication with Secord, navigating both projects with great thoughtfulness, rigor, and care. She received crucial assistance from Shalini Le Gall, Chief Curator, Susan Donnell and Harry W. Konkel Curator of European Art; Molly Papows, Exhibitions Manager; Erin Damon, Director of Collections and Head Registrar; Kirk Hoffman, Lead Preparator; and Lark Wicinas, Exhibitions Specialist. Heidi Dikeman, Director of Design, provided stunning exhibition design, and Christian Adame, Peggy L. Osher Director of Learning and Community Collaboration, devised vibrant community engagement programs with his team. Additional talented members of the PMA staff, including Brian Arundel, Senior Manager of Grants, Foundations, and Government Relations; Emma Sullivan, Curatorial Administrator; Tim Burns, Assistant Preparator; Conrad Carpenter, Preparator; Julie Warchol, Associate Registrar; Amy Doyel, Associate Registrar; Elena Henry, Deputy Director and Chief Financial Officer; Elizabeth Jones, Senior Deputy Director; Ashleigh McKown, Director of Philanthropy; and many others, helped make this project a resounding success.

This project is integral to the PMA's commitment to *Art for All*. As a vision for our institution, *Art for All* supports the PMA's endeavor to offer accessible and inclusive exhibitions that support our diverse communities. We strive to create a central gathering place where a strong artistic vision and the collection drive conversation, creativity, and cultural vitality.

We are delighted to join forces again with Rizzoli Electa to produce this unique, thoughtful, and dazzling publication. Senior editor Isabel Venero steered the project with great insight and brought a sensitivity to the subject matter that was invaluable throughout. The scholars who contributed essays to this volume, including Andrew James Hamilton and Dakota Hoska, along with Secord, DeSimone, and Mize, all demonstrated deep engagement with Frey's work, and we thank them for their invaluable perspectives. We also thank Richard Slovak for attentively copyediting the manuscript and the many talented photographers across the country who documented Frey's works so beautifully, especially Jared Lank and Eric Stoner. The effusive catalogue design—as vibrant and inventive as Frey's own weavings—emerged from the brilliant eye of Kimberly Varella of the award-winning Content Object Design Studio. Varella went above and beyond to experience Frey's work and process firsthand. Her trip to northern Maine from Los Angeles took place in early February 2023; she journeyed with Mize to meet Frey, braving an arctic blast of minus twelve degrees Fahrenheit in the process!

Many institutions and individuals contributed to this exhibition; indeed, you will be hard-pressed to find more dedicated, generous advocates of an artist's career than Frey's supporters. The faith, collaboration, and generosity of our venue partners—the Art Institute of Chicago and the Bruce Museum—have brought this exhibition into the national spotlight that Frey's work so deeply deserves. James and Peter Pettengill of Wingate Studio offered invaluable expertise, collaborating with Frey to produce an unprecedented series of prints for the exhibition, with spectacular results. The team at Karma gallery in New York provided guidance as we prepared for this project, and their debut presentation of Frey's work in April 2023, *Out of the Woods*, was an unforgettable and historic moment that PMA staff were honored to witness. In particular, we are grateful to Brendan Dugan for introducing Frey to New York audiences and for Karma's support of this publication. Major support for the exhibition has been provided by Bank of America. We are also grateful for the generous support of Isabelle and Scott Black, Adam and Diana Lee, The Crewe Foundation, The Bear Bookshop of Marlboro, VT, and Furthermore: a program of the J. M. Kaplan Fund.

Gratitude is owed to the exceptional lenders who have offered enthusiastic generosity and serious commitment to Frey's success every step of the way. We thank the many private collectors who graciously parted with their works for the duration of this exhibition tour and supported this project in countless other ways. We are likewise thankful to the institutional lenders to the exhibition, all of whom have shown tremendous support for Frey's remarkable career, including the Abbe Museum, the Art Institute of Chicago, the Autry Museum of the American West, the Bowdoin College Museum of Art, the Colby College Museum of Art, the Farnsworth Art Museum, the Denver Art Museum, the Hood Museum of Art, the Hudson Museum at the University of Maine, the National Museum of the American Indian, the Smithsonian American Art Museum, and the Virginia Museum of Fine Arts.

Finally, we can't overstate our admiration and appreciation for Jeremy Frey himself. He embraced this immense undertaking with vision, courage, and dedication. Jeremy, thank you for entrusting your awe-inspiring art and story with us. It is humbling to have the opportunity to partner with a visionary artist to mount an exhibition of such historic magnitude and profound beauty.

— Mark H. C. Bessire
Judy and Leonard Lauder Director

Index of Art

Deception, 2014
Ash, braided cedar bark, spruce root, and dye
17 ⅛ × 16 × 16 inches
Virginia Museum of Fine Arts, Richmond, 2016.11a-b
Pages 124–25

Fine Weave Vase, 2015
Ash and braided cedar bark
9 × 4 ½ × 4 ½ inches
Collection of Dr. and Mrs. Ari and Lea Plosker
Pages 126–27

Loon, 2015
Ash, cedar bark, porcupine quill on birch bark, and dye
19 × 10 × 10 inches
Collection of Dr. Marc and Lynn Appelbaum, New Mexico
Pages 68–69

Green Urchin Basket, 2015
Ash, sweetgrass, and dye
4 × 5 ½ × 5 ½ inches
Abbe Museum, Bar Harbor, ME. Museum purchase, Native American Festival 2015, 2015-06-004
Page 108

170

Covered Vase, 2016
Ash, cedar bark, cherrywood, sweetgrass, and spruce root
14 ¾ × 7 × 7 inches
Portland Museum of Art, ME. Gift of Barbara M. Goodbody, 2021.19.6a,b
Pages 128–29

Blue Point Urchin, 2016
Ash, sweetgrass, and dye
5 × 9 × 9 inches
Collection of Dr. and Mrs. Ari and Lea Plosker
Page 108

Fine Weave, 2016
Ash and sweetgrass
6 × 5 × 5 inches
Collection of Dr. and Mrs. Ari and Lea Plosker
Pages 64–65

Untitled, 2017
Ash and braided cedar bark
16 ¾ × 9 ½ × 9 ½ inches
Collection of David and Sue Halpern
Pages 132–33

Phoenix, 2017
Ash, cedar, sweetgrass, spruce root, and dye
8 × 6 × 6 inches
The Buker Collections
Pages 130–31

Muwin (Bear), 2017
Ash, sweetgrass, porcupine quill on birch bark, and dye
13 × 7 × 7 inches
The Buker Collections
Pages 70–71

Urchin, 2017-18
Ash, sweetgrass, and dye
4 ½ × 5 ¼ × 5 ¼ inches
Portland Museum of Art, ME. Gift of Barbara M. Goodbody, 2021.19.7a,b
Pages 106–7

Caged, 2018
Ash, sweetgrass, and dye
13 × 7 × 7 inches
The Buker Collections
Pages 134–35

Cathedral, 2018
Ash, sweetgrass, and dye
21 ¼ × 10 × 10 inches
Portland Museum of Art, ME. Museum purchase with support from the Peggy and Harold Osher Acquisitions Fund, Bernstein Acquisition Fund, and Barbara Goodbody, 2018.15a,b
Pages 136–37

Double-Walled Point Basket, 2018
Ash, cedar bark, and dye
12 × 18 × 18 inches
Private collection
Pages 138–39

Ghost Bear, 2018
Ash, sweetgrass, moose antler, and dye
21 × 10 × 10 inches
The Buker Collections
Pages 140–41

Cubs, 2018
Ash, sweetgrass, porcupine quill on birch bark, and dye
19 × 10 ½ × 10 ½ inches
The Buker Collections
Pages 72–75

Cihpolakon (Eagle), 2019
Ash, cedar bark, birch bark, porcupine quill on birch bark, and dye
10 × 7 ½ × 7 ½ inches
Collection of Carole Katz
Pages 76–77

Color in Winter, 2019
Ash, sweetgrass, porcupine quill on birch bark, and dye
16 × 12 × 12 inches
Colby College Museum of Art, Museum purchase from the Bruce C. Drouin '74 and Janet L. Hansen '75 Maine Art Endowed Fund and Friends of Art, 2019.026
Pages 78–79

Large Turquoise Urchin Basket, 2019
Ash, sweetgrass, and dye
5 ¼ × 11 ½ × 11 ½ inches
Smithsonian American Art Museum, Washington, D.C., Museum purchase through the Kenneth R. Trapp Acquisition Fund, 2020.55
Page 109

Loon, 2020
Ash, cedar bark, porcupine quill on birch bark, and dye
36 × 23 × 23 inches
Private collection of Catherine Stiefel, California
Pages 80–81

Quilted Cedar Bark Multi-Top, 2020
Ash, braided cedar bark, sweetgrass, and dye
18 × 9 × 9 inches
The Buker Collections
Pages 142–43

Blue Point Vase, 2021
Ash, sweetgrass, and dye
11 ½ × 8 × 8 inches
Collection of Dr. and Mrs. Ari and Lea Plosker
Pages 144–47

Malsom (Wolf), 2021
Ash, sweetgrass, porcupine quill on birch bark, and dye
16 × 10 × 10 inches
The Buker Collections
Pages 82–83

Symphony in Wood, 2022
Ash, sweetgrass, and dye
18 ½ × 11 ½ × 11 ½ inches
Collection of Dr. Marc and Lynn Appelbaum, New Mexico
Pages 156–57

Green Point Urchin, 2022
Ash, sweetgrass, and dye
4 × 6 × 6 inches
Collection of Dr. and Mrs. Ari and Lea Plosker
Pages 110–11

Defensive, 2022
Ash, sweetgrass, and dye
12 ½ × 7 ½ × 7 ½ inches
Collection of Carole Katz
Pages 150–51

Watchful Spirit, 2022
Ash, sweetgrass, porcupine quill on birch bark, and dye
27 ⅜ × 22 ¼ × 22 ¼ inches
Denver Art Museum: Purchased with the Nancy Blomberg Acquisitions Fund for Native American Art, 2022.51A-B
Pages 84–85

Observer, 2022

Ash, sweetgrass, porcupine quill on birch bark, and dye
13 ½ × 10 ½ × 10 ½ inches
Collection of Carole Katz
Pages 86–87

Dawnland, 2022

Ash, sweetgrass, and dye
17 ½ × 11 ½ × 11 ½ inches
Collection of Jim and Sara TenBroek
Pages 148–49

Nearly Monochrome, 2022

Ash, braided ash, cedar bark, and dye
31 ½ × 16 5/16 × 16 5/16 inches
Art Institue of Chicago. Mrs. Leonard S. Florsheim Jr. Fund; purchased with funds provided by the bequest of Fred E. Spreitzer, 2022.1824a-b
Pages 152–55

Navigating Tradition, 2023

Ash, sweetgrass, and dye
6 ¾ × 9 ½ × 9 ½ inches
Portland Museum of Art, ME. Museum purchase with exchange funds from the gift of Joseph and Ruth Sataloff, 2023.35
Pages 160–61

First Light, 2023

Ash, sweetgrass, porcupine quill on birch bark, and dye
11 ¼ × 16 ½ × 6 inches
Farnsworth Art Museum, Rockland, ME. Museum purchase, Lynne Drexler Acquisition Fund, 2023.10
Pages 88–89

Aura, 2023

Ash, sweetgrass, and dye
21 × 12 × 12 inches
Pages 158–59

Permanence, 2023

Ash, cedar bark, birch bark, sweetgrass, and dye
19 ½ × 11 ¼ × 11 ¼ inches
Bowdoin College Museum of Art, Brunswick, Maine, Museum Purchase, Jane H. and Charles E. Parker, Jr. Art Acquisition Fund
Pages 162–63

Biography

Born 1978, Passamaquoddy Indian Township Reservation, Maine.
Frey lives and works in Maine.

Education

2007–present Traditional Arts Apprenticeship Program (Master Basketmaker), Maine Indian Basketmakers Alliance

2010 AA in Automotive Technology and General Technology, Washington County Community College

2002–04 Traditional Arts Apprenticeship Program (Apprentice), Maine Indian Basketmakers Alliance

Selected Awards

2022 Best of Basketry, SWAIA | Santa Fe Indian Market, NM

2022 Judge's Choice, Heard Museum Guild Indian Fair and Market, Phoenix, AZ

2021 Best of Basketry, SWAIA | Santa Fe Indian Market, NM

2019 Cummings Award for Artistic Excellence, Colby College Museum of Art, Waterville, ME

2018 Best of Basketry, SWAIA | Santa Fe Indian Market, NM

2015 Best of Show, Heard Museum Guild Indian Fair and Market, Phoenix, AZ

2014 Best of Basketry, SWAIA | Santa Fe Indian Market, NM

2014 Native Arts and Cultures Foundation (NACF) Artist Fellowship

2013 Best of Basketry, First Place, American Indian Arts Marketplace at the Autry Museum of the American West, Los Angeles, CA

2012 Best of Basketry, Heard Museum Guild Indian Fair and Market, Phoenix, AZ

2012 Artist in Business Leadership Fellowship, First Peoples Fund

2011 Best of Show, SWAIA | Santa Fe Indian Market, NM

2011 Best of Show, Heard Museum Guild Indian Fair and Market, Phoenix, AZ

2010 United States Artists Ford Foundation Fellow

2004 and 2005 First Place in Basketry, Celebration of Basketry, Heard Museum Guild Indian Fair and Market, Phoenix, AZ

Solo Exhibitions

2023 *Jeremy Frey: Out of the Woods*, Karma, New York, NY

Selected Group Exhibitions

2023 *Threads: Artists Weave their Worlds*, Bowdoin College Museum of Art, Brunswick, ME

2023 *Spark of the Eagle Dancer: The Collecting Legacy of Lambert Wilson*, Western Carolina University Fine Art Museum, Cullowhee, NC

2023 *A Summer Arrangement: Object & Thing at LongHouse*, East Hampton, NY

2022–23 *This Present Moment: Crafting a Better World*, the Renwick Gallery of the Smithsonian American Art Museum, Washington, D.C.

2022 *The New England Triennial*, deCordova Sculpture Park and Museum, Lincoln, MA

2021 *Always Home: Traditional Wabanaki Arts*, Monson Arts, ME

2019–20 *Wiwənikan . . . the beauty we carry*, Colby College Museum of Art, ME

2019 *Open-Ended: New Acquisitions at the PMA*, Portland Museum of Art, ME

2019 *Carry ME*, Space Gallery, Portland, ME

2017 *Hear My Voice: Native American Art of the Past and Present*, organized by Virginia Museum of Fine Arts (VMFA), Richmond, VA; traveled in 2018–19 to Museum of the Shenandoah Valley, Winchester, VA, and Taubman Museum of Art, Roanoke, VA

2015 *You Can't Get There from Here: The 2015 Portland Museum of Art Biennial*, Portland, ME

2015 *Baskets from the Dawnland: Weaving the Past and Future Together*, Maine Historical Society, Portland, ME

2015 *Maine Indian Basketry Exhibition*, Maine Fiberarts, Topsham, ME

2012–13 *Rethink! American Indian Art*, Berkshire Museum, Pittsfield, MA

2012 *Changing Hands: Art without Reservation 3*, Museum of Arts and Design, New York, NY

2011–12 *Transcending Traditions: The Next Generation and Wabanaki Basketry*, co-organized by Maine Indian Basketmakers Alliance and the Hudson Museum, University of Maine, Orono, ME; traveled in 2012, with the subtitle *The Next Generation and Maine Indian Basketry*, to the Abbe Museum, Bar Harbor, ME

2008 *Spirit of the Basket Tree: Wabanaki Ash Splint Baskets from Maine*, Hood Museum of Art, Dartmouth College, Hanover, NH

2003–5 *The Language of Native American Baskets: From the Weavers' View*, National Museum of the American Indian, New York, NY

Public Collections

Abbe Museum, Bar Harbor, ME
Art Institute of Chicago, IL
Autry Museum of the American West, Los Angeles, CA
Bowdoin College Museum of Art, Brunswick, ME
Colby College Museum of Art, Waterville, ME
Denver Art Museum, CO
Farnsworth Art Museum, Rockland, ME
Heard Museum, Phoenix, AZ
Hood Museum of Art, Dartmouth College, Hanover, NH
Hudson Museum, University of Maine, Orono, ME
Michigan State University Museum, East Lansing, MI
National Museum of the American Indian, Smithsonian Institution, Washington, D.C.
Portland Museum of Art, ME
Robert S. Peabody Institute of Archaeology, Phillips Academy, Andover, MA
Smithsonian American Art Museum, Washington, D.C.
Virginia Museum of Fine Arts, Richmond, VA

Teaching, Talks, Juries, and Demonstrations

2023 Interview by Toshiko Mori, "Jeremy Frey: Interweaving Nature with Tradition," *Domus*

2023 "A Conversation: Jeremy Frey and Jaime DeSimone," Karma, NY

2022 Faculty, Wood/Baskets, Haystack Mountain School of Crafts, ME

2021 Juror for *Untitled, 2020: Art from Maine in a ___ Time*, Portland Museum of Art, ME

2019 "Jeremy Frey: Basketry Demonstration," Portland Museum of Art, ME

2017 "Hear My Voice," artist panel with Molly Murphy Adams, Jeremy Frey, and Virgil Ortiz in conversation with Dr. Johanna Minich, exhibition curator and consulting curator for the Native American Collection, Virginia Museum of Fine Arts, Richmond, VA

2015 "Jeremy Frey Baskets," demonstration and discussion, Mingei International Museum, San Diego, CA

2014 "Saved by Creativity," TedxDirigo Talk

2007–present Maine Indian Basketmakers Alliance, Traditional Arts Apprenticeship Program, Master Basket Maker

2006 Demonstrator, Featured Artist, Smithsonian Folklife Festival, Washington, D.C.

Contributor Biographies

Theresa Secord (Penobscot Nation) is a traditional basket maker and the founding director of the Maine Indian Basketmakers Alliance (MIBA). During her twenty-one years of leadership, the MIBA was credited with saving the endangered art of ash and sweetgrass basketry. Secord received a lifetime achievement award for artistic excellence from the National Endowment for the Arts (2016) and the Prize for Creativity in Rural Life from the Women's World Summit Foundation at the United Nations (2003), for helping basket makers rise out of poverty. Among more recent honors, she is a 2021 Luce Indigenous Knowledge Fellow. Secord has worked with Indigenous artists nationally to help them achieve their own goals of art and economic self-sufficiency through a long association with First Peoples Fund. She is a member of the governing board of the Colby College Museum of Art and a trustee at the Portland Museum of Art in Maine, where she continues to advocate for Indigenous and underrepresented artists. A basket maker for thirty-five years, she has won a number of awards for her art, including Best of Basketry at the 2020 Santa Fe Indian Market. Her baskets reside in many private and museum collections.

Andrew James Hamilton is associate curator of Arts of the Americas at the Art Institute of Chicago. He helps steward the collections of Native and Indigenous art of the Americas, from ancient periods to the present, as well as colonial Latin American art. He is also a lecturer in the Department of Art History at the University of Chicago, where he teaches classes on the ancient Andes, among other topics. He is the author of *Scale & the Incas* (Princeton University Press, 2018), which he also illustrated with more than seventy color plates. His second book, on a royal Inca tunic in the collection of Dumbarton Oaks, Washington, D.C., is forthcoming with Princeton University Press. His work has been supported by a Getty/ACLS Postdoctoral Fellowship in the History of Art, the Princeton Society of Fellows, a postdoctoral fellowship from the Fondation Fyssen at the Collège de France, the Musée du Quai Branly, Dumbarton Oaks, the Sainsbury Research Unit at the University of East Anglia, and the Fulbright-Hays Program. He was previously a lecturer at Princeton University. He received his PhD and MA from Harvard University and his BA from Yale University. He is a practicing artist; in addition to illustrating his scholarship, he often works in fiber, textiles, and weaving, as well as other media and techniques.

Dakota Hoska (Oglála Lakȟóta Nation, Pine Ridge, Wounded Knee) serves as the associate curator of Native arts at the Denver Art Museum, where she has been employed since 2019. Previously, she was a curatorial research assistant at the Minneapolis Institute of Art, supporting the groundbreaking exhibition *Hearts of Our People: Native Women Artists*. Hoska completed her MA in art history, focusing on Native American art history, at the University of St. Thomas, St. Paul, Minnesota (2010). She also completed two years of Dakhóta language at the University of Minnesota (2016) and received her BFA in drawing and painting from the Minneapolis College of Art and Design (2012). Hoska has participated in multiple curatorial programs such as the EPIC international curatorial exchange program sponsored by the Association of Art Museum Curators, the Otsego Institute Workshop (Summer 2017), organized by the Otsego Institute for Native American Art History and sponsored by Fenimore Art Museum, the Shakopee Mdewakanton Sioux Community (SMSC) Native American Fellowship at the Minneapolis Institute of Art, and the American Indian Museum Fellowship at the Minnesota Historical Society. She frequently presents on issues related to curating Native North American art collections. She currently serves on multiple national advisory councils and continues to contribute essays like the one in the present volume to catalogues and blogs related to Native artists and artistry.

Jaime DeSimone is the chief curator at the Farnsworth Art Museum in Rockland, Maine. Prior to joining the Farnsworth in summer 2022, DeSimone served as the Robert and Elizabeth Nanovic Curator of Contemporary Art at the Portland Museum of Art in Maine from 2018 to 2022, where she curated the exhibitions *Flying Woman: The Paintings of Katherine Bradford* (2022), *Down North: North Atlantic Triennial* (2022), *Richard Estes: Urban Landscapes* (2021), *Carrie Moyer and Sheila Pepe: Tabernacles for Trying Times* (2020), and *Ragnar Kjartansson: Scenes from Western Culture* (2019–20). In 2019, she was a recipient of the prestigious Curatorial Research Fellowship from the Andy Warhol Foundation for the Visual Arts for research and travel in connection with the *North Atlantic Triennial*. DeSimone was also a scholar in the Fulbright Arctic Initiative III (2021–23). She served in other curatorial positions at MOCA Jacksonville (2014–18) and the Addison Gallery of American Art (2005–12). She holds degrees in art history, with a specialization in contemporary art, from American University (MA, 2005) and Bates College (BA, 2001).

Ramey Mize is assistant curator of American art at the Portland Museum of Art. She specializes in art of the Americas from the nineteenth century to the present day, with a focus on cultural exchange, expressions of place, and the intersections between U.S. and Indigenous art. Her curatorial practice is dedicated to expanding the field, notably through the reinstallation project *Passages in American Art* (2023). Before joining the PMA, Mize was the Lois and Arthur Stainman Research Assistant in the Metropolitan Museum of Art's American Wing, where she supported the exhibition *Winslow Homer: Crosscurrents* (2022). In 2020–21, she was the Met's Douglass Foundation Fellow and a participant in the Center for Curatorial Leadership/Mellon Foundation Seminar in Curatorial Practice. Previously, she held curatorial positions at the Colby College Museum of Art, the Philadelphia Museum of Art, and the Pennsylvania Academy of the Fine Arts. Her research and curatorial work have also been supported by the National Endowment for the Humanities, the Andrew W. Mellon Foundation, and the Terra Foundation for American Art, among others. She holds a BA from the University of North Carolina, Chapel Hill, an MA from the Courtauld Institute of Art, London, and a PhD from the University of Pennsylvania.

Glossary

Compiled by Andrew James Hamilton
Translations by Theresa Secord*

When he made baskets, they were very beautiful.
Neke eposonutehke, eci-wolinaqahk 'toposonutihil.

The Passamaquoddy terms in this glossary can be located in the Passamaquoddy-Maliseet Language Portal: https://pmportal.org/. Portions of text within quotation marks derive from the Passamaquoddy-Maliseet Dictionary. This important online resource includes audio files presenting the correct pronunciation of these terms.

basket
posonut

The Passamaquoddy word for basket.

basket maker
posonutehke

The Passamaquoddy word for basket maker.

binding (also lashing)
lakopehtikon

In basketmaking, the binding is the thin ash splint used to lash the rim, often made of sweetgrass, to the top edge of the basket.

birch bark
masq

The bark of the white birch tree (*Betula papyrifera*), which can be removed in papery sheets.

braided sweetgrass
latokonikon

The Passamaquoddy word for braided sweetgrass is the same word for braided hair and other materials. Frey often uses braided sweetgrass to create X-weaves. (See *sweetgrass*; *over-weaves*; *X-weaves*.)

braided wood
latokonikon

Braided strips of very fine ash are one of Frey's inventions, which he often uses to create X-weaves. (See *over-weaves*; *X-weaves*.)

brown ash (black ash)
wikp

Fraxinus nigra is a species of ash native to the northeastern United States and Canada. It is called brown ash in Maine, but black ash in other regions. The medium-sized deciduous tree often grows in swamps. Its wood has been used to make baskets since time immemorial; however, the species is threatened by an infestation of a non-native, parasitic insect known as the emerald ash borer. (See *ring-porous*; *emerald ash borer*.)

cedar bark
kakskusimus wolokasq

Frey uses the fibrous bark of the northern white cedar (*Thuja occidentalis*) in the rims of some baskets, as well as in braids, which he uses like braided ash and braided sweetgrass.

chase weaving

When a basket has an even number of standards, a single weaver worked over and under them will simply repeat its original path row after row—leaving the standards unincorporated. In chase weaving, two weavers are inserted simultaneously. One goes over a standard while the other goes under. As the pair pass into each subsequent row, they create the alternation of weavers that successfully incorporates the standards.

chase weaving/twining
toqanokonomon

"S/he folds it in two, holds on to it with two hands, braids it using both hands."**

collar (also rim)
kecalokahk

The top edge of the body of a basket, often elaborated with sweetgrass held in place by a binding. (See *rim*; *sweetgrass*; *binding*.)

dye
cossikon

The pigments used to stain ash wood various colors. While basket makers historically used dyes from botanical sources, chemical commercial dyes manufactured by companies like Rit are now commonly used.

emerald ash borer

A green beetle (*Agrilus planipennis*) that is native to northeastern Asia. First identified in North America in Canton, Michigan, in 2002, it has become a widely invasive species that is decimating populations of ash trees throughout the Great Lakes region and now Maine.

fancy basket
amalhikon or amalhi-posonut

Passamaquoddy artists developed more elaborate baskets in the 1700s and 1800s for use in colonial homes—especially as sewing baskets. These were further refined in the late 1800s with even more fanciful shapes in order to be sold to tourists visiting the large so-called cottages of Maine's coastal and inland resorts.

fine braiding
apsatokonomon

"S/he braids it into [a] fine or thin braid."

fine weaving
apsoskonuwe

"S/he does fine weaving."

fuzzies
piyehsuwiw

"It is hairy or fuzzy." Frey's term for the small strands of wood that form on the edges of splints when they are split. He carefully removes them.

gauge
likpesawakon

A wooden hand tool with a number of evenly spaced metal blades used for cutting ash splints into multiple strips with consistent widths.

growth ring (or grain)
wolikpeksu

"Tree, ash splint; wood has good grain for splitting, use in basketmaking." A growth ring is the amount of wood that a tree grows in circumference during a single growing season.

Hong Kong cord
hankan

A pre-braided grass cord that was imported from Asia and used in some baskets in the mid-1900s instead of braided sweetgrass.

* Secord, a Passamaquoddy language learner, realizes there are likely errors in translation and no disrespect is intended.
** In reference to the usage of "s/he" below, the authors acknowledge and understand more than two genders, but here we share the existing translations in the Passamaquoddy dictionary, as compiled and written by their community in 2008.

lid
kpihikon

The Passamaquoddy word for (basket) lid, cover.

mold (also form)
tuwihtikon

The wooden shape over which a basket is woven.

hollow rib mold / *tuwihtikon*
A mold made of wood, built similarly to a barrel. Because it is hollow, it weighs less, and is used by Frey to make extremely large baskets.

puzzle mold / *tuwihtikon*
A mold made of solid wood, turned on a lathe, and cut into seven pieces, each small enough to be extracted through the opening of the finished basket.

over-weaves
amalhakopehtahsu

"S/he weaves fancily." Supplemental, nonstructural weavers that are added to a basket and manipulated into a variety of three-dimensional shapes.

curls / *cokiqisok*
"Warts or, in basketmaking, decorative loops woven onto the sides of the basket." A supplemental weaver that is formed into a small, open, circular loop.

diamond-curl loops / *t-apucehlal*
"S/he turns (animates it) inside out, folds back." A supplemental weaver that is inserted into the row above or below to create a diagonal curl. Often, four of these curls are configured to create a diamond shape.

points / *qinusqikon*
"It is pointed." A supplemental weaver that is twisted to create a sharp point.

X-weaves
A supplemental weaver that affixes two crisscrossing braids to the exterior of the basket.

pounding
likpehtihike

"S/he pounds ash . . . to obtain basket splints." The process of hitting an ash log, often with the back of an axe, to crush the layers of spring wood and separate the growth rings into splints.

quillwork
kawiyik; 'tamalhakopekhikhawa kawihi

"Porcupine quills; s/he weaves quills in fancy designs." An art form in which porcupine quills are dyed and used for embroidery to embellish objects.

rim

Frey most often uses the term "rim" to describe the top edge of a basket. (See *collar*.)

ring-porous

A tree with larger and more numerous vessels in its spring wood, making it more spongy and less dense than its summerwood.

sapwood
wapikp

The sapwood is located near the outer part of an ash log. Whitish in color, it is flexible and used for fancy baskets.

splints
monikpehlal

"S/he strips splints from (an ash log)." A general term for strips of ash wood, encompassing both standards and weavers.

splitter
pihtuhtamut

The wooden device used for splitting splints of ash wood in half.

standard (sometimes also called "stander")
nemotahkapit

Although "standard" is now the most commonly used word for the vertical element of a Passamaquoddy basket, it is possible that the original English term was "stander." The Passamaquoddy word *nemotahkapit* describes a person sitting upright. The standards or standers bend at the bottom of a basket like a person's waist.

tapered standards
Standards that are shaped to be wider and narrower at different points along their lengths in order to create a basket's curved form.

sweetgrass
suwitokolasol (anglicized noun), wolimahaskil or welimahaskil

Hierochloe odorata is an aromatic grass that grows in coastal areas of Maine. In basketmaking, it is often braided as well as lashed to the rim. (See *braided sweetgrass*; *rim*; *collar*.)

urchin basket
musahkuhs posonut

A traditional form of Passamaquoddy basket with a low, round shape resembling a sea urchin.

weavers
loskonuwakonok (plural)

The horizontal element woven over and under the standards to form a basket. Weavers may have an additional decorative and three-dimensional weaver added on top of them, called an over-weave. (See *standards*; *over-weaves*.)

weaving board
tuwikcihikon

A square board placed on one's lap and used as a surface on which to form the flat bottoms of baskets.

Published on the occasion of the exhibition *Jeremy Frey: Woven*, organized by the Portland Museum of Art, Maine.

Major support for the exhibition has been provided by:

BANK OF AMERICA

Generously supported by:

Isabelle and Scott Black

Adam and Diana Lee

The Bear Bookshop, Marlboro, VT

CREWE
THE CREWE FOUNDATION

Exhibition catalogue support provided by:

KARMA, New York

Furthermore: a program of the J. M. Kaplan Fund

Furthermore:
a program of the J.M. Kaplan Fund

MIX
Paper | Supporting responsible forestry
FSC
www.fsc.org
FSC™ C023053

Portland Museum of Art, ME
May 24–September 15, 2024

The Art Institute of Chicago, IL
October 26, 2024–February 10, 2025

Bruce Museum, Greenwich, CT
June 1–September 7, 2025

First published in the United States of America in 2024 by

Rizzoli Electa, A Division of
Rizzoli International Publications, Inc.
49 West 27th Street
New York, NY 10001
www.rizzoliusa.com

in association with

Portland Museum of Art
Seven Congress Square
Portland, ME 04101
Portlandmuseum.org

FOR PORTLAND MUSEUM OF ART
Editors: Theresa Secord and Ramey Mize

FOR RIZZOLI ELECTA
Publisher: Charles Miers
Editor: Isabel Venero
Copy Editor: Richard Slovak
Production Manager: Kaija Markoe
Designer: Kimberly Varella, Content Object

Printed in Hong Kong
2025 2026 2027 2028 / 10 9 8 7 6 5 4
Hardcover ISBN: 978-0-8478-9970-8
Paperback ISBN: 978-0-8478-3851-6
Library of Congress Control Number: 2023948237

Visit us online:
Instagram.com/RizzoliBooks
X: @Rizzoli_Books
Facebook.com/RizzoliNewYork
Youtube.com/user/RizzoliNY

The authorized representative in the EU for product safety and compliance is Mondadori Libri S.p.A., via Gian Battista Vico 42, Milan, Italy, 20123, www.mondadori.it

PHOTO CREDITS

Theresa Secord—*Evolution of an Artist and the Oldest Art Form in New England*
Page 8: Photograph by Jared Lank
Page 10, Figure 1: Image courtesy University of Maine
Page 10, Figure 2: Image courtesy Theresa Secord
Page 11, Figure 3: Image courtesy Theresa Secord
Page 11, Figure 4: Photograph by Jared Lank
Page 12, Figure 5: Image courtesy Jeremy Frey
Page 14, Figure 6: Image courtesy Theresa Secord
Page 16, Figure 7: Photograph by Eric Stoner
Page 16, Figure 8: Photograph by Luis Sánchez Saturno. *The Santa Fe New Mexican* © 2011. Reprinted with permission. All rights reserved
Page 18, Figure 9: Image courtesy Colby College Museum of Art and Luc Demers
Page 20, Figure 10: Photograph by Eric Stoner
Page 21, Figure 11: Image courtesy Theresa Secord

Andrew James Hamilton—*Weaving Wood*
Page 22: Photograph by Jared Lank
Page 23, Figure 1: Image courtesy Andrew James Hamilton
Page 24, Figure 2: Photograph by Jared Lank
Page 24, Figure 3: Image courtesy Andrew James Hamilton
Page 25, Figure 4a–c: Images courtesy Andrew James Hamilton
Page 25, Figure 5: Image courtesy Andrew James Hamilton
Page 26, Figure 6: Photograph by Jared Lank
Page 26, Figure 7: Image courtesy Andrew James Hamilton
Page 27, Figure 8: Photograph by Jared Lank
Page 28, Figure 9: Image courtesy Jeremy Frey
Page 29, Figure 10: Image courtesy Jeremy Frey

Dakota Hoska—*Transforming Trees: Jeremy Frey and Materiality Beyond Expectations*
Page 30: Photograph by Jared Lank
Page 31, Figure 1: Photograph by Eric Stoner
Page 31, Figure 2: Image courtesy Owen Clarkin, some rights reserved (CC BY-NC), iNaturalist.com
Page 32, Figure 3: Image courtesy Alamy Photos
Page 33, Figure 4: Image courtesy Denver Museum of Natural History. © Denver Museum of Nature and Science
Page 33, Figure 5: © Don Johnston. Image courtesy Denver Art Museum
Page 34, Figure 6: Image courtesy Vancouver Art Gallery
Page 35, Figure 7: Image courtesy Jennie Hord and Denver Art Museum
Page 36, Figure 8: Image courtesy Archives of American Art, Smithsonian Institution
Page 36, Figure 9: Image courtesy Addison Doty and Clark & Del Vecchio, Santa Fe, NM

Ramey Mize—*Jeremy Frey: Full Circle*
Page 44: Photograph by Jared Lank
Page 45, Figure 1: Image courtesy Dr. Ari Plosker
Page 46, Figure 2: Photograph by Jared Lank
Page 47, Figure 3: Photograph by Jared Lank
Page 48, Figure 4a–b: Images courtesy the artist and Karma. Photographs by Max Lee-Russell
Page 49, Figure 5a–b: Images courtesy the artist and Karma. Photographs by Max Lee-Russell

Plates
Pages 53–55: Images courtesy NMAI photo services
Pages 56–59: Photographs by Luc Demers
Pages 60–67: Photographs by Eric Stoner
Pages 68–69: Photographs by Addison Doty
Pages 70–75: Photographs by Saygo Studios
Page 77: Photograph by Eric Stoner
Pages 78–79: Images courtesy Colby College Museum of Art
Page 80: Photograph by Eric Stoner
Pages 82–83: Photographs by Saygo Studios
Pages 84–85: Images courtesy and © Denver Art Museum
Pages 86–87: Photographs by Eric Stoner
Pages 88–89: Photographs by Jared Lank
Pages 90–93: Photographs by Jared Lank
Page 94: Image courtesy Hood Museum of Art
Pages 95–97: Photographs by Eric Stoner
Pages 98–99: Photographs by Addison Doty
Pages 100–101: Images courtesy David Halpern
Page 103: Photograph by Luc Demers
Pages 104–05: Photograph by Jared Lank
Pages 106–07: Photographs by Luc Demers
Page 108 (top): Photograph by Jared Lank
Page 108 (bottom): Photograph by Eric Stoner
Page 109: Image courtesy Smithsonian American Art Museum
Pages 110–11: Photographs by Eric Stoner
Page 113: Image courtesy Hood Museum of Art
Page 115: Image courtesy Kitty Leaken
Page 116: Image courtesy NMAI photo services
Pages 118–19: Courtesy the artist and Karma. Photographs by Addison Doty
Pages 120–21: Photographs by Eric Stoner
Page 123: Image courtesy Autry Museum of the American West
Page 124: Image courtesy David Stover. © Virginia Museum of Fine Arts
Pages 126–27: Photographs by Eric Stoner
Pages 128–29: Photographs by Luc Demers
Pages 130–31: Photographs by Saygo Studios
Page 133: Image courtesy David Halpern
Page 134: Photograph by Saygo Studios
Page 137: Photograph by Luc Demers
Pages 138–39: Photographs by Genevieve Hanson
Pages 141–43: Photographs by Saygo Studios
Page 144–47: Photographs by Eric Stoner
Page 148–49: Photographs by Paul-David Young
Page 150: Photograph by Eric Stoner
Pages 153–55: Images courtesy Art Institute of Chicago, Art Resource, NY
Page 157: Photograph by Addison Doty
Page 158: Image courtesy the artist and Karma
Page 160–61: Images courtesy the artist and Karma. Photographs by Max Lee-Russell
Page 162: Image courtesy the artist and Karma
Pages 164–65: Courtesy the artist and Karma. Photograph by Max Lee-Russell

Pages 164–65: *Jeremy Frey: Out of the Woods*, 2023, Karma, New York, installation view.

Front and back covers and endpapers (detail of interior): *Defensive*, 2022. Ash, sweetgrass, and dye. 12½ × 7½ × 7½ inches. Collection of Carole Katz. Photographs by Eric Stoner

Pages 50–51 and 164–65: *Jeremy Frey: Out of the Woods*, 2023, Karma, New York, installation view

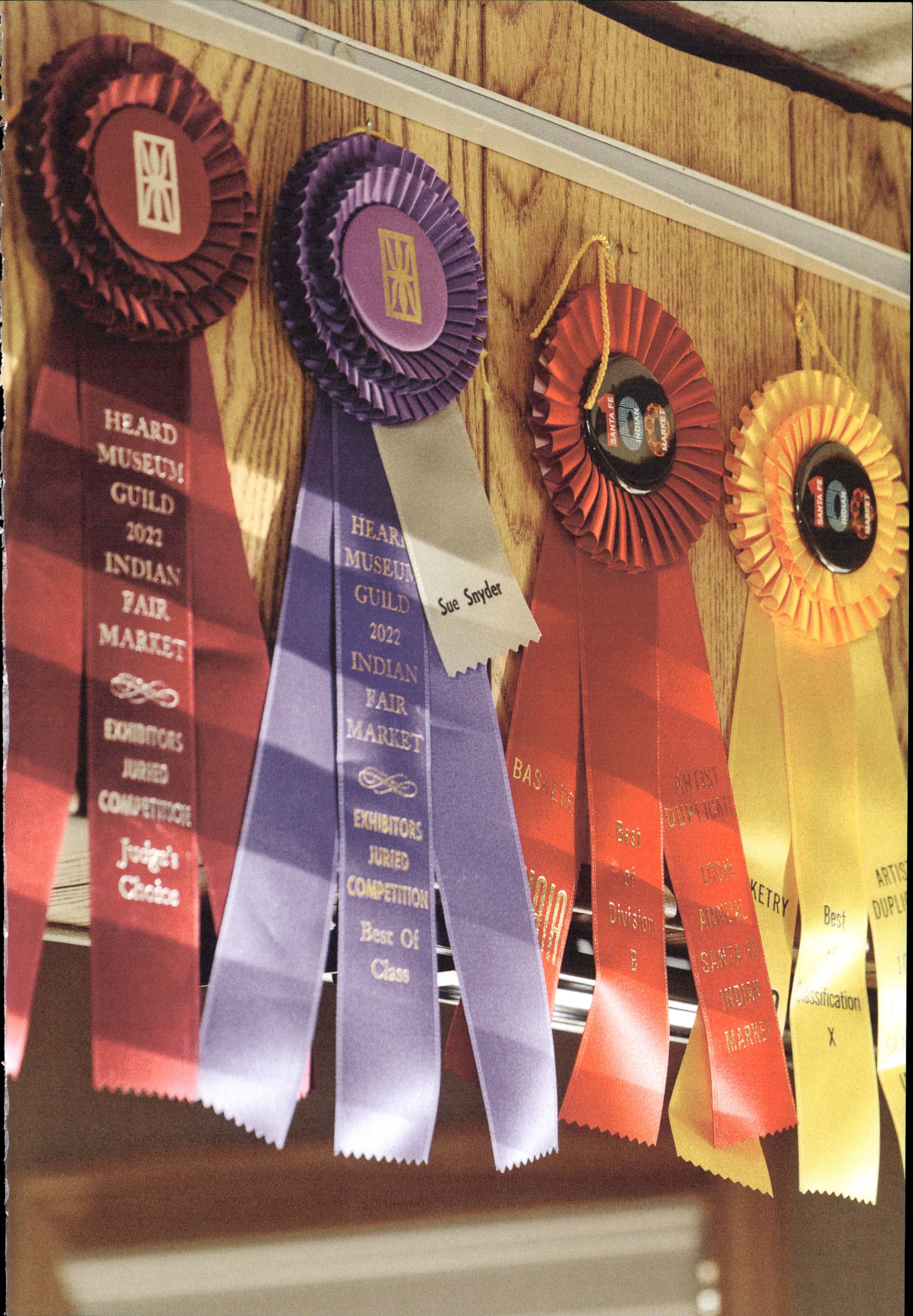
HEARD MUSEUM GUILD 2022 INDIAN FAIR MARKET
EXHIBITORS JURIED COMPETITION
Judge's Choice
GUILD 2022 INDIAN FAIR MARKET
EXHIBITORS JURIED COMPETITION
Best Of Class
Sue Snyder
SANTA FE INDIAN MARKET
Best of Division B
ARTIST
ANNUAL SANTA FE INDIAN MARKET
SANTA FE INDIAN MARKET
Best
Classification X

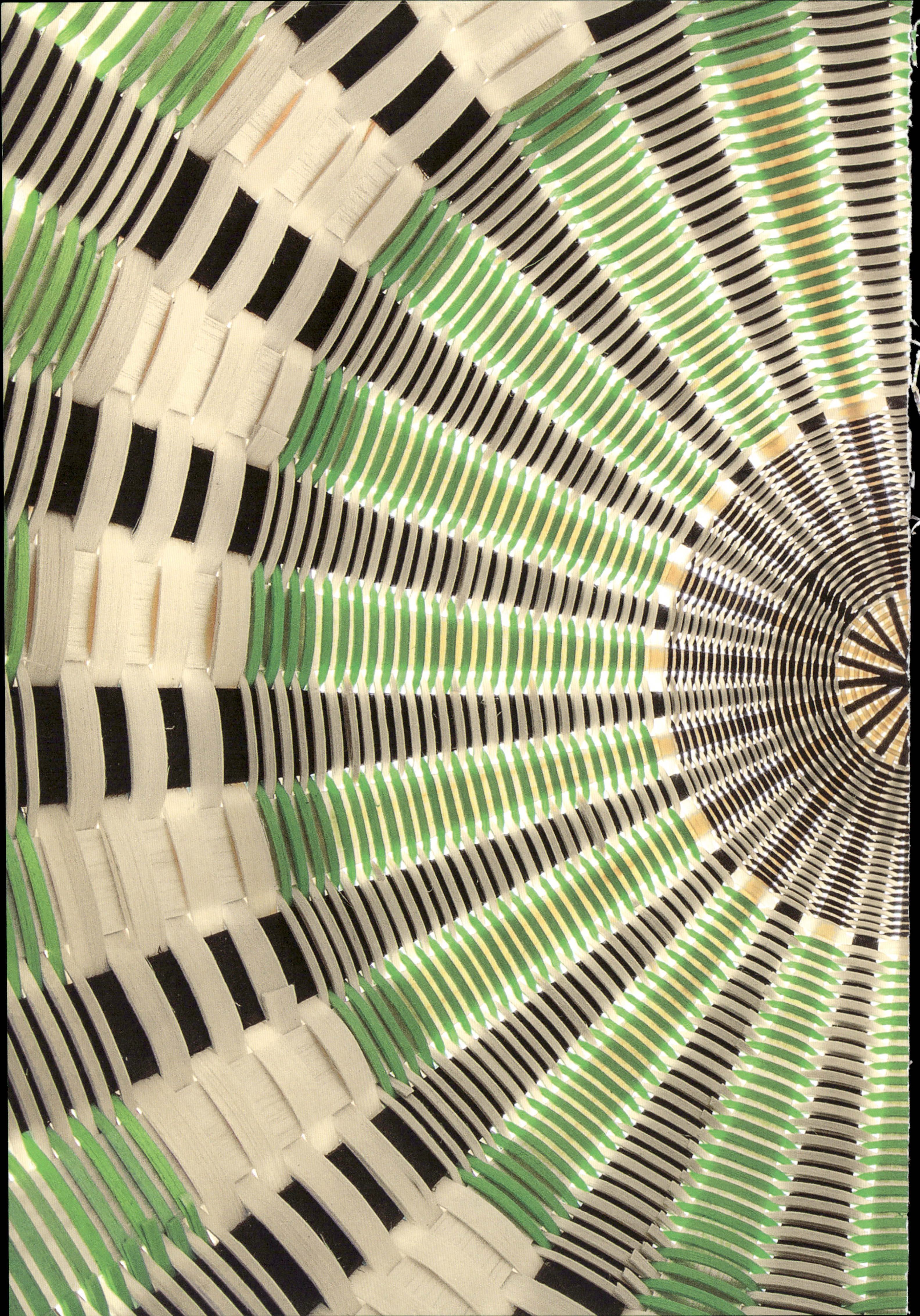